KT-369-586

The Sovereign State
The Secret History of ITT

Anthony Sampson

CORONET BOOKS
Hodder Fawcett Ltd., London

Copyright © 1973 by Anthony Sampson
First published by Hodder and Stoughton Ltd 1973
Coronet Edition 1974

This book is sold subject to the condition that
it shall not, by way of trade or otherwise, be
lent, re-sold, hired out or otherwise circulated
without the publisher's prior consent in any
form of binding or cover other than that in
which this is published and without a similar
condition including this condition being
imposed on the subsequent purchaser.

Printed and bound in Great Britain for
Coronet Books,
Hodder Fawcett Ltd,
St. Paul's House, Warwick Lane,
London, EC4P 4AH
by Hazell Watson & Viney Ltd,
Aylesbury, Bucks

ISBN 0 340 18284 9

THE SOVEREIGN STATE

'How did such a company come about, and how had
it so inexorably increased its scope? How can
one man dominate a corporation and hold
together an industrial empire making thousands
of products across half the world? How can
governments ever control such an organism
which is, like a jellyfish, both everywhere and
nowhere? And how does the multinational
corporation, of which ITT is a convenient
caricature, fit in with modern notions of politics
and diplomacy?' – from the book

'A work of questionable scholarship based on a
grave misstatement of facts, omission of
important material and just plain factual
errors.' – *J. D. Barker*, ITT PR officer, writing
to *Der Spiegel*.

'*The Sovereign State* represents massive research
in and around a corporation that dislikes being
researched.' – *Daily Telegraph*

'Sampson has put together a readable and revealing chronicle. . . . He has unearthed a lot of previously unpublished material.' – *Financial Times*

'An engrossing book.' – *The Scotsman*

'The book is very, very good . . . and unquestionably the best book ever written about ITT. In this very important work Anthony Sampson brings to his subject a rare blend of business and political acumen.' – *New York Times*

'Excellent.' – *Irish Press*

'Mr Sampson has produced a superbly researched work . . . which will enlighten, expand the perception and chill the blood of anyone who reads it.' – *Baltimore Sun*

'Anthony Sampson has written an entertaining book about the most disreputable member of the conglomerate club. Mr Sampson goes into all this in considerable depth and has arranged his material excellently.' – *The Observer*

'Mr Sampson's book is extremely readable.' – *The Economist*

'A good and disturbing book which should be read.' – *Daily Mirror*

'It is a history both fascinating and sinister.' – *The Illustrated London News*

'It is largely in his narrative that Anthony Sampson excels, and his plot and characters provide pure theatre for a riveted reader. . . . Here is the stuff of best-selling novels: double agents and electronic bugs; confabs with Hitler and Peron; Communist show trials and executions. . . . Sampson, to be sure, has mined a rich vein of documentary material here.' – *New York Times Book Review*

'Engrossing and sobering.' – *Sunday Express*

'*The Sovereign State* contains a great deal of matter for students of economics and politics to ponder on.' – *Times Literary Supplement*

'Remarkable.' – *Glasgow Herald*

'It is a muckraking work of great significance and an exposé of the modern multinational corporation.' – *San Francisco Chronicle*

A Note on Sources

In writing this book, I have made use of a large number of off-the-record conversations with present and past officials of ITT, and I am most grateful to the candour of many of those who have co-operated. My formal relations with the company have deteriorated since my first conversations with Geneen and other directors, when it became clear that my account was likely to be very critical; and eventually all official enquiries, I found, were sent on to the ITT public relations department in New York. But the informal contacts have always been more illuminating, and I am grateful to many rebels within the ITT system who continued to have talks which were both revealing and entertaining. I am also indebted to many of the critics of ITT who have made it their business to accumulate information, and who have been generous with their time and their files; most notably Ralph Nader and Reuben Robertson of the Centre for Responsive Law in Washington; Jack Anderson and Brit Hume; Morton Mintz of the *Washington Post;* Professor Abraham Briloff of Branch College; Bob Olstein and Thornton O'Glove of Coenen and Co.; Ray Dirks of Dirks Brothers; and to countless other journalists, bankers and diplomats, many of whom would prefer not to be named. Outside America, I have found that a study of a multinational corporation requires multinational contacts and sources, and I am grateful to the numbers of colleagues and friends who have provided me with information from London, Brussels, Paris, Milan, Stockholm, Santiago, Madrid and Moscow.

Any student of multinational corporations must be grateful to ITT for the quantity of confidential memoranda that it has allowed to become public, whether through subpoena, through court cases or through leakage; thus providing a collection of primary sources, which must be unique among big companies. I have taken full advantages of them with references in footnotes wherever possible. The most important collections include the Hearings before the Anti-Trust Sub-Committee, presided over by Emmanuel Celler, in 1969; (*Conglomerate Hearings*). Part 3 provides 1476 pages of hearings and memoranda, giving copious details of ITT acquisitions and policies. The hearings were followed by the Report of the Staff of the Anti-Trust Sub-Committee, published in June 1971 (*Conglomerate Report*) which analyses the general arguments about conglomerates and includes 90 pages of analysis of ITT's policies and financial stability. The most formidable body of information is contained in Parts 2 and 3 of the hearings before the Senate Committee on the Judiciary, on the nomination of Richard Kleindienst in 1972 (*Kleindienst Hearings*). These 1660 pages contain both the Senators' long enquiry, and a mass of additional ITT memoranda, notes and reports. After the hearings the individual views of Senators Kennedy, Bayh and Tunney were published separately in May 1972 as a 284-page book (*Kennedy Report*), providing an analysis of the hearings, a detailed chronology, and an appendix of documents and newspaper articles including important references to ITT.

On the ITT operations in Chile, the major evidence is contained in the collection of memoranda made available by Jack Anderson (*Anderson Chile Papers*) and since published by the Chilean government who have made available several documents, including their own version of the breakdown of their talks with ITT.

On the early history of ITT, including Colonel Behn's wartime activities, a number of documents recently declassified provide reports and evidence of ITT's Nazi affiliations and Latin American manoeuvres : the most important of which are the files referring to Dr. Gerhardt Westrick and Kurt von Schroeder, and the report of January 1943 by Allen Sayler of the Interdepartmental Committee on Hemisphere Communications (*Sayler Memorandum*). Further details of ITT's wartime links, and of the activities of Colonel Behn and Dr. Westrick, are available in a staff memorandum for members of the Interdepartmental Advisory Committee, produced as a confidential document on November 14, 1942. Among the many books dealing with Nazi connections with America, two are specially relevant to ITT: *All Honourable Men,* by James Martin (1950) and the biography of Sir William Stephenson by Montgomery Hyde, published in Britain as *The Quiet Canadian,* and in America as *Room 3603.* Some hints of Colonel Behn's trust in Hitler are contained in three articles by Maurice Deloraine, published by the ITT magazine *Sigma* in 1970, as *An ITT Memoir;* a fuller version of which has been promised in book form, but not published.

For the Budapest Spy Trial, the only major published source is the Communist transcript, published in Hungarian and English by the Hungarian State Publishing House in 1950, under the title: *Robert Vogeler and Edgar Sanders and their accomplices before the Criminal Court.* For the background to the trial, I am specially grateful to Lajos Lederer and Lazlo Veress.

In preparing and writing this book at high speed I have owed much to people who have eased the strain. To my assistant Alexa Wilson for her miraculous organisation, and for producing an ordered typescript out of chaos. To Bettie du Toit, for listening to chapters and helping to unscramble confusions. To my publishers, Robin Denniston and Alan Gordon Walker in London, and Sol Stein and Pat Day in New York, for their encouragement and suggestions. To my agent, Michael Sissons of A. D. Peters, for his reassurance and customary efficiency. And finally to my wife, Sally, for her valuable research and advice, and for her tolerance of this absorbing pursuit.

For this paperback edition, I have made some additions and excisions, and I have also added a new penultimate chapter, The President's Doorstep, bringing the story of ITT's troubles in Washington up to date, with the help of evidence from the Senate Watergate Committee and other documentation that has come to light.

Anthony Sampson
January 6, 1974

Contents

THE INTERNATIONAL TELEPHONE AND TELEGRAPH CORPORATION (ITT) is the eighth biggest American company by sales, and the biggest American company in Europe, where it has forty percent of its business. It employs 400,000 people, half of them in Europe. It was founded in 1920 as a telephone company by Sosthenes Behn, who was its chief executive for thirty years. For the last fourteen years its president and chief executive has been Harold S. Geneen, who enlarged it by a series of spectacular acquisitions, which turned it into the biggest and most controversial of the new multi-industry 'conglomerates'. Its American-based subsidiaries now include (with numbers of employees):

Hartford Fire Insurance (15,000).
Sheraton Hotels (19,300).
Continental Baking: Wonderbread, Hostess Cakes etc. (34,000).
Rayonier: Cellulose, Timber (6,110).
Cannon Electric (2,577).
Federal Electric (5,320).
APCOA and Service Industries (9,829).
World Directories (2,875).
Grinnell: fire-extinguishers (14,255).
Levitt: houses (2,701).
Canteen: feeding systems (10,869).
Avis: hire-cars (7,591).
(The last four are in process of being divested.)

Its European interests include hotels, insurance, teleprinters, cosmetics, automotive parts, lamps, pumps, food, and the following major telecommunications companies (with numbers of employees):

Germany: Standard Elektrik Lorenz (37,072).
Britain: Standard Telephones and Cables (22,189).
France: CGCT and LMT (15,313).
Italy: FACE telecommunications (6,522).
Spain: Standard Electrica CITE and Marconi (23,182).
Sweden: Standard Radio (1,633).
Belgium: Bell Telephone (13,666).
Norway: Standard Telefon (3,814).

I

The Barbecue

That inscrutable thing is chiefly what I hate—
                                    Captain Ahab: *Moby Dick*

It was in Brussels, at the annual ITT barbecue of managers
from all over the world, that I first felt the full impact. It
was just after the ITT scandal had broken in Washington
and Chile, after the giant corporation had been accused of
bribing the Nixon government to drop an anti-trust suit,
and of trying to undermine the elections in Chile. I was
already interested in multinational corporations, and I had
become specially curious about this conglomerate, with its
astonishing jumble of world interests, from telephones to
cosmetics, from hire-cars to hams, with an apparently unstoppable power to operate beyond the reach of governments. I had been talking to people both inside and outside
the company, and to my surprise I had been invited, as a
solitary journalist, to attend this self-contained company
function.

It was a strange setting, which seemed outside time or
place. It was at the 'Executive Mansion', a big bourgeois
house in a suburb of Brussels, which ITT maintains as a
company club and a centre for entertainment. A marquee
had been put up in the garden, draped with blue-and-white
ITT bunting, and Belgian waiters were cooking steaks and
sweet corn on the charcoal grills, while the polyglot managers queued docilely with their plates. The American
contingent, sixty of them, had flown over two days before,
for their monthly inspection of the European accounts:
they had the dazed, sleep-walking look of people still con-

fused by the jet-lag, and some of them (I confirmed) still kept their watches on New York time, in case they had to ring up the head office.

It was not immediately easy to tell the Europeans from the Americans, except perhaps from the shoes and trousers; for the Europeans, too—whether Swedish, Greek or even French—had a hail-fellow style and spoke fluent American, joking and reminiscing about old times in Copenhagen and Rio. I soon had a sense of being enveloped by the company, by its rites, customs and arcane organogram, of being swept right away from Brussels, or Europe, or anywhere.

After a good deal of back-slapping, shoulder-punching and story-telling, the executives sat down to their meal at trestle-tables in the marquee. There was no special seating plan; the atmosphere was determinedly democratic and unsnobbish. But in the middle a bald hearty man was pointed out to me, the young president of ITT Europe, Mike Bergerac; and next to him looking small by comparison was an owlish figure in a neat dark suit. This, I recognised, was the master-mind behind the whole corporation—Harold Sydney Geneen.

After the meal, there were speeches. An Italian manager told a long funny story in comic Italian–American about marriage and sex. There were references to how famous ITT had become in the past weeks, and how they no longer needed to read company reports to learn news of their company; they could read it in the newspapers. Then Mike Bergerac made another humorous speech, in praise of Geneen, speaking in a Californian drawl, with an easy-going, open-air casualness which made it hard to believe that he had ever been French. The climax of his joke came when he revealed that Geneen had recently been to London, where he had been observed—improbably enough—enjoying watching a game of cricket at Lord's. Bergerac then suddenly brandished a cricket-bag, out of which he produced a cricket bat, stumps and pads (they had been flown over at the last moment, I was told by my neighbour, by ITT's advertising men in London). He held them up, one by one, while the executives rocked with laughter, and Geneen too laughed with an impish grin which lit up his face.

Then Geneen stood up. He continued the joke, swinging the bat with remarks about batting for business, bowling fast balls and needing strong pads. But the picture of Geneen as the cricketer never really seemed convincing; and he quickly went on to talk about ITT, with more jokes about the terrific publicity, and how this was a 'non-sandwich evening' (most of the evenings when the Americans come over are spent in late-night conferences, with only time for a sandwich).

As soon as he spoke, for all the informality, it was clear that he dominated the whole gathering, like a headmaster at the end of term pretending to be one of the boys, but fooling none of them. He talked about record profits, continuing expansion, successful delegation and multinational co-operation. His eyes gleamed as he went on about ITT's brilliant performance. He ended by saying, 'I want you to know that I'm having a lot of fun, and I want you to have fun, too.'

There was a surge of applause. It seemed clear that he really was having fun; though I was less sure that the rest were. Yet listening to the jokes and the speeches, one would not think that this company had just been through a barrage of public criticism, examination and censure. I asked the head of public relations, Ned Gerrity, what effect he thought the scandal had had on ITT's business. He said it had really established the company's corporate identity: 'The bookings for Sheraton hotels have been a record.'

After the speeches, the managers walked around the garden and the house, drinking and chatting about turnover and inventories. They were hearty in a rather tense way, like a reunion of alumni who are not quite sure how well they know each other. The tension was heightened by the presence of the bosses—the senior vice-presidents who had flown over from New York, who wandered round warily. There was Tim Dunleavy, a big jolly Irishman with tousled hair, who had the cosy look of a teddy-bear, but whose jollity was said to be only a smokescreen for a steel-trap mind. There was Jim Lester, inscrutable with his narrow eyes and circumflex mouth, like a sad mandarin; his implacable exterior, I was told, concealed an implacable interior. There was Ned Gerrity, regarded as the eyes and ears of his master, Geneen; a leathery man with pebble glasses, loping round the lawn with his cigar rolling round his mouth.

The gathering was as emphatically masculine as a regiment or a football club; there was not even a waitress. The whole *esprit* was one of challenge and ordeal, with a whiff of grapeshot in the air : the appearance of a girl would have shattered the spell.

Later in the evening I was taken to meet Geneen, who was standing talking in the now almost-empty marquee. It was a surprising encounter. I was introduced as an English writer, and he told me immediately how much he liked England, where he had been born, and how he loved coming back to London. Then he went on to explain how he had admired the British Empire, and was sorry it had been given up so hastily. Why didn't the British government support the White Rhodesians? Didn't they realise that four-fifths of the British people were behind Ian Smith? He went on to talk about America's difficulties with the rest of the world —how her oil supplies were in danger, and how eventually she might need to move into the Arab countries to protect them. As he warmed to his tirade, his whole frame came to life; he began gesturing, pointing, and laughing, his fingers darting around, touching his nose, his ear, his chin, as if weaving some private spell; his greeny-brown eyes twinkled, and he grinned and laughed like a gargoyle. He seemed no longer a dark-suited owlish accountant, but more like an imp or a genie : almost like Rumpelstiltskin, magically turning thread into gold. I noticed that a clutch of vice-presidents were standing round listening, watching him carefully : they laughed when he laughed, and nodded when he nodded.

Businessmen, he explained, are the only people who know how to create jobs, and make work for people; he was responsible for 400,000 employees, all over the world, and it was his duty to lobby governments on their behalf, as effectively as he could. What do governments know about providing jobs? Why does the American government waste time with anti-trust questions, when it should be supporting the big corporations which are battling with the Japanese, and contributing to the balance of payments? As for these liberal newspapermen who attack big business, what do *they* know about making jobs? I interrupted him to say: 'Perhaps *I'm* a liberal newspaperman!' He looked at me in disbelief and roared with laughter, with the others in chorus.

He argued for three-quarters of an hour in the marquee, treating me patiently, with amused tolerance, as a wayward sceptic who would soon see the true light of reason: he even sent a message afterwards, saying how much he'd enjoyed the talk. We parted amicably, with mutual incomprehension. But in this marquee, like a nomad's encampment, I had begun for a moment to get the feel of being inside this amazing corporation, to glimpse it through the eyes of the master and followers. From their camp they looked out onto a world benighted with prejudice and unreason; where governments were merely obstructing the long march of production and profit; where nations were like backward native tribes, to be placated, converted, and overcome.

That barbecue evening aroused my curiosity, more than it satisfied it. It seemed like a caricature, exaggerating all the characteristics of these new organisms, the multinational corporations, and raising in an extreme form the question: who, if anyone, can control them? Here was a giant company which had just undergone this extreme public battering, apparently emerging all the prouder and more unified from the ordeal, as if it were a pirate ship that had slipped through a naval engagement. Its duality looked baffling; on one side it presented itself as a highly responsible world organisation, constantly mindful of its 200,000 shareholders, its 400,000 employees, its seventy host nations, and held together with an accounting system of the strictest control: in the words of its advertisements 'serving people and nations everywhere'. Yet on the other side, in the marquee I had the powerful impression that here was a company that was accountable to no nation, anywhere; and held together and inspired by one man, against whom no-one cared to argue. A man, moreover, who in spite of his famous accounting skills and discipline, yet had the unmistakable style of a buccaneer—who could stir up others with purpose and excitement, luring them away from their families and homes into a world of hectic travel, late-night meetings, constant pressure and outrageous demands.

How did such a company come about, and how had it so inexorably increased its scope? How can one man dominate a corporation and hold together an industrial empire making thousands of products across half the world? How can governments ever control such an organism which is, like a jellyfish, both everywhere and nowhere? And how does the multinational corporation, of which ITT is a convenient caricature, fit in with modern notions of politics and diplomacy? How does it, or should it, relate to the nation-state, to the Common Market or to the models of world trade?

It was with such questions in my mind that I decided to write a book about ITT. Its special fascination lay partly, of course, in the recent succession of ITT scandals—the subsidising of the American Republican convention, the dropping of the anti-trust suit, the proposed intervention in Chile. But ITT also has a special attraction for the student of the long trail of evidence that it has left behind it, in the form of memos, letters and hearings. Most studies of multinational companies are necessarily generalised and theoretical; for very few companies have revealed details of their disputes with governments or each other. But ITT is a company that has always tried to go to the limits; and in doing so, like an elephant, it has trampled a wide path behind it. At each stage of its advance it has offended governments or employees enough to bring more documents into the open, thus providing primary sources for its workings. Delving through the mountains of ITT memos I have begun to get some of the feeling of what it is like to work inside this enveloping giant.

'He's Captain Ahab, really,' said one Geneen-watcher, and I could see what he meant—the monomania and obsession, the magnetic ascendancy he cast over his crew in the hunt for the whale. But as I continued my own travels, I came to think that Geneen and his corporation resembled not so much the crew of the *Pequod*, as the white whale itself; a leviathan secretly encircling the world, usually detectable only by the turbulence of the water, but suddenly showing one side of its huge strange shape, or spouting dark water, first in one corner of the globe, then a few days later at the opposite end; becoming a legend for ubiquity, immortality, and supernatural strength. As I myself began to follow the whale, I soon realised that this mysterious creature, this Moby Geneen, had provoked a whole flotilla of Ahabs, some infuriated by some ghastly injury, and determined to harpoon it, some merely fascinated by the challenge of the creature and its manifestations, obsessed only by the desire to behold it or circumscribe it. The quest still continues, and what will happen to the whale remains a tantalising question.

In the story that follows, I trace the development of this remarkable company from its beginnings fifty years ago, and show how it has raised political problems at each stage of its career. I describe how its buccaneering character was first set, long before Geneen arrived, by its adventurous founder, and how he pursued his own intrigues and foreign policy through the Second World War, and through the cold war that followed. I show how Geneen then took it over, to convert it into an industrial conglomerate, but still with its defiant independence of governments; how Geneen's ambitions and rough tactics brought it up against the trust-busters; how his battle against them created a major American scandal and opened up an enquiry into corruption in government; how the scandal then shifted to Chile, and the CIA, and thus provoked a new debate, about the role of multinational companies. Throughout, I try to show how ITT has been not just a maverick company, but also in some ways a forerunner of a new kind of industrial animal, which has a significance which will affect our whole picture of politics and diplomacy. It has been a revealing pursuit, which has changed my ideas in the course of it, and I hope I can convey some of the excitement to the reader.

2

The Buccaneer

I may analogise the present situation in the communications field to that in ocean transportation in the past. There was a time when the master of a vessel was in effect the diplomatic representative of his country in contact with the governments in the foreign ports where he touched. That situation is not altogether unlike our present situation in which the managements of international communications companies are in a position to shape our international communications policy through their ability to negotiate and make arrangements with the representatives of foreign governments. Indeed, managements of communications companies may at times be in the position of serving interests other than their own national interests.

> Paul Porter,
> Chairman of the Federal Communications
> Commission, 1945

The International Telephone and Telegraph Corporation — to give ITT its full name [1] — is nowadays considered essentially a contemporary phenomenon, the creation of Harold Geneen, who transformed it in the last decade, and turned it into a dynamic and masterful conglomerate. But many of its deepest characteristics, I believe, can be traced back to its earlier history, and to a formative period which established strengths and flaws to its character which have survived all subsequent changes.

ITT was one of the first of the multinational corporations, in the modern sense, establishing factories and man-

---

1. Until the fifties, its official abbreviation was IT&T. To avoid confusion, I call it ITT throughout.

agement all over the world. But from its foundation in 1920, it was always a maverick company. Dealing with the newest form of instant communications, the telephone, it could circle the world with a speed and mobility that, like the old adventurers' ships of Drake or Columbus, left nations and politicians lagging behind it : it created not only a new kind of business, but a new kind of diplomacy. The opportunity was taken to the limit by a daring and many-sided entrepreneur, who saw the new technology as the means to operate with new-found freedom above, or beneath, nations. He gave the company a reckless spirit which has never left it.

The true character and career of Sosthenes Behn, the founder of ITT, still presents an enigma. During his lifetime, his dominating personality was the object of awe and affection; he was the Prince of Telephones, a brilliant industrial diplomat, who presided over banquets and regally entertained foreign potentates at the Plaza Hotel, where he lived. When he died in 1957, his friends mourned a vanished age of adventure and style. But he left behind him buried secrets which are only now beginning to come to the surface, showing his personality in a more complex and sinister light; it is only now, with the help of recently declassified papers, that the range of his activities is beginning to emerge.[1]

Most companies, even the biggest of them, have corporate characters that have emerged partly from the places on which they were first based—from Detroit, Endicott, or Turin—even though they may long since have outgrown them. But ITT, from the first, had a unique placelessness. Its origins were not so much multinational, as a-national, in a group of offshore islands. Sosthenes Behn was born in the Virgin Islands when they were still owned by Denmark; his father was Danish and his mother was French, and he was brought up with a polyglot background. His father was French Consul, and sent him to be educated first in Corsica,

1. Five feet of files on ITT between 1930 and 1945, in the Washington National Archives, provides a unique source of detailed information about the company's wartime activities, including several boxes of transcripts of Colonel Behn's wartime telephone conversations, which provide material for a complete book in themselves. (Record Group 259—Records of the Board of War Communications.)

then in Paris. When the United States acquired the Virgin Islands from Denmark (for $30 million, in 1917), it acquired the Behn family, too. The young Sosthenes, with his brother Hernand, quickly looked to larger horizons.

They began their career as sugar brokers in the nearby island of Puerto Rico, and it was only by accident that they became involved in the new gadgets, telephones, when they acquired a tiny Puerto Rican telephone business as a bad debt. But young Sosthenes realised the scope of this growth industry, at a time when telephones were sweeping across America; and he soon bought more telephones, first in Puerto Rico, then in Cuba. After the war—when he rose to be a colonel in the U.S. Signal Corps—Sosthenes and his brother founded a small company with the high-sounding name of International Telephone and Telegraph—deliberately named to confuse it with the big company, AT&T, which operated the telephones inside America (with which it has been confused ever since). The first annual report emphasised—as did the reports for the following fifty years—that there were far more telephones per hundred population in America than in the rest of the world. On that difference lay ITT's opportunity.

It was Behn's ambition to build up an international telephone network to rival and complement the American system : there were both idealism and profit in that concept, and anyone who laments the backwardness of telephones outside America might wish that Behn had succeeded. But Behn's grand desire soon came up against the obstacles of nationalism and the insistence of governments on controlling their own communications; and in trying to hold his system together, Behn gradually wove a web of corruption and compromise which left the idealism in ruins, and his company with deep kinks in its character.

Behn's first major expansion came in Spain, where in 1923 the dictator Primo de Rivera invited private companies to apply to run the telephone service, which was then chaotic. Behn saw his chance, rushed to Madrid, and set himself up in grand style at the Ritz, appearing much richer than he was. With his fluent Spanish diplomacy and his capacity for working all night, he eventually got the contract, and Spain became the jewel in the ITT empire. Behn set up the Compañía Telefónica de España, with the Duke of Alba as chairman, and hurriedly mustered American engineers to fulfil the contract. It was the first triumph of Behn's chameleon business philosophy—enthusiastically to support the regime, whatever it might be. Or, in the words of the annual report of 1924, 'to develop truly national systems operated by the nationals of each country'.

In 1925, there was a still greater opportunity. The Western Electric Company, which was making telephones all over the world, split off its international holdings, anticipating an anti-trust action. The Behn brothers, backed by Morgan's bank, offered $30 million for International Western Electric, and got it; overnight they became owners of a network of manufacturing companies, now renamed International Standard Electric (ISEC), including a big one in Britain, renamed Standard Telephones and Cables (STC). The network was safeguarded by a cartel agreement with the American Western Electric and its operating company, AT&T, who promised not to compete with ITT abroad, in return for using them as their export agents; and ITT promised not to compete with AT&T in America.

With this International System, as he called it, Behn set himself up in style. He knew very little about technology but he did know how to negotiate, and how to impress. In 1928 he moved into a new thirty-three storey gothic skyscraper at 67 Broad Street, New York, which still stands there—still partly inhabited by ITT—as a monument to Behn's peculiar vision. Above the entrance a mosaic depicts an angel with a flash of lightning between his outstretched hands, and two hemispheres concealing his private parts : the symbolism might be appropriate.

In this new gothic palace, Behn soon established a reputation as a princely host, with a panache that most tycoons lacked. He was an aristocrat among businessmen; he had married Margaret Dunlap, related to the Berwind coal-owning family, and a Berwind duly appeared on the board. He worked in a Louis XIV salon, with a portrait of Pius XI on the wall, and in the penthouse dining room his French chef could concoct banquets for two hundred guests. Behn loved to show off his telephone conversations in several languages, and visitors would be invited to pick up an earphone and listen. He had a commanding appearance, with his tall ramrod back, his strong eyes and hawk nose : he had great charm, and he took care with his image, furnishing the press with stories of his hospitality and valour.[1] He was the unchallenged master of the company, the more so after 1933, when his brother Hernand died : Sosthenes would describe how Hernand used to be known in Spanish as *Behn bueno*, the good Behn, while he was *Behn male*, the wild Behn.

The European network lacked a central piece in the jig-saw, Germany, and Behn soon filled the gap. In 1930 he formed a holding company called Standard Elektrizitäts Gesellschaft (SEG), jointly with one of the German giants, AEG, who soon after sold out; and then bought another company, Lorenz, from Philips. The companies brought him into outright competition with his biggest world rival, Siemens, who fought back by going into partnership with Ericsson, the Swedish telephone company then controlled by the fraudulent financier Ivar Kreuger. Behn swiftly retorted by making a deal with Kreuger, buying a block of Ericsson shares in return for $11 million, plus some ITT shares, which would give Kreuger a place on the ITT board.

To celebrate the deal, Behn gave a Swedish banquet in Broad Street for two hundred guests. Then the auditors, Price Waterhouse, checking the Ericsson accounts, found certain 'manipulations' which could not be explained : it was the first indication of Kreuger's colossal fraud.[2] Behn communicated his suspicions to his bankers, and soon afterward Kreuger committed suicide (Behn sent seventy-five dollars' worth of flowers to the funeral). He was left with a block of Ericsson shares and a directorship of Ericsson; but without the grand alliance that he had hoped for. But Behn

---

1. A reporter from the *Washington Post*, Lemuel Parton, described (September 24, 1936) how he had once been interviewed by Colonel Behn for a public relations job in Spain : 'Talking with nervous, aggressive, hard-driving Mr. Behn across his desk, it seemed to me that, baldly, what he wanted was a press agent, but the last thing in the world he wanted was publicity.'

2. 'How it is possible that the management of the ITT, which included some of America's foremost bankers, did not discover this until then, appears inconceivable.' (George Soloveylchik, *Ivar Kreuger*, London, 1933, p. 142.)

consolidated his position with a succession of cartel agreements, carving up Europe and Latin America among ITT, Siemens, Ericsson, and General Electric.

In America in the meantime, Behn's International System was beginning to arouse the jealousy of his rivals and the suspicions of the government, who distrusted his involvements with foreign governments. When the new Federal Communications Act of 1936 was being prepared—which brought into being the Federal Communications Commission—one section of it, 310(a), was specifically aimed at ITT. It stipulated, among other things, that licences for radio stations should not be granted to any corporation of which any officer or director was an alien, or of which more than one fourth of the capital stock was owned by aliens. At that time, about a fifth of the ITT stock was owned by non-Americans, and Behn protested vehemently to the Commerce Committee of the House of Representatives: 'International trade and good will,' he said, 'should not be stifled and throttled by a bugaboo of national defence.' In fact the foreign share ownership was not necessarily very relevant; even with an increasing majority of American ownership, ITT was to become more suspect.

A NAZI NETWORK

A more far-reaching cause for distrust was largely unnoticed at the time: on August 4, 1933, *The New York Times* reported in a small news item that the new Chancellor of Germany, Herr Hitler, had for the first time received a delegation of American businessmen at Berchtesgaden. It consisted of two men: Colonel Sosthenes Behn and his representative in Germany, Henry Mann. The meeting was the beginning of a very special relationship between ITT and the Third Reich.

Behn was eager to work closely with the new Nazi government. He asked Hitler's economic adviser, Wilhelm Keppler, for names of reliable men acceptable to the Nazis who could join the boards of ITT's German companies. Keppler suggested several, including the banker Kurt von Schroeder, of the Stein Bank, who was to become a general in the SS, and the crucial channel of funds into Himmler's Gestapo.

Schroeder joined the board of one of the ITT companies, SEG, and became the safeguarder of ITT's progress in Germany. He reorganised the company, cancelling its debts, and soon bringing massive new contracts for armaments for SEG and Lorenz. In return for his co-operation, Behn through Schroeder was soon able to get special treatment from the Nazis: in 1935 and 1936 Schroeder persuaded the Reichsbank to pay off outstanding bills held by Lorenz, which carried with them contingent liability, at a time when other companies were refused payments. As the pace of re-armament quickened, so ITT in Germany rapidly expanded; Behn was appreciative of Schroeder's help, and offered him 250,000 Reichsmarks in recompense.[1]

Behn's other important Nazi ally was Dr. Gerhardt Alois Westrick, of the famous law firm of Albert and Westrick, who acted for many American companies in Germany: he became a director of the ITT companies, and Behn's personal contact; he came several times to New York staying at the Plaza Hotel and paid for (the FBI noted) by Colonel Behn.

Behn also had meetings with Hermann Goering, the head of the German Air Force, and it was not long before ITT did Goering an important service. In 1938 Lorenz acquired a 28 per cent share in the Focke-Wulf company, whose bombers were to wreak havoc on Allied convoys: a remarkable diversification for an electrical company. When Schroeder was interrogated after the war, he was confident that Colonel Behn had approved the Focke-Wulf purchase, and he went on:

> From 1933 till the outbreak of war, the great bulk of the profits of ITT German companies could have been transferred to Colonel Behn's companies in the United States; but he never asked me to do that for him. Instead he appeared to be perfectly content to have all the profits of the companies in Germany which he and his interests controlled reinvested in new buildings and machinery and in other enterprises engaged in production of armaments.

He was asked:

1. Interrogation of von Schroeder, November 15, 1945.

Did you know of, or did you hear of, any protest made by Colonel Behn or his representatives against those companies engaged in these activities preparing Germany for war?

He replied : No.[1]

Behn was so confident in Hitler that he was prepared to strengthen ITT's companies in Germany at the cost of its companies elsewhere. In 1935 Hitler forbade the export of patents and technical information from Germany, except under special licences; but ITT continued to supply its German subsidiaries with patents, and to build up the exports from Germany.[2] As the Nazis increased their control over industry, the German directors of ITT companies became more anxious to assert their loyalty; visitors from America were discouraged, and even Colonel Behn was not allowed to see the extension of the ITT factories for war work. But he still insisted that, by dealing with Hitler, he could protect the investments for his stockholders. After the Anschluss with Austria in 1938, the Austrian ITT company, Czeija-Nissl, was put under the management of the Berlin headquarters, and all Jews were ejected, including the chairman, Frank Nissl. The Nazis wanted to expropriate the Austrian company as being foreign-owned, but Behn went to see Hitler again. Hitler reassured him about the prospects of ITT in the Reich, and told him that he had no further territorial ambitions. Behn remarked afterward how well dressed Hitler was, and how much of a gentleman.[3]

In the meantime in Spain, Behn had an awkward time during the Civil War, with parts of the telephone service in Republican hands, and parts taken over by Franco; he himself stayed for a long time in Madrid, establishing himself in the company's thirteen-storey headquarters, the Telefónica, bringing with him the chef from the Ritz, and providing shelter for refugees and for the press, who used the Telefónica both to file their stories, and to observe the war, with bombs falling all round it. The American staff of the telephone company anxiously avoided words like 'the enemy' which would appear to commit them to one side and talked about the 'home side' and 'the visitors'. Colonel Behn him-

1. Interrogation of von Schroeder, November 19, 1945.
2. Sayler Memorandum, 1943.
3. Maurice Deloraine: *An ITT Memoir*, 1970.

self presided calmly over the building, plying the journalists with coffee and excellent brandy.[1] Eventually, Madrid got too hot even for the Colonel, and he retreated to France, to return later to negotiate successfully with Franco for the reinstatement of the concession.

By September 1939, when Hitler invaded Poland, the German ITT companies, now effectively run by Dr. Westrick, controlled also the subsidiaries in Austria, Hungary, and Switzerland. It was clear that, in return for its help to Hitler, ITT in Germany had an especially favoured position : Schroeder intervened with the Economics Ministry to enable the ITT companies to be the first foreign companies declared by the Reich to be German, and thus exempt from the Custodian of Alien Property.

In the spring of 1940, while the continent of Europe was falling to the Nazis, Dr. Westrick arrived in grand style in New York, staying at the Plaza, again at ITT's expense, with an entourage including his two sons and a mysterious secretary, the Baroness Ingrid von Wagenheim. Dr. Westrick and the baroness talked to a succession of American businessmen, including Henry Ford, to persuade them to cut off supplies to Britain—which, they said, could bring the war to an end in three months. Westrick gave glowing accounts of the prospects of German-American trade after Britain had been cleaned up.[2] Westrick kept in touch with the ITT factories in Berlin and occupied Europe, and also with Colonel Behn, who was then in Lisbon; he arranged through Berlin (as the FBI later reported) for Behn to travel to Biarritz to collect some belongings from his house there.

But by the end of July 1940, the *New York Herald Tribune* had been alerted to Dr. Westrick's presence by William Stephenson, who was running British intelligence in America. Westrick, it emerged, was the personal emissary of Ribbentrop, acting under Hitler's instructions; his visit had been planned by Colonel Behn, on visits to Germany

1. Geoffrey Cox (now Sir Geoffrey Cox), *The Defence of Madrid*, 1937.

2. *The Times*, August 11 and 20, 1940. The Confidential Staff Memorandum for the Hemisphere Communications Committee, dated November 14 1942, said of Westrick : 'it was reliably reported to the FBI that on his 1940 visit to New York, when his status was that of a Nazi official, Colonel Sosthenes Behn made his hotel reservations'.

and Holland.[1] Westrick was forced to leave, travelling across America with his entourage; he set sail from San Francisco to Japan, and thence went via Siberia to Germany, where he again took charge of his ITT empire, which now included most of Europe.

Back in Berlin, Westrick showed Schroeder the power of attorney he had been given by Behn, which authorised him to do whatever he thought was in Behn's interests, with a contract allowing him 100,000 Reichmarks a year. Behn continued on good terms with the Nazis. He saw Goering several times to discuss ITT's financial problems, and Goering once asked him to transmit peace feelers to Britain, which, Behn said, he communicated to Churchill, Chamberlain, and Eden. Goering discussed with Behn the possibility of buying the German companies, paying for them through goods or raw materials in Switzerland. ITT tended to acquire in exchange the mysterious and prosperous company General Anilin and Film Corporation (GAF), an offshoot of the I. G. Farben cartel, which made Agfa films, dyestuffs, and chemicals, whose true ownership was effectively concealed through Swiss banks; but GAF was seized by the United States Treasury Department.[2]

Behn's high-powered contacts, both in Europe and elsewhere, helped to provide an unrivalled private intelligence service—which was perhaps the greatest asset of his company. When foreign leaders came to America, they often lunched with Behn in his penthouse before they talked to the State Department, and his information was often better than his government's. Its effectiveness was shown in Rumania in 1941, when the Iron Guard leader Ion Antonescu insisted on taking over the telephone system from ITT. With the help of the German economic agent, Behn negotiated compensation of $13.8 million, which included accumulated profits : the deal excited much comment, for it was the first time that a big American company had extracted dollars from a Nazi-controlled country since the war.[3] And it was at the last moment; for a few days later

1. See Ladislas Farago : *The Game of the Foxes*, Hodder and Stoughton, 1971, p. 403.
2. FCC Inter-Office Memorandum, February 27, 1943.
3. *New York Times*, July 9, 1941.

31

the Nazis took over completely. This and subsequent deals showed how well Behn was informed; but the information went only to him, and it was characteristic of ITT—as it still is today—that only the man at the top knows the full story of the company's operations.

It is important to put Behn's Nazi sympathies in perspective. Countless American industrialists believed until the last possible moment that Hitler and Mussolini were good for business, and had only limited territorial ambitions. Sosthenes Behn had more excuse than many of them for condoning the dictators. His International System of communications was, he maintained, by its nature, a peace-making influence; its survival depending on accepting each local regime; and he could not afford to be too fussy about his friends. In private, his former colleagues maintain, he was very critical of the dictators; but he had to keep in with them, he explained, in the interests of the stockholders. It was not ITT's fault that the world was splitting apart.

But Behn's system had long since ceased to be a peace-making influence, or to carry honest communications; he had himself fallen into the habit—which became so characteristic of his company—of saying one thing in one part of the world, and another in another. His eagerness to keep in with each regime served to exacerbate, rather than moderate, the conflict, for he was prepared to do almost anything to avoid his companies' being expropriated. He helped to build up the Nazi war machine, extending from communications into armaments, and he allowed the neutral companies to become interlocked with the Nazi system.

For the employees of the British ITT company, Standard Telephones and Cables, the wartime situation would have been especially poignant, if they had known about it. Standard had always appeared all-British, particularly after 1931, when the American chief executive, Henry Pease, had been succeeded by a succession of Englishmen, most notably Sir Thomas Spencer and Sir Frank Gill. Sosthenes Behn would arrive on the *Queen Mary*, set himself up in the elegant suite in the company's Aldwych headquarters, and give magnificent lunches at the Ritz. No-one apparently was aware of his German activities across the channel.

It was not until Pearl Harbour that the United States government became urgently concerned with ITT's links with the Axis powers. In January 1943 a secret report was produced by Allen Sayler, of the Federal Communications Commission, which outlined the full ramifications of the ITT network, for the wartime body called the Interdepartmental Advisory Committee on Hemisphere Communications. Sayler's memorandum began by showing how ITT before the war had allowed its German companies to become increasingly interlocked with neutral countries, and how:

> Far from halting these dealings and breaking up the relationships of these neutrally located subsidiaries with the Axis, ITT in the United States has made repeated and persistent efforts to obtain licenses for such dealings with the enemy. In addition, ITT has sought ever since December 1941 to export materials from the United States to its subsidiaries in neutral nations which are producing for the Axis.

The main concern of the FCC report was with Latin America, where ITT continued to maintain links with the enemy countries after America entered the war, and was strongly suspected of allowing its lines to be used to pass information to German submarines. The most crucial country was Argentina, which had strong pro-Nazi sympathies, and where ITT was associated with German interests, including the cable company TTP, which they shared with Siemens. The danger was described by Behn's nephew, Nando Behn, in an intercepted message to New York (June 29, 1942):

> It is about time something is done down here to cut out the sole communication center in the Americas with Berlin. Our competitors, Transradio, have a direct circuit with Berlin and you can be pretty sure that every sailing from Buenos Aires is known in Berlin before the ship is out of sight. This is no secret, but it is certainly a situation that ought to be brought under control.

But (as the FCC report pointed out) the ITT companies in the Argentine were also maintaining communications with the enemy; in the first seven months of 1942, for instance, the United River Plate Telephone Company (which ITT had bought from the British) handled 622 telephone calls between Argentina and Berlin. Moreover the influence of ITT in Argentina was extending itself through the continent rather as ITT Germany had expanded through Europe. Argentinians supervised the ITT companies in Brazil and Peru, which were on the side of the Allies, and in 1942 three local directors of the Montevideo Telephone Company in Uruguay were replaced by three Argentinian directors. Throughout Latin America ITT was unwilling to stop dealing with people on the 'proclaimed list' of banned companies and evaded export controls and licences by fabricating stories and by smuggling, though, as one message from Argentina admitted, 'perhaps some of our stories have not been convincing'. The All-America Cables Office (another ITT company in Argentina) was believed to have obtained confidential information about tungsten ore through its cables, and to have passed it on to the Havero trading company, and thus to the Nazis. And elsewhere too —in Chile, Colombia, Cuba, and Ecuador—messages were passed via ITT to enemy countries; when Bolivia cut off diplomatic relations with the Axis in 1942, the business of the ITT subsidiary CIRBOL dropped by fifty percent.

The State Department was watching Colonel Behn and his ITT network with remarkable thoroughness, intercepting letters and cables between ITT officials and friends, showing the pervasive influence of the Axis. From all over Latin America came the evidence of ITT's playing along with the Nazis. A letter in April 1942 from ITT New York to Pinkney, the chief executive in Brazil, described the ITT links with German-owned companies, and warned : 'Failure to furnish service to enemies via such connections would render the companies affected liable to litigation and forfeiture in the countries in which they operate.' A report from an ITT man in one Argentine company, the Compañía Unión Telefónica (CUT) had an examiner's note saying :

Records indicate this CUT has in its employ Ruys de Behrenbrouch, who speaks five languages and pretends to be anti-Nazi but frequently visits the German embassy and works at night in the CUT office, where he quite possibly listens to conversations to and from foreign countries.

A letter from 'Mildred', who worked for an ITT company in Brazil, complained of the number of German staff in the company, and described how the boss, 'Harry,' 'has been so busy he left the line in charge of a German. . . . The police have picked up so many of the good workers, both in the office and in the field, that at present they are greatly understaffed. But I guess all these worries are part of being on the staff of ITT.'

ITT's support of the pro-Nazi governments in Argentina brought them into head-on collision with the State Department, particularly after 1944, when the new regime came to power; Behn and his local manager, Henry Arnold, insisted on defending Perón, to the fury of the American ambassador, Spruille Braden, who believed in an outright confrontation. Braden may have been crude and arrogant in his attitudes, but ITT, as in pre-war Germany, had its own pressing reasons for appeasement; they knew they were likely to be nationalised, and they wanted to be sure of good terms; eventually in 1946 they got them, with a remarkable settlement of $90 million, including (as in Rumania) accumulated profits. Certainly, Behn's friendship with Perón had been worthwhile. As in Rumania, the settlement was not a moment too soon; for shortly afterwards, the Argentine government was broke.

In this transaction, as in many other ITT deals, there were widespread suspicions of graft : Ambassador Braden, who deeply distrusted Behn, alleged that Behn gave a payoff of $14 million for the Argentine settlement. Behn's ex-employees insist that the Colonel specifically forbade them to deal in graft; and the lawyer who negotiated the Argentine settlement denies that any private money was paid. But Behn, in all big deals, kept secrets to himself. Braden describes how, when he was ambassador to Cuba, he once argued with Behn about graft in the ITT penthouse. Behn insisted that no company could do business in Latin America without paying bribes, and when Braden protested, Behn promised to pay only 'a little graft' in Cuba, by which he meant $30,000 a year.

In all his negotiations Behn was greatly helped by his private intelligence service; and part of this can be seen in the complete transcripts of his wartime telephone conversations, which were monitored and filed away by the State Department. He was discreet on the telephone, for he knew that the American censor was listening, and probably the censor abroad, too; he talked in a primitive code, referring to cities by the names of the local ITT managers—like, Pete's Town (Lisbon, where Pete O'Neill was in charge), Spencer's Town (Thomas Spencer in London), or Arnold's Town (Buenos Aires)—perhaps the code also fitted Behn's view of the world, as a chain of ITT outposts. But no-one was much fooled by it : the censor scribbled the name of the town in the margin, and sometimes interrupted to ask for an explanation when the Colonel talked about 'potatoes' with Caldwell, his man in Madrid, the censor asked what he meant, and the Colonel explained that potatoes meant pesetas.

The conversations show how thoroughly Behn could keep in touch with every political swing on the continent and how he held together the company by the sheer force of his personality—staving off nationalisation and controls, fixing the local politicians, dominating and reassuring his deputies across the crackling line. He was always unflappable, always relaxed, philosophically quoting Spanish proverbs, describing the meals he'd just eaten; but determined to know everything, and if necessary to intervene personally. He was a master of the human touch, concerned about his managers' wives, children, and health; talking about celebrations and holidays, sending cigars, flowers or medicines, ending up with 'God bless you, old man.' He knew how to keep them on their toes, and he was always one step ahead of them. 'Tomorrow is always late,' he told Henry Arnold in Buenos Aires. 'I tell you what I've always found : that when a vice-president didn't want to see me, that was just the time for me to go.' But he was also a calming father figure, as he showed for instance in November 1943, when Arnold was alarmed by the new Argentine government, in which Perón first came to power.

BEHN: Hello, Bill—good morning.

ARNOLD: Good morning, Colonel. . . .

BEHN: I'm sorry I couldn't talk to you from Washington yesterday. I was tied up. . . .

ARNOLD: This is a good circuit and we can talk freely. . . . Colonel, I've got a lot of things to talk to you about today—have you time to talk to me?

BEHN: Go ahead, but don't kid yourself about your circuit being free.

ARNOLD: Our circuit is in pretty good shape at this end!

BEHN: Well, I know, but—

ARNOLD: The general situation here is becoming worse instead of better. The government interferes in our business every single day. The intervention is increasing in every way and the policies appear to be definitely anti-American.

BEHN: . . . You mean the policy of the ruling group.

ARNOLD: That's right—yes—we have a lot of alarming evidence that our company, in particular, is being subject to persecution. . . . The desire seems to be that these people wish to take over control in one way or another. . . . There are many projects of nationalisation and government ownership and things of that kind under consideration. . . .

BEHN: You're somewhat under a strain, my dear Bill—I know how it is—I know you're down there and all these things are happening, but don't let it get you, don't let it get you, old man.

ARNOLD: I'm perfectly calm.

BEHN: Well, I don't say you're not perfectly calm, but I gather that you are definitely under a strain—one can be calm and still under a strain you know, and you know there's no black cloud that hasn't a silver lining, you know, and the Spaniards have a proverb which says: 'There's no bad that lasts a thousand years.'

ARNOLD: I'm not excited, Colonel, I simply want to take advantage of this circuit and give you the latest information.

BEHN: That's all right, old man, that's all right . . . are you still of a mind that I shouldn't visit you at the moment?

In Europe in the meantime, even after Pearl Harbour, Behn continued to keep in touch with his companies in Switzerland and Spain, and through them with the Axis powers. In Switzerland (as the FCC memorandum complained) the ITT factory continued to collaborate fully with the Nazis, at a time when its Swiss-owned rival, Halser, refused to make equipment for Germany; and in Spain, the ITT company provided Germany with raw materials, including zinc sulphate and mercury, and made equipment 'apparently for the German army'. The State Department had complained that ITT in Spain 'had not made a genuine effort to seek ways and means of carrying out the desires of this government'; but Colonel Behn insisted with his usual argument that if the Spanish company did not collaborate, Franco would expropriate it. The Spanish operation was crucial to ITT. In May 1940, just before the fall of France, Franco had announced that ITT would again take over the telephone system. In September 1943, Behn himself went to Madrid, to negotiate closer ITT control of the properties. He gave a succession of elaborate dinner parties with vodka and champagne for Franco's officials, and came back to report a new investment of $60 million.

Spain was the chief means of contact with wartime Germany, and in Madrid the ITT executives from New York could still meet with their Nazi equivalents: a mysterious meeting early in 1942 was reported by RCA officials, in which Kenneth Stockton, an ITT vice-president, discussed the future of ITT properties with German officials. Behn was able, through Spanish intermediaries, to arrange a meeting with Westrick in Switzerland; its object, it seems, was to sell the ITT Lorenz company to Siemens—an amazing proposition which, like the earlier Rumanian deal, suggests that Behn still commanded much influence with the Nazis. But Siemens would pay only with their funds which were blocked in America, and the State Department refused to unblock them.

Where, if anywhere, did Colonel Behn stand, as he telephoned and flew across the frontiers of war? In Washington, there were differing views of his loyalties; the State Department had grave doubts and watched him closely; the FCC thoroughly distrusted his foreign connections and stockholders; and the Justice Department was preparing antitrust action to break up the combine. Among many politicians and journalists, the unreliability of ITT was well known,[1] and Colonel Behn was aware enough of his reputation to appoint after the war Thomas Blake, a former press secretary for Roosevelt, to be his Washington lobbyist: Blake's main job, as he told me, was to dispel the 'bad smell' that ITT had left behind.

But at the same time, the Colonel had very good friends in politics and especially in the Pentagon, which had several ex-ITT men and future ITT men in high places. General Stoner of the Signal Corps later paid tribute to Behn's help in teaching him about communications, and after the war Behn received the Medal of Merit, the highest civilian honour, for providing the Army with land-line facilities. The wartime annual ITT reports were full of patriotic references, and pictures of the American flag flying over ITT's plants: Behn was building up a stronger base in America, and in September 1942 he announced a great new ITT plant in New Jersey. ITT laboratories in America, helped by a contingent of refugee French engineers from Paris, achieved some valuable inventions, including the High Frequency Direction Finder, nicknamed Huff-Duff, which was used to detect German submarines attacking the Allied convoys in the Atlantic.[2] Thus while ITT Focke-Wulf planes were bombing Allied ships, and ITT lines were passing information to German submarines, ITT direction finders were saving other ships from torpedoes.

CONQUERING HEROES

When the tide of war turned, and Europe was invaded, Colonel Behn emerged in new chameleon colours. On the very day of the liberation of Paris, August 25, 1944, the French ITT workers were celebrating in the laboratories, hoisting French flags on the roof, when who should arrive at the door but the Colonel, wearing a mud-stained battle dress, sitting in a jeep with his son William at the wheel. Supposedly he was a communications expert, advising the

1. In November 1947, an internal *Time* magazine memorandum from Washington reported: 'We know that Sosthenes Behn has been watched and used by U.S. intelligence agencies for a long time. All of this is in the Department of Cloak and Dagger and we could never defend ourselves in court with G2 records.'

2. Deloraine: *An ITT Memoir*, 1971.

American Army; but his preoccupation was to inspect and re-establish the ITT factories in Western Europe; he went from Antwerp to Brussels and then back to Paris, insisting on magnificent meals en route; he stopped at Epernay, and loaded up the car with champagne.[1] The arrival of Behn and other American tycoons in France caused bitter resentment in London, where the government was refusing to give permits to civilians. The *Daily Mail* of September 20 described how a planeload of American businessmen had come over, including one 'in the electrical goods trades'. The American Secretary of State, Cordell Hull, indignantly denied it, but Behn in the meantime was inspecting all his French plants.

It became clear, as the Allies pushed into Germany, that ITT now had a very close relationship with the American army. ITT officials mysteriously appeared in brigadier-general uniforms, including Kenneth Stockton, who had been chairman of ITT's European board, alongside Westrick and Hofer. The situation led to some angry questions, and in Congress, Representative Jerry Voorhis made the comment:

> Here we have a great international corporation with the most definite kind of property interests in Germany having its own vice-presidents in positions of power with regard to deciding what is to be done to prevent the reconstruction of Germany's warmaking power. . . .

It was a time when the Allied military operations in Germany were becoming overlaid and confused with commercial operations; it was a surrealist nightmare (I witnessed part of it in the British Navy near Hamburg at the time), and the military governments were in no position to understand and control it. In the postwar rubble there were all kinds of business marauders, picking up what they could; but ITT were in the forefront. In October 1945, they even managed to dismantle two Focke-Wulf aircraft plants in Mühlhausen, in the Russian Zone, and to move them to Nuremberg, in the American Zone; with the help of Dr. Westrick, who was now helping ITT to recover its business, and in return was protected by ITT. Alexander Sanders,

1. Deloraine: *An ITT Memoir*, 1971.

who had worked for ITT in Germany and later became its German finance director, returned to Berlin in October 1945 as a colonel in the U.S. Bombing Survey, and got in touch with his old boss, Westrick, whom he had last seen in Tokyo in 1940. They spent two days together on Lake Constance, and Westrick arranged to subpoena Sanders in his defence.[1]

Schroeder in the meantime had been found in June 1945 in a prison camp in France, wearing the battle dress of an SS corporal. He was questioned at length by two investigators about all aspects of his career, including his dealings with Westrick and Behn over the ITT companies, and about ITT's contributions to Himmler's SS; he went through a succession of trials, sentences, and appeals for the rest of his life.[2]

What lay behind this remarkable transmogrification of Behn the supporter of Hitler into Behn the Allied hero? Part of the story is still buried in secret files; but it is clear that Colonel Behn, at some stage of the war, became very close to American intelligence agencies, and realised that he could perform useful services for them, with his own private information network. While the Justice Department and the FBI continued to distrust him, military intelligence found him and his telephones indispensable. In Latin America, American agents were placed in the ITT offices in Bolivia, Paraguay, and Argentina, among others; and Behn, on his visits to Europe, could bring back information through Switzerland and Spain about the state of the Axis. Allen Dulles, who was working for intelligence in Switzerland, may have played a key role in the rehabilitation of ITT : Westrick, who often visited Switzerland, was reported to have been in touch with Dulles in the middle of the war, to discuss ITT's problems; Dulles duly made contact with Behn, and helped to arrange for ITT's return to Europe, via the American Army, and for Westrick's protection.

Whether Behn was ultimately more helpful to the Allies than he had been to the Axis may never be known, even after the intelligence records are available; perhaps only he knew whether he was ultimately an agent or a double agent.

1. *Washington Post*, November 1, 1945. Also private information.
2. James Stewart Martin: *All Honourable Men;* Little Brown, 1950, p. 54.

But certainly there could be little doubt where his first loyalty lay; the only power he consistently served was the supranational power of ITT.

In the immediate postwar period, denazification policies were closely linked with anti-trust policies, and for a short time the Allies were determined to break up the concentrations of German industry. The Department of Justice set up a very active decartelisation branch, run by a forceful attorney, James Stewart Martin. But the big corporations were busily reasserting their influence, with growing support from Washington, and the plans to denazify and break up the cartels were already being mysteriously postponed and defeated; in the end only the chemical combine I. G. Farben was successfully divided. ITT was soon able to retake possession of their factories, and in the summer of 1946 one of ITT's vice-presidents, Gordon Kern, arrived in Germany on a thirty-day permit, which was endlessly extended, and took control of the Lorenz factory, making telephone equipment for the American Army. Among his other activities, Kern arranged for a German attorney acting for ITT to visit Switzerland, to discuss patents with the Swiss ITT company, a connivance that was then strictly against the rules; but Kern pretended that the attorney needed medical treatment in Switzerland. The decartelisation branch discovered the plot through the postal censorship, and demanded that Kern's permit be cancelled; but he was let off with a caution.

The Department of Justice in Washington was actively preparing an anti-trust suit against both ITT and AT&T; and in 1946 a comprehensive complaint was drafted, in the name of the Attorney-General Tom Clark, and his anti-trust chief, Wendell Burge.

It made a powerful case against the interlocking monopolies. It maintained how ITT after 1925 had 'established a foreign monopoly channelising all orders for communications equipment and kindred products placed by many firms, through the ITT system, thus denying to other manufacturers . . . access to this foreign market'. It described how, 'under the 1925 agreements, the world would be divided up to prevent and eliminate competition between component companies of the ITT and AT&T systems . . .' and maintained that many of the agreements had continued up to the present :

> During the period of the war, relations under some of the agreements were maintained between defendant ISEC [1] and its contracting partners located in Great Britain and neutral countries. During said period relations under some of the agreements were also maintained, to the extent that conditions permitted, between ITT's system companies and ISEC's contracting partners in enemy or enemy-occupied countries, under the supervision of one Gerhardt A. Westrick. Westrick, an agent of the Nazi government, was during the period of the war placed in charge of the ITT system companies in various countries of Continental Europe by Sosthenes Behn, president of the defendant ITT, and was empowered to represent the interest of the ITT system in Germany.

The complaint was never signed; the last note on the unsigned draft is dated March 10, 1947. The carve-up between ITT and AT&T has tacitly continued until today: ITT is only a minor competitor in the American telephone market, and AT&T still does not sell telephones in Europe. The anti-trust drive was frustrated by the pressure of the large corporations, who wanted a strong German industry. And the fear of Nazism very rapidly gave way to the fear of Communism. Colonel Behn, as we see in the next chapter, soon appears as a key anti-Communist.

In Latin-America as in Europe, ITT re-emerged as the champion of freedom against foreign infiltration. In 1946 the company even asked the Truman administration for financial help to buy up its rivals in Mexico, owned by the Swedish company Ericsson, who were thought to be politically unreliable, being neutral. In the end the request was turned down, but President Truman's Secretary of War, James Forrestal, had given strong support.[2]

1. The International Standard Electric Company was the European subsidiary of ITT, the successor to International Western Electric.

2. On April 25 Forrestal wrote to the Secretary of State, George Marshall, stressing that it was of 'the utmost importance to the national interest and security that all communication facilities in the western hemisphere be owned by hemispheric interests and, if possible, by companies controlled by citizens of the United States.' (Documents released by the State Department; see the *Guardian*, July 19, 1972.)

In Europe, when it was clear that the decartelisation policy had changed, James Martin sent in his resignation, and later summed up his own conclusions in phrases which have a familiar ring. 'We had not been stopped in Germany by German business. We had been stopped in Germany by American business. . . . We have to enable the government to control economic power instead of becoming its tool. . . . We have been slow to recognise the inherent dangers in corporate empires because we have had a theory that business does not need to be governed.'

It is important again to put this wartime story into perspective. ITT was only one of scores of corporate empires, British as well as American, which used all their muscle to restore their prewar interests, to defy the governments' attempts at denazification. And with hindsight the more extreme decartelisation theories of that era now seem irrelevant or vindictive. The German steel cartel, which then seemed so menacing, is now an ailing semi-nationalised industry; and the Common Market has since been more concerned with making combines than in breaking them.

But the history of ITT was a special case of corporate crime : for the telephone cartel, as the anti-trust complaint suggested, had been used to give secret support to the Nazis from neutral and hostile powers, and to reinforce the German war machine, in a way that was made much more effective by the existence of the cartel; while Behn protested that he was only acting in the interests of stockholders, to avoid expropriation, the interests of peace would have been better served if the cartel had broken up, and the Nazi companies *had* been expropriated. Behn exploited his mastery of communications not—as his mosaic symbol implied —to spread truth across the world, but to suppress it, and to say different things in each country. Being so multinational and mobile, his company could be everywhere and nowhere at once. Behn's whole personal approach, and his own benign despotism, was suited not to democracies but to dictatorships. He liked dictators, and they liked him; for he made his telephones their instruments.

Perhaps the most interesting part of the story was its burial. Other big German combines, like Krupp, Siemens, or Mercedes, while they regained their own dominance, went through an ordeal of public recrimination and questioning which (I believe) fundamentally affected their corporate character[1]; and a new generation forced them to undergo some kind of corporate self-analysis. But ITT buried its history in a mountain of public relations, so that scarcely anyone on its staff now knows that it was ever associated with Focke-Wulf bombers or with Hitler's SS.

Most remarkable of all, ITT now presents itself as the innocent victim of the Second World War, and has been handsomely recompensed for its injuries. In 1967, nearly thirty years after the events, ITT actually managed to obtain $27 million in compensation from the American government, for war damage to its factories in Germany, including $5 million for damage to Focke-Wulf plants—on the basis that they were American property bombed by Allied bombers.[2] It was a notable reward for a company that had so deliberately invested in the German war effort, and so carefully arranged to become German. If the Nazis had won, ITT in Germany would have appeared impeccably Nazi; as they lost, it re-emerged as impeccably American.

1. William Manchester would disagree. See *The Arms of Krupp*, 1969.
2. *Foreign Claims Settlement Commission of the United States*.: Final Decision, May 17, 1967, and Proposed Decision, March 27, 1967. The commission, in the Proposed Decision, decided that because the German government after 1942 obtained full control of ITT's subsidiaries through superimposing a new government holding company, this was 'tantamount to the placement of these companies under an enemy property custodian'. In view of the earlier insistence of Westrick and Schroeder on making the companies German, and Behn's connivance in this, this decision seems surprising.

3

The Cold Warriors

The influence of Colonel Behn on the company continued for long after the Second World War; but it was more in the field of diplomacy than in finance. For as a commercial operator he had lost a good deal of his reputation. The war had left the International System in some disarray, and the profits had slumped. The Russians were taking over Eastern Europe. In Spain, Franco nationalised the operating company in 1945, while leaving ITT with the monopoly to supply the equipment. In Argentine, the Perón regime nationalised the system in 1946—though with generous compensation of $95 million.

Behn decided that ITT should diversify, buying other industries in America, where the political climate was safer. But the Colonel's skills were those of an individualist, and he was not at home in the more humdrum problems of management. He bought two American companies which looked promising. One of them, Capehart-Farnsworth, made TV sets and radios; the other, Colderator, made refrigerators; but both investments were disastrous.

The shareholders were becoming restive, observing the lack of dividends, and Behn's own lavish way of life. In 1947, a group of rich shareholders decided to organise a revolt—led by Clendenin Ryan, the grandson of one of the robber barons, Thomas Fortune Ryan, who with his family and friends owned a sixth of the ITT shares. He complained that in nine years the shareholders had got nothing out of ITT, while Behn and the other directors had got $3.7 million in salaries and fees. Behn, breaking his customary silence, replied that the real question was not why had ITT done so badly, but why it hadn't gone under altogether. After a dramatic proxy fight, a compromise was agreed, with the help of another very tough customer, J. Patrick Lannan, a tall cold Irishman from Minnesota. Seven new directors would join the board, including Ryan and Lannan (who is still a director today). A new president was elected, General Harrison, a fine-looking white-haired executive from AT&T. Behn would continue as chairman and chief executive officer. The new arrangement, in the tactful words of the announcement in June 1948, 'will allow Colonel Behn to devote more time to pressing international problems and leave him free to spend more time abroad'.

But the double harness of Harrison and Behn was an unsatisfactory solution; for the General was a weak man, and the Colonel was strong, and being still chief executive officer he could still keep his hands on the controls. Moreover the 'pressing international problems' were, as it turned out, more than an excuse for getting Colonel Behn out of the way. For by 1948, three years after the end of the world war, Europe was already in the throes of the cold war, and ITT was in the midst of it. Colonel Behn was playing once again a shadowy role. In this context his position was much closer to American policy; for he was indisputably anti-Communist. Yet here, too, there is great doubt as to how far ITT was following American foreign policy, how far creating its own; and two remarkable stories can now be pieced together which throw a slanting light on the ambiguous relationships between the company and the governments.

SABOTAGE IN HUNGARY

The first story emerged in a most dramatic and melancholy setting, in a darkened courtroom in Communist Hungary in February 1950, where an American and a British businessman, together with several Hungarians, were accused of sabotage and espionage. The trial was a grim charade; one of the 'show trials' that were then beginning, a year after the arraignment of Cardinal Mindszenty, to advertise the wickedness of the West. One by one the accused

47

admitted their errors, incriminated each other, prompted by the presiding judge who led them through a carefully-rehearsed story. It was a historic event, a new stage in Stalin's grip on Eastern Europe. But the trial has a special relevance in this narrative, for the three principal accused, Robert Vogeler, Edgar Sanders and Imre Geiger, were all officials of ITT.

The true story remains very incomplete, and will probably always be so. The British and American files remain secret, and the main sources, apart from private information, are the account of Vogeler in his book,[1] and the Hungarian 'white book' which gives a verbatim report of the trial, with its own commentary.[2] The evidence from the trial, the enthusiasm of the confessions, and the blatant simplifications, are clearly untrustworthy. But they give some indication, not only of ITT's relationship to Western intelligence, but of the Communist portrayal of that connection—a portrayal that is specially ironic in the light of events twenty years later.

The story revolved round the Hungarian subsidiary of ITT, the Standard Electric Company, which had been set up in 1928 as part of Colonel Behn's international system. It had become part of the Nazi network, and during the war, working under the supervision of Dr. Westrick in Berlin, it had expanded rapidly, so that after the war, in spite of being stripped of equipment, both by the Germans and the Russians, it was the most important exporter of telecommunications and electronics in Eastern Europe. Potentially it was a key part of ITT's European empire; but as the cold war got colder, its future became increasingly doubtful.

Gradually, by the 'salami tactics' of their leader Rakosi, the Hungarian Communists were able to discredit and eliminate their rivals; and after the peace treaty of 1947 they were able steadily to take command of the country, and to press ahead with nationalisation.

1. Robert Vogeler: *I Was Stalin's Prisoner*, Harcourt Brace (New York), 1952.
2. Hungarian State Publishing House: *Robert Vogeler and Edgar Sanders and their accomplices before the Criminal Court*, Budapest, 1950.

The ITT factory was in a very anomalous position, both for the Americans and the Russians. The Communists, on their side, could not easily expropriate the ITT factory, for they needed Western expertise to run it, and in terms of the peace treaty they had to pay compensation for any nationalisation. For the Americans, what was most maddening was that Hungary, as one of the former Axis powers, was required to pay $200 million reparations to Russia; and Russia wanted part of her reparations in the form of ITT equipment, much of it with military uses. The Americans thus had to watch one of their own factories exporting quite advanced telecommunications equipment to Russia, just when relations were rapidly worsening. The irony of the situation was illustrated by an incident in 1947, when American diplomats in Budapest discovered that a small office in their legation had eight microphones concealed in the walls and ceiling. It turned out (as one of the diplomats later recounted) that the equipment had all been secretly made in the Budapest ITT factory.[1]

Hungarian telephones and telegraphs had suffered from the ravages of the war, and in 1946 one of ITT's vice-presidents, Ogilvie, came to Budapest with the 'Telecom Plan' to re-equip Hungary's telecommunications controlled by the post office; a committee of Americans would supervise the plan, and the cost would be repaid in ten years. But the plan, not surprisingly, was rejected by Ernö Gero, the Communist minister, and the ITT factory continued in limbo, while the Communists looked to non-American suppliers, and eventually made an agreement with Philips of Holland. But since the ITT factory was the main supplier inside Hungary, and they needed its technical know-how, they still had to deal with ITT. Their resentment with the Americans was increased by the fact that the Hungarian company was not allowed to export to the hard-currency areas of Europe, to avoid competing with other ITT factories. But the Russians had considerable awe for ITT, which they regarded, very exaggeratedly, as a key part of the American power system.

ITT were thus in a tricky situation, which called for all

1. Christopher Felix (pseudonym): *The Spy and his Masters*, London, 1963.

Colonel Behn's diplomacy. But the ITT factory may have had importance far greater than its commercial potential; for it could provide indispensable help to Western intelligence, in a country where 'cover' was increasingly difficult to find.

The story began as early as 1945, when, according to the Communists, Colonel Behn was working closely with American intelligence. In New York he was visited by an electrical engineer, Robert Vogeler, who had also been a major in the Marine Corps. Behn appointed Vogeler to be area manager for the ITT companies in Eastern Europe, based on Vienna, but told him also to establish contact with American intelligence in Vienna. Vogeler did so, and in Vienna he moved between the offices of ITT and the ODI, the military intelligence organisation for Eastern Europe, where he had his own room, number 15, in the Allianz building. For the next four years Vogeler played this double role, going to Hungary for short visits—eight weeks in all. In 1946, Colonel Behn himself arrived in Vienna, and he and Vogeler visited Hungary together.

In 1947, according to the trial, Behn recruited another suspected spy, this time a British one. Edgar Sanders, then aged forty-one, was a half-Russian accountant who had been born in Leningrad; he was a cousin of George Sanders, the film star, and had some resemblance to him—handsome with sleek black hair. He had (he confessed) begun to work for British intelligence during the war in the middle east and after the war had joined the British military mission in Budapest as an intelligence officer with the rank of Captain. Then, when the Hungarian peace treaty was signed, which cut down the scope for espionage, he had to be demobilised in London : but he was soon told by a Captain Barkley (?) in the War Office to return to intelligence. He was recruited, as cover, into ITT, for which his brother, Alexander Sanders (see page 40), worked in Germany. He saw Colonel Behn who sent him back to Budapest to run the ITT factory. But he was also told to report to Major Hanley in the British legation; and he was instructed to try to isolate Hungary from the rest of the Communist world.

The third villain in the Communist drama was a Hungarian, the chief engineer at the ITT factory in Budapest. Imre Geiger, then forty-eight, came from a middle-class Jewish family; he had joined the ITT company when it was formed, and had (he said) been in contact with American intelligence before the war. He was inducted into intelligence by Ogilvie, and in the autumn of 1947 he went to New York for talks with ITT where (he said), he found there was close contact between the company and the U.S. General Staff. Then in 1948 Colonel Behn came to Hungary, and promoted him to be general manager of the ITT company—with the understanding that he could undertake sabotage and espionage. Behn promised that he would help Geiger to escape, when it was necessary, and would then get him a good job with ITT, in the West.

A fourth accomplice came from outside ITT, but was very important to the others. Zoltan Rado had an important position in the Ministry of the Interior, supervising the ITT factory. He had, he said, been brought up in Czechoslovakia, and came to Britain during the war, where he was mixed up with Trotskyites and used by the British intelligence to inform against Communists; then he came to Hungary, still working for the British, but pretending to be a local Communist, so that he got quick promotion in the ministry, where he could fix permits and visas for the ITT men.

In October 1948, only four months after his demotion from president, Colonel Behn came to Budapest, and presided over a crucial meeting in the sitting room of the Gellert Hotel, a grand tourist hotel; with him were Pinkney, Vogeler, Sanders, and Geiger. They waited till the secretary, Mrs. Zador, had left, disconnected the telephone in case it was bugged, and Behn then explained his master-plan. A third world war, he said, was now imminent, and Hungary would be on the enemy side. It was therefore against American interests that an American corporation should develop Hungary's telecommunications. Therefore, they must slow down production and sabotage production, in every possible way. Behn, according to Sanders, explained that this ITT policy was 'not exactly from the authority, but with the understanding of the U.S. General Staff'. Geiger pleaded with Behn that he wanted to get out of Hungary, to get a job in the West; Behn said that he must stay, to carry out the plan.

Thereafter, according to the confessions, the 'sabotage and espionage' were intensified. Orders intended for Russia were despatched instead to Turkey. Accounts were fiddled (said the state auditor), to belittle the assets and thus evade taxes. Machinery was moved round the factory, from one corner to another and then back again, to interfere with production. Production was down to forty per cent of its previous figure; the equipment was shoddy, orders delayed. The factory was instructed to take new blueprints only from London; but when London was asked, they endlessly delayed.

At the same time, the accomplices passed any information they could find, through the American legation, to ITT in New York and thus to intelligence in Washington. Sanders, though working for British intelligence, went through the American legation. Rado, having started by working only for the British, was recruited in 1949 by the Americans too, who could pay him more money (he complained that the British only paid him £120 in 1948). They provided plans of the telephone network and other installations, which were duly laid out by the British air attaché, Bisdee, with blue circles and flags on a map.

But Vogeler, it seems, had been rash. He had become friendly with a young baroness, quite attractive, called Edina Dory, who worked as a barmaid at the Astoria hotel. She seemed a natural ally : her father was a big landowner who had been dispossessed of his land by the Communists, so that Edina was forced to find a lowly job. Her sister had married an American intelligence officer, Colonel Kovach, who had earlier worked at the American mission, and she herself wanted to get out to the West. Vogeler met Edina at the Astoria, trusted her, and used her to pick up odd bits of information; for she sometimes worked on the telephone exchange at the Astoria. Vogeler was possibly already under surveillance, but his closeness to Edina seemed incautious; for the secret police, the AVP, carefully watched such places as the Astoria.

At the end of October Vogeler began to suspect that he was being shadowed, when he met with the American intelligence chief, Colonel Kraft. He warned Geiger and Edina Dory, and told them that he would get them out. He sent a signal to the American legation in Vienna, who promised to organise the escape. On November 10, Geiger and his wife, with Edina Dory, boarded a train as instructed at Budapest East, then changed trains at Gyor, heading for the frontier town of Pinnye, on the line to Vienna. Then, at Pinnye, the frontier police arrested the three of them. Nine days later Vogeler was picked up by the police on a charge of espionage. Two days later Sanders, too, was stopped in the street and bundled into a police car.

Three months after the arrests, after extensive interrogation by the secret police, the suspects were brought to trial in Budapest; the fourth major figure, Rado, had been arrested just before. Appearing in court, the accused, as *The Times* correspondent described them, sounded composed and relaxed as they gave their confessions to the presiding judge, with only occasional promptings. The evidence, apart from the detailed confessions of guilt, dwelt at some length on the relations between ITT and the American government.

Vogeler went on to explain that 'the co-operation between the company and the military was such that the military could control the operations and policies of the company, and that was not only true of our company but of other companies that have large foreign subsidiaries.'

Imre Geiger, the Hungarian general manager, talked about Behn's Nazi connections. Behn, he said, had come to Hungary in 1938, when it was already under Nazi influence; a dinner was given for him, at which he said that production should be doubled. Then the judge began asking him about ITT in wartime : but here, for the first time, Geiger seemed reluctant to answer the promptings :

JUDGE: Did the Americans have any indirect contact with the factory during the war against the Fascists?
GEIGER: They had contact.
JUDGE: How?
GEIGER: They sent here the representatives who previously worked at the Berlin Standard subsidiaries and it was the representative of the former Berlin Stan-

	dard factory who controlled and directed the Budapest factories.
JUDGE:	Was this person in touch in any way with the Americans during the war as well?
GEIGER:	According to my knowledge, yes.
JUDGE:	Where?
GEIGER:	Abroad.
JUDGE:	Where?
GEIGER:	In Germany, and then . . .
JUDGE:	Americans could not very well get there.
GEIGER:	They couldn't after the Americans had entered the war.
JUDGE:	But there is data here showing that they were in touch even then. Did you not know that they met Colonel Behn in Switzerland on several occasions?
GEIGER:	After America entered the war.
JUDGE:	And even then instructions did not change to develop the output of this factory?
GEIGER:	This lasted to the very end, to the end of the war.

The trial lasted for four days. The accused again admitted their guilt, and thanked the court. The defence counsel pleaded for leniency; the accused, one of them said, were 'only marionettes in the hands of the monopoly capitalists; the banker-colonels, railway-king generals, and cigar-trust magnates . . . these intricate connections are characteristic of the United States of America'. But Vogeler was sentenced to fifteen years, Sanders to thirteen years. Two other accused, a priest and an accountant, were given ten years; Edina Dory, five years. Geiger and Rado were sentenced to death, and were executed soon afterwards.

As for the ITT company, it was expropriated soon after the first arrests, without compensation; the uncovering of the plot had given the Communists the excuse that they needed. The name Standard was eradicated, and it was renamed BELOYANNIS after a Greek Communist guerilla leader.

Vogeler only served a year of his sentence. The State Department took reprisals, closing Hungarian consulates and restricting visas, and Vogeler's pretty wife Lucile campaigned ingeniously on his behalf, befriending Russian agents to discuss terms, and then bearding Dean Acheson himself, then Secretary of State, in London. ITT pressed the State Department to bargain with the Communists, and eventually in April 1951 Vogeler was released, in return for reopening the consulates and relaxing travel restrictions: ITT may also have agreed to supply the Communists with some licences and blueprints.

At first, Vogeler said there was 'some truth' in his confessions, but later he wrote a book describing how they were made under duress, and giving his full version of the story. Neither he, nor anyone else, he said, had been a spy : his instructions from Colonel Behn were simply to do what he could to prevent confiscation of the ITT properties. The Hungarians were trying to force the company into bankruptcy—the technique known as 'creeping expropriation'; and Behn, when he came to Hungary in 1948, was desperately trying to reach an agreement that ITT would provide licences and blueprints for the Communists, in return for prompt payments and reasonable profits. The negotiations were suspect by the State Department, and by the American commercial attaché in Budapest, Jule Smith, who reckoned that ITT could only forestall expropriation by giving the Communists technical information which they ought not to have. Vogeler insisted that the officers of ITT were loyal American citizens; if they did not come to terms with the Communists someone else (like Philips from Holland) would. By July 1948 Behn had actually reached a draft agreement with the Communists, which would give them new technical information including navigational aids for airports; but while they were waiting for approval by the State Department, the atmosphere became increasingly dangerous. Vogeler was refused a visa to return to Hungary —an ominous sign—and Sanders warned him that the bubble was about to burst. But Colonel Behn was impatient and cabled : 'I AM SURPRISED AT DELAY AND URGE YOU ARRANGE TO GO TO BUDAPEST AS SOON AS POSSIBLE.' So Vogeler went back to Budapest, only to discover that the State Department had refused to approve the agreement, and that the Communists had signed up with Philips. They now had no further use for ITT, and the police closed in: Vogeler tried to escape in the ITT car, and was arrested at the frontier.

Vogeler denied that he was an agent; all he did was to

help some Hungarian friends to escape, to pass some information to American intelligence, and to keep in touch with his friend Fish Karpe, a daring American agent who was later pushed out of the Arlberg Express. It is hard to believe that Vogeler was engaged in very serious espionage, for he and his wife were both rash and outspoken. With his virulent anti-Communism, he was more calculated to infuriate the Hungarians than to deceive them : after his release, he became increasingly embarrassing to ITT too, and ended up by suing them for $500,000. Sanders, on the other hand, was a more serious character, who had certainly earlier worked for British intelligence : he was not released until two years later, and retired quietly to Southend.

What kind of dangerous game Colonel Behn was really playing remains obscure. The prospects of an agreement with the Communists after 1947 must have been very slender; but (as Vogeler explains) Behn was hoping that Hungary might be detached from the Soviets, as the Yugoslavs had been; and he may have thought that by maintaining an ITT presence he would have a better chance of eventual compensation.[1] Behn was as usual making his own intricate foreign policy, maintaining an ambiguous attitude to the Russians in his attempt to make a bargain, and incurring the distrust of the State Department. He was running his own intelligence service, rather than working for anyone else's; but it would be surprising if he were not keeping in touch with American intelligence. What is clear is that he was relentless in pursuit of his own business interests, risking the lives of his staff, and sending two men to their death, at a time when the danger was clear, and providing the Communists with a useful pretext. The ruthless Budapest adventure has some resemblance to the Chile caper, twenty years later.

THE OLD BOY NET

While ITT were thus busily engaged on the frontier of the cold war, they were also very active in America and

1. Twenty-four years later, in March 1973, the Hungarians agreed to pay $19 million for nationalised American property, of which a large share will go to ITT.

56

Western Europe, in building up transatlantic communications; and four years after the Hungarian trial they were specially concerned with an ambitious project to lay a new submarine cable. It was a much more straightforwardly commercial venture than the Budapest business; but it was put forward in the name of NATO and the Atlantic alliance; and the details of this transaction, which emerged in a very accidental way, revealed a careful confusion between ITT's interest and the British or American interest. The detailed documentation that has become available gives a vivid picture of ITT's lobbying tactics.

The company's special emissary for the project was an intrepid admiral, Ellery Stone, who had been an important figure in ITT before the war; in 1933 he had welcomed the Italian aviator, Italo Balbo, in New York, on behalf of ITT. During the war Stone had risen to be Rear-Admiral, and Chief Commissioner of the Allied Control Commission in Italy, while keeping close links with ITT (his aide was one of Behn's sons): he always seemed, as one colleague recollected, more like a businessman than an admiral. In Italy he worked closely with many top Englishmen, and he emerged from the war covered with honours, Knight Commander of the British Empire, Grand Officer of the Crown of Italy, with a Legion d'Honneur and the Order of Leopold II. He stayed in Italy after the war at Allied Forces Headquarters, and married a young Italian countess, his third wife. Then he went back to ITT, as president of its subsidiary Commercial Cables, and became specially active in Europe, rushing around contacting his old friends, name-dropping everywhere, entertaining in the Savoy or in his special suite at the Hotel Metropole in Brussels, and (as one ITT official complained to me) 'treating every office as his quarterdeck'.

In 1954 the admiral was made responsible for trying to arrange 'landing rights' for a transatlantic cable which ITT wanted to lay from the United States via Canada and Greenland to Britain, which was code-named 'Deep Freeze'; eleven per cent of the cable capacity was to be leased by the U.S. air force and for this reason the American government contracted to help ITT in acquiring landing rights abroad. Eventually the project was abandoned, and ITT—with astonishing nerve—sued the U.S. government for $800,000 for breach of contract, for not helping them enough.[1] ITT eventually lost the case, as late as 1968; but in the course of the argument the Justice Department acquired a pile of Admiral Stone's correspondence, and other ITT documents (classified as the J261 documents) which thus became public —giving the evidence for this remarkable story.[2]

The admiral's chief job was to persuade the British government to allow the landing rights, even though the cable would be in direct competition with the British nationalised company, Cable and Wireless, and the British were already committed to another new cable. Nevertheless, he set about his lobbying with remarkable persistence, exploiting his wartime friendships to the limit. Before moving into action he wrote from New York to Sir Thomas Spencer (then chairman of Standard Telephones and Cables, ITT's London subsidiary) a characteristic name-dropping letter:

> I know Sir Roger Makins,[3] your Ambassador here, very well, and also Sir Harold Caccia [4] who is now in the Foreign Office. Caccia was my British political adviser in Italy for one year. Also Harold Macmillan, who is being mentioned over here as successor to Mr. Eden if and when Sir Winston retires. I served with General John Harding in Italy when we were both under Alex,[5] and Admiral McGrigor, First Sea Lord, served under me in Italy, so I am hoping at least to be received by these gentlemen should we run into serious trouble.

When Macmillan became defence minister four months later, the admiral saw his opening; he sent a letter of congratulation, and Macmillan's secretary replied that the Minister would like to see him. So the admiral called on Macmillan on November 3, 1954 and explained Deep

1. See U.S. Court of Claims: Commercial Cable v the U.S., April 1968, p. 3.
2. Some of the documents are reproduced in *America Inc.*, by Morton Mintz and Jerry Cohen: London, Pitman, 1972, p. 330–337. I have added further extracts from the J261 documents.
3. Later Lord Sherfield.
4. Later Lord Caccia, now chairman of ITT in Britain.
5. Field-Marshal Lord Alexander.

Freeze to him for twenty minutes. Then (as Stone reported to ITT in New York) :

> half way thru our meeting he dictated memo to permanent secretary of his ministry, advising him of his relationship with me during the war, my present position, the cost and route of Deep Freeze and the JCS [Joint Chiefs of Staff] support saying that he understood our application had been pending for some time . . . I asked for an opportunity to be heard at highest level if there should be possibility of a negative or restrictive decision; I really feel much good was accomplished becos of Macmillan's strong position in Government.

At the same time the Admiral, amazingly enough, had obtained the apparent support of another war veteran who had served in Italy, Major-General Sir Leslie Nicholls, who was none other than the chairman of Cable and Wireless. Two days after he had seen Macmillan, the admiral wrote to New York :

> I am writing—not cabling—this because I'm always afraid of getting Gen. Nick into trouble—he is so very frank with me and tells me much more than I'm sure he should. I called him this a.m. to see if he had received the new P.O. paper. He had and said—'They're still "agin" you. But I've got my staff shooting holes in it and of course I'll go back at them again.' . . . The big guns in our favour will have to come from Defence and Treasury. The latter own and receive dividends from C&W and are the ones who will appreciate our $17,000,000 expenditure and the saving of expense on the proposed NATO–UK–Iceland cable . . .

Nicholls and Macmillan remained useful contacts; five months later, in April 1955, Stone reported to the president of ITT, General Harrison, that he had seen Macmillan again and referred to his 'extreme friendliness and helpfulness'. He added that 'the military person [General Nicholls], did a fine job in briefing Mr. Macmillan in our favour two days before I saw him yesterday'.

In the meantime ITT in New York were applying pressure on Washington and Ottawa. For dealing with Canada ITT deployed their high-powered lawyer in Ottawa, Gordon Maclaren, who knew several members of the Canadian cabinet personally, including Lester Pearson, then Foreign

Minister. One of the items in the bill from Maclaren's law firm (which later came into the hands of the Department of Justice) mentioned : 'Telephone call from L. B. Pearson and will he try to stir things up and let us in on the great difficulty they have run into and bring us into the picture if possible (Confidential).' The day after that call, the ITT man in Canada dealing with Deep Freeze had a very confidential call from Pearson (whose contents were quickly passed to Stone), giving news of a message from the Canadian High Commission in London, saying that Britain was opposing Canada's application and that 'it might be desirable for Canada to hold off making an immediate decision pending further exchanges between the two governments'.

At the same time ITT were using the American government in Washington to press the British—by pretending that the cable was primarily a defence project, not a commercial one. Forest Henderson of ITT in New York cabled Stone in London on September 14, 1954 :

FEEL WOULD BE ABLE TO GET ASSISTANCE FROM JOINT CHIEFS IN WASHINGTON BY HAVING THEM CALL ATTENTION TO DEFENCE OFFICIALS UK OF THE URGENT NEED HERE FOR SPEED FOR MILITARY REASONS TO COMPLETE CABLE ON TARGET DATES WITHOUT BRINGING INTO PICTURE ANY OF COMMERCIAL ASPECTS.

The next month Henderson told Admiral Stone : 'We feel that it is high time for our State Department to step into this picture with a strong message to the FMs [Foreign Ministers] of all countries involved requesting immediate attention to our project and favourable action on same,' and he told Stone that he would go to Washington to work on it, making use of information that ITT had received from Lester Pearson, but not divulging it.

The following May, there was a meeting in Paris of the NATO foreign ministers including Dulles and Macmillan, who had been recently promoted from Defence Minister, and Admiral Stone now had the chance to take up Deep Freeze at the very top level. He asked to see Dulles' assistant, Livingston Merchant, about Deep Freeze saying, 'It is my hope that Mr. Dulles will find opportunity to mention the matter to Mr. Macmillan as I have twice discussed it informally with him as Defence Minister, having known and served with him during World War II.' Stone then reported a 'satisfactory' meeting with Merchant, who promised to urge Dulles to talk to Macmillan, and also to take up the question with Sir Harold Caccia, who was now Macmillan's deputy and whom (as the admiral hastened to remind ITT in New York) ITT had recently been able to help 'on a personal matter'.

Dulles duly obliged. The same evening Douglas Dillon, the Under Secretary of State who was also in Paris, sent a cable to Washington which gives some insight into the government-business relationship :

ADMIRAL STONE SAW MERCHANT MORNING MAY 12 LEAVING MEMO WITH ATTACHMENTS BEING POUCHED DEPARTMENT. URGENT SECRETARY [Dulles] MENTION PROBLEM TO MACMILLAN WHICH SECRETARY DID LATER IN MORNING. SECRETARY TOLD MACMILLAN HE PROBABLY RECALLED FROM DEFENCE MINISTRY DAYS MATTER COAXIAL CABLE AND MILITARY IMPORTANCE ATTACHED TO IT. HE SAID WE WERE STILL AWAITING REPLY MID-MARCH NOTE TO UK AND ASKED HIM TO GIVE MATTER PUSH ON RETURN TO LONDON. MACMILLAN AGREED TO DO SO. IN SUBSEQUENT FOLLOW-UP WITH CACCIA BY MERCHANT FORMER STATED ORIGINAL POSITION BASED ON CABINET DECISION AND CONSEQUENTLY NO FURTHER OR MODIFIED ANSWER COULD BE EXPECTED BEFORE BRITISH ELECTIONS. LEAVE DISCRETION EMBASSY LONDON HOW MUCH FOREGOING TO COMMUNICATE TO ADMIRAL STONE WHO BELIEVED ENTITLED TO AT LEAST MINIMAL REPORT. DILLON.

The Admiral's bombardments continued. The next month Sosthenes Behn himself—now aged seventy-two—arrived in London, and Stone arranged a interview for the Colonel with the American Ambassador : 'Because of friendship with the Ambassador and extensive acquaintance with many prominent personages in London, he would like to see if there is aything he can do to break the "log jam".' Not even the Colonel could break the jam. As early as 1956 Stone was still hopeful, after a talk on February 28 with the Postmaster-General, Dr. Charles Hill. But there was still heavy resistance from London and Ottawa, and eventually the project was abandoned.

Though they did not suceed, the Deep Freeze papers show how skilfully ITT could manoeuvre between the Western governments. It was only by chance that these papers came to light : how many other interventions occurred will never be known. The project was all along primarily a moneymaking one, competing directly with the British company, with only a secondary defence interest : yet ITT could apparently persuade officials and ministers on both sides of the Atlantic to help them and pass them secret information, while keeping their own operations secret from the governments. They could co-ordinate their pressure on Ottawa, Washington and London through their own high-speed intelligence service.

These two diplomatic adventures, at the opposite ends of Western Europe, throw some light on the nebulous character of ITT. The operations in Budapest and in London were of course of quite different kinds; but both suggest that the company's own diplomatic and intelligent service were more effective, and also more ruthless than those of the Western nations it dealt with. It could be argued that this was just as well; that a multinational industry should have a more global perspective than national bureaucrats. But Colonel Behn's record hardly supports this. He depended on governments, while he defied them; he was able to appear as one moment the guardian of national security, the next as the true buccaneer. And in spite of his wartime record, the pirate ship which he had launched was still riding high, and the navies could not catch up with it.

How continuous are the characters of corporations? Certainly ITT was to experience great convulsions and transformations in the years to come, with new industries, a very new kind of president, and a new geographical spread. But in two central respects it still resembles Behn's invention. Firstly, is is still constructed round a single dominating head. No-one on the board or in management, then or now, has been strong enough to stand up to the mistakes of the president. The great mass of managers are—as one current director put it to me—'like second-lieutenants, action-oriented, waiting to be told what to do'.

Secondly, ITT still regards itself as above governments, above controls, and above morals. It presents itself still as an American company in America, British in Britain, German in Germany; but it owes loyalty to none of them, and regards each government as an unnecessary obstruction. It

would be absurd, I believe, to compare ITT's recent mis-
deeds with its wartime performance. But throughout its
five decades, it has acted in a way which raises doubts both
about its character and its constitution.

4

The Geneen Machine

It was not until 1956 that Colonel Behn finally left ITT, thirty-six years after he had founded it. In April General Harrison died in harness, and the next month Behn retired at the age of seventy-four: he died the following year. Between them, they bequeathed a vacuum, and the board were bewildered as to who should fill it. They appointed a caretaker president, another general called Edmund Leavey, a West Pointer who looked grave and dignified, but had little idea what to do with ITT. In the meantime, the board elected a sub-committee of three directors, led by a gentlemanly banker from Kuhn Loeb, Hugh Knowlton, to find someone to pull the company together. They put out feelers through consultants, or 'bodysnatchers', and eventually heard of a restless executive in Boston, with a legendary reputation for making profits.

Harold Sydney Geneen was at that time executive vice-president of Raytheon, the giant electronics company, working under the aristocratic president, Charles Francis Adams, of the proud Adams family. It was clear that Adams had no intention of leaving the presidency, and Geneen, at the age of fifty, was impatient for power. The ITT directors asked Geneen to lunch. He put on a dazzling performance, showing total mastery of the facts and figures; and he made it clear (as Knowlton recollects) that if he came to ITT he would run a tight ship. The sub-committee quickly recommended him to the board, and in 1959 Harold Geneen became president of ITT.

The directors had knowingly made a bold choice, but they did not realise the full potency of the genie that they had let out of the bottle. The phenomenon of Geneen was already well-known to experts on management and investment; when he left Raytheon, the shares dropped by 6½ points. But he had never yet been his own boss; and even to those who knew about him, he was an inscrutable man. There was even a good deal of doubt as to how to spell or pronounce his name, and still today the public relations men complain that it is apt to appear in the press as Geheen or Green. There is an ITT joke which goes: 'is the G hard as in God, or soft as in Jesus?' (It is soft, as in Genie.)

The new president of ITT had little obviously in common with Sosthenes Behn: no commanding presence, no high living, no cosmopolitan panache, no anecdotes about his exploits. He looked, as he was, a master-accountant. But Geneen liked, from time to time, to compare himself to Behn ('He was a man of his time; I am a man of my time') and there were resemblances. In the first place, Geneen like Behn had come from outside any traditional hierarchy or power-structure; he was a loner who seemed to have come from nowhere; he, too, was an appropriate head of a multinational corporation. And he was, like Behn, a despot.

Geneen's life has always been nomadic, and his tracks are still difficult to trace. He was born, surprisingly enough, in Bournemouth, the conservative seaside resort on the south coast of England, where his Russian father was a concert manager. His father and uncle had come over to England from Russia in the eighteen-eighties, and there are still Geneens in England, some of them in the antique trade in Bournemouth and Southampton. But the connections are not close; one first cousin only heard about his rich relation a few years ago. Geneen's father married Aida da Cruciana who, in spite of her name, was regarded as very English, and who remained very close to her son until she died. Geneen retains an undoubted affection for Britain: he feels safe in London, and can walk in the street without worrying about kidnapping. Above all, he associates London with his mother. There is a teak bench in the Mount Street gardens opposite the Connaught Hotel, where many Americans are commemorated, which has the inscription: IN MEMORY OF AIDA GENEEN, WHO LOVED THE GARDENS OF HER NATIVE ENGLAND, FROM HER SON HAROLD S. GENEEN.

But Geneen left England at the age of one, when his parents took him to America. Soon afterwards they separated, and young Harold was left with his mother. She sent him to a boarding school at Suffield, Connecticut, where he spent nine years of his life, from the age of seven to sixteen. In a reminiscence forty years later he described how :

> I spent the entire time either boarding at the school or again at camps, except for the occasional holiday vacations, when I got home. Even a number of the lesser ones of these, i.e. Thanksgiving or Easter, being short, and for family reasons, I spent at school. So far more than most people, I have reason to remember and appreciate what I got out of this school . . .

It was an old Baptist foundation, with a hundred students from very different backgrounds. He was clearly a lonely child. But he looks back on Suffield nostalgically as the school which turned him into an American, where he unconsciously absorbed the 'values and principles that were still fundamental, and pretty close to those which have made the country . . .'

He left school at the age of sixteen, instead of going on to day college as he had planned; and from then onwards his ambition and much of his emotion were channelled into accountancy. He got a job as a page at the New York Stock Exchange, where he worked during the Great Crash—a searing experience—and soon began evening classes at New York University. He soon realised his special aptitude with figures, and he had the imagination so rare in accountants to see beyond the figures—to visualise how business could be run. He joined the accountancy firm of Lybrand Ross and Montgomery (now Lybrand Cooper) in New York. His colleagues were struck by his enthusiasm, and bubbling ideas.

Geneen wanted to get inside the big companies and after eight years with Lybrand Ross he moved into a succession of jobs in industry. But though he could work wonders, he felt himself up against constant frustrations. At Bell and Howell, the electronics company in Chicago, he would work till midnight, setting up a strict system of financial control, but he felt he got very little recognition. He moved to Jones and Laughlin, the Pittsburg steel company, but Geneen felt that his boss, Charles Austin, was destroying his self-confidence; and when Austin became president, Geneen left.

In 1956 he saw his opportunity in Raytheon. The company was not doing well—it was before the electronics boom that followed the Sputnik—and the senior jobs were held by engineers who were not profit-minded. The president, Adams, hired Geneen as executive vice-president. Geneen was now forty-seven, and it was his first real break. He moved in with abrasive energy; he stirred up the senior executives, brought in his own men, acquired new companies, set up a control system. He gave a pep-talk to the engineers, and told them : 'This is a commercial company, and our epitaph is written in dollars per share returned to stockholders.' In three years, he increased the earnings per share from $2 to $3.50. He had become known as a master-manager. But he was still not the boss : 'I was driving at high speed,' he said later, 'when every so often, without warning, somebody else would try to put their hand on the wheel.'[1]

He had become very conscious of his power to move and motivate other people, with carrots and sticks. But he had developed along that channel only; and accounts were his life. He had married twice, the second time to his ex-secretary at Bell and Howell, who is his present wife : but he had no children, and his life was his company. In his rapid progress from Suffield to Manhattan to Chicago to Pittsburg to Boston and back to New York, he never seemed settled : his restless ambition seemed part of his search for identity.

Moving into the Gothic ITT skyscraper, Geneen took quick and drastic action. The company was making good profits, it was true, since the recovery of Europe—a fact which was rather hushed-up by subsequent public relations. But Geneen was appalled by the lack of management and discipline; ITT was really no more than a holding company, investing in factories thousands of miles away, and hoping for the best. 'Management must manage,' he told a meeting of security analysts soon after he arrived, by which he meant, as he explained later, 'a philosophy of aggressive *anticipation* of goals and problems and of effective advanced counter-

1. *Forbes Magazine*, May 1, 1968.

actions to insure our attainment of final objectives'.[1] Or, to put it another way, in the phrase which re-echoed through the company : 'I want no surprises.' Geneen determined to build up, on a much larger scale than he had done at Raytheon, a system of control and surveillance which would ensure that he could oversee his scattered empire, and rule it through logic, not hunch. There would be none of Behn's inspired gambles, his eccentrically personal style.

By 1961 the headquarters of ITT had appropriately moved out of Behn's pinnacled palace into a shapeless grey skyscraper in Park Avenue, with no mosaics, no Louis XIV furniture, no French chef; only floor upon floor of managers' offices. From his office on the twelfth floor, Geneen gradually set up the most intricate and rigorous system of financial control that the world has ever seen. Weekly meetings, monthly meetings, annual meetings, were summoned to keep check on the managers; a special room with a great horse-shoe table was constructed, where Geneen could inspect and question the managers and their accounts. The head of each company was required to submit to headquarters a monthly report of such complexity that it required a special department to compile it; five-year plans were prepared, targets set, profits compared. Each detail was analysed and cross-checked, so that Geneen, poring over his books in Park Avenue, could tell exactly which of his products, in any part of the world, was failing to reach expectations. He made it clear that he had to know about everything, to be warned of any likely disaster. He insisted that, 'You can't hide mistakes—even from yourself.' And to all his managers he repeated his ominous warning : 'I don't want any surprises.'

Above all, Geneen did not want surprises outside America, where eighty-two percent of ITT's business still lay. Soon after he became president, Fidel Castro nationalised the telephone company in Cuba, which ITT had owned since Colonel Behn bought it in one of his earliest ventures. It was a traumatic shock for Geneen, confirming his worst fears about foreigners. Geneen surveyed the international scene with considerable distrust, though he was confident,

1. Annual Report, 1967; commenting on Geneen's speech to New York security analyists, March 1960.

at least on the surface, that ITT could weather every storm. In a somewhat tactless report to the stockholders in 1962, he boasted that ITT :

> has in its time met and surmounted every device employed by governments to encourage their own industries and hamper those of foreigners, including taxes, tariffs, quotas, currency restrictions, subsidies, barter arrangement, guarantees, moratoriums, devaluations—yes, and nationalisations.

But he was determined that ITT must redress the balance between its investments outside and inside America—as Behn had already tried and failed to do.

By 1963, having transformed the management, he was ready, and in March he prepared an internal document for the board, headed ACQUISITION PHILOSOPHY [1] which outlined the proposed transformation of ITT. The memorandum gives a vivid picture of Geneen's pessimistic view of the world at that time. 'For the first time in four decades,' he said, 'the tides of U.S. prestige are admittedly running lower than ever before throughout Europe in particular . . . in back of this is the further possibility of changing European recognition of the Russian situation.' Europe seemed to him thoroughly unstable. In France there was strong anti-American sentiment. In England 'the new labor movement [sic] has set for its goal a nationalistic policy and to a degree an anti-U.S. policy. Last week a socialist document called for the nationalisation of certain companies including our STC company.' In Belgium, 'the general thought will be much like France.' In Italy, 'we have seen a continuous wave for some six months now of ill-founded strikes which if not aided by Government have been at least allowed to continue.' The Italian Government was 'committed to a semi-Leftist approach'. Only the German government seemed friendly.

Furthermore, Geneen warned, two-thirds of ITT's income in Europe came from the PTT departments (postal telegraph and telephone) which were becoming better organised under the Common Market : 'More and more, the PTT ministers are comparing notes, cost quotations and pricing . . . the Common Market pronouncements, if and when followed,

1. *Conglomerate Hearings* : Vol. 3, p. 258 ff.

would call for complete compulsory international bidding for all PTT supplies without reference to source country of manufacture.'

Geneen reckoned, therefore, that ITT's foreign earnings would 'be subject to increasing pressures pricewise, source-wise and ownershipwise', and recommended an immediate policy of acquiring American companies. In five years time, he proposed, ITT should have fifty-five percent of its earnings coming from America, instead of eighteen percent. They would have to buy large companies as well as small ones, in any field where there were prospects of high growth, including chemicals, pharmaceuticals, insurance and food. Two years later, when acquisitions were already under way, Geneen enlarged further on his aims.[1] He stressed that service industries would be specially suitable for ITT management, as would industries where know-how can be transferred from America to Europe. He foresaw that ITT could become the forerunner of a new generation of multinationals, combining global activities with rigid controls.

> In the past five years we in the company have seen the development of a demonstrated and proven approach THAT WORKS to the complex problem of managing a fully world-wide organisation of the type of ITT. . . . We have done it by necessity some several years ealier than will be later experienced by many expanded U.S. companies who will operate around the globe as true international companies.

Geneen's plans were approved by the directors, and ITT thus embarked on its expansion and diversification. But it is interesting at this point to note how wrong were the European predictions and judgments on which Geneen's policy was based. It is true that Europe looked rather more menacing at that time than it proved to be; but the picture of semi-Leftist Italy, of pro-Russian sentiment, or of Belgium being like France, was not well-informed, and as it turned out the ITT companies in Europe were to continue to be the most profitable part of ITT's business. From the point of view of the shareholders, ITT would have been as profitable —if not more so—if Geneen had never embarked on his acquisitions. The question arises : was Geneen's acquisition

1. *Conglomerate Hearings*: Vol. 4, p. 266.

programme really motivated by a distrust of Europe, or was it motivated primarily by Geneen's simple desire for aggrandisement?

Whatever his motives, Geneen's new policy was to have great significance, not only for ITT but for the whole pattern of industrial development. For in swallowing a succession of companies, and imposing his ingenious system of control, he helped to create a new kind of industrial animal, a conglomerate which was also multinational; a company that could make anything anywhere. The examples that follow show some of the strains and conflicts of this process. But while other financiers had similar ambitions, the Geneen machine was unusually powerful. He was able, through a subtle system of centralisation, to present ITT, as it suited him, either as one big company, or as hundreds of small ones. The huge range of industries made ITT much harder to tie down than the more monolithic and visible industries of General Motors or Du Pont. ITT, like Geneen himself, seemed both everywhere and nowhere. It was almost as if Colonel Behn's elusiveness in world politics had transferred itself to Geneen's American operations. Was it Geneen who transformed ITT, or ITT who transformed Geneen?

LAZARDS

MR. CELLER: If there were no Lazard Frères, would there be less mergers?

MR. ROHATYN: I think there would have been a few less, Mr. Chairman.[1]

Geneen's acquisition programme was a colossal undertaking; for ITT was already a very big corporation, and he was proposing to more than double its size in five years. For his grand design he needed the expert help of an investment bank, to help find him companies, woo them, and marry them (the language of mergers is always strongly sexual, as if it were a substitute excitement; companies are always romancing or raping each other, getting into bed, perhaps three-in-a-bed). Geneen already had the venerable advice of Kuhn Loeb, the Wall Street firm which had helped to appoint him. But Geneen needed also a more aggressive ally, a master of mergers; and he found it in Lazards. For the

1. *Conglomerate Hearings:* Vol. 3, p. 236.

next decade ITT's fortunes and Lazards were to be interlocked.

Lazards has a long cosmopolitan history, going back to
New Orleans in 1848, where it was founded by two French-
Jewish brothers. There are important Lazards in London
and Paris; in London it is controlled by Lord Cowdray, one
of the richest men in Britain, and run by a former chairman
of the Tory party, Lord Poole : in Paris it is run by Pierre
David-Weill, of the old French banking family. Before the
last war, Lazards in New York was little more than a branch
office for the London and Paris banks; but in the last thirty
years all three banks have been quietly dominated by the
shrewd and masterful head of the New York office, André
Meyer.

Meyer, now seventy-four, is the most influential private
banker in America and a man of indomitable will-power.
He lives at the Carlyle hotel, never goes to parties, preserves
a deep detachment. After thirty years in America, he still
seems very French, with a strong French accent. He once
worked in Indo-China, and prefers the North Vietnamese
to the South. His son teaches physics at the Sorbonne in
Paris. He works at the top of the Rockefeller Plaza, a wizened
brown nut of a man, with a pulled-in mouth which can
suddenly turn to a grin; he switches suddenly from apparent
passivity to bursts of energy, striding across the room or
picking up the telephone, gripping it like a gun, muttering
'yes' or 'no' and plonking it down. He rules by the telephone;
he gets up at five in the morning, and does his business with
Europe before reaching the office; bankers complain that if
they ring him up at 5.30 a.m. the number is likely to be engaged. He is rung up by august clients, like President Pompi-
dou, Mrs. Onassis, Gianni Agnelli, Senator Kennedy, or by
other bankers seeking advice. When there is a currency crisis,
he is followed to wherever he is. A friend describes how he
was talking to Meyer in a garden in Switzerland during a
crisis; a telephone suddenly appeared from the bushes, for
Meyer to seize.

Since Meyer first came to New York, he has made a fortune estimated at $200 million for himself, and he runs a
syndicate for a group of multi-millionaire families, including
the American Rockefellers in America, the Belgian Boels,

and the British Pearsons (Cowdrays) : 'Lazards isn't really a bank,' someone complained to me, 'it's a damn great money-making machine for a few very rich men.' But Meyer's money-making comes from his banking expertise, a combination of international connections, and mastery of detail. His speciality is mergers, from which much of the recent profits of Lazards have come : they received fees of $10.5 million for mergers and acquisitions between 1964 and 1968. Meyer arranged the merger between Fiat and Citroen, and between Douglas aircraft and McDonnell (for which Lazards' fee was a million dollars). In spite of these vast clients, Meyer's own organisation has remained compact and very personal : he seems almost offended by the giants that he has created. Part of the value of Lazards to industry lies in Meyer's ability to think large and small. Lazards' directors are on the boards of sixty American corporations, and Meyer's directorships include Allied Chemicals, Fiat, Montecatini, and RCA.

It was not surprising that Geneen should look to Lazards as allies in buying up companies. He approached Meyer, who agreed, but insisted that Kuhn Loeb should still share the underwriting (there is still a man from Kuhn Loeb on the ITT board—Alvin Friedman, a cautious banker of measured words who took over from Hugh Knowlton). Meyer thus became an important influence on Geneen : he was a much subtler, and more rounded man than his client. But another Lazards partner was much more directly involved with Geneen : a phenomenal financial brain called Felix Rohatyn. (There is endless confusion, as with Geneen, about how to pronounce it; the stress should be on the first syllable.) Rohatyn is in total contrast to Meyer, with none of the traditional bankers' smoothness and deep camouflage, and a stimulating openness of manner. He has crew-cut hair, a piercing expression, talks fast in a high voice, drives a small Toyota, wears an old raincoat, seems oblivious to surroundings. He is a Democrat, and helped Muskie with his campaign in 1972. He comes from right outside any establishment; he was born in Vienna, of Polish-Jewish parents, who brought him to America in the 'thirties, fleeing Hitler. He graduated in physics, and was then taken up by Meyer, who trained him and regarded him almost as a son.

Rohatyn had total mastery of figures, and enormous drive; like Meyer, he never gave up, and hates to lose. He negotiates, as one witness describes it, like a terrier with a rat. He, too, was to become an expert on mergers; he married Kinney to Warner Brothers. Loew's to Lorrilard.

Rohatyn's first assignment for Lazards was to arrange an acquisition for Geneen, just after Geneen had taken over; it was a small electronic company, called Jennings in California. It was the beginning of an important relationship for both of them. Geneen liked Rohatyn's tough intelligence and enthusiasm; Rohatyn was excited by the sense of challenge and adventure, and appreciated Geneen's friendship. Together, with Geneen's single-minded obsession with ITT, and Rohatyn's range, they made a winning team.

AVIS TRIES HARDER

The first big company that Lazards found for Geneen was Avis Rent-a-Car—a lively enterprise which showed most resistance to Geneen's discipline. It had been set up in 1956 by Warren Avis, and raced ahead with air travel, but its management could not keep up, and it was outbid by its giant rival Hertz: so that by 1962 it was making a loss of $648,000. Then Lazards bought it up: Meyer and Rohatyn realised the potential, and brought in a dynamic young showman from American Express, Robert Townsend, to run it, together with Bud Morrow from Avis and Donald Petrie from Hertz. The four young men revived the bankrupt company with shrewdness and flair: not least through the famous cheeky advertising campaign knocking Hertz (devised by Doyle Dane and Bernbach) proclaiming the slogan: 'We're number two. We try harder.' Townsend ran it with cheerful irreverence, wearing a red Avis coat in the office and projecting the notion that Business Is Fun. In three years, the Avis image was transformed, and so were its profits; by 1965 it was making $5 million; and Townsend and his colleagues had got rich through a generous incentive scheme, paying themselves small salaries and large share options.

Lazards, having rehabilitated Avis, wanted to sell it; and Geneen was looking round for fast-growing service industries. Geneen commissioned an exhaustive investigation into Avis, which showed an expected growth of twenty to twenty-five percent, and large scope for expansion. By July 1965 the deal was done; ITT bought Avis for $52 million.

But Townsend himself had no desire to become part of a conglomerate; as he later put it, 'I would like it on my tombstone, "Townsend never worked a single day for a company like ITT".' Those words specially infuriated Geneen; in fact Townsend stayed several months on the ITT payroll. But eventually he did leave, to enjoy himself as a business entertainer, explaining how he had transformed Avis, which was now feeling the dead hands of bureaucracy. Eventually he wrote a best-seller explaining it all, *Up the Organisation,* which antagonised Geneen still further. He described his unorthodox business methods, which were the opposite of the austere ITT discipline; he told how he had sacked all his public relations men, worked without a secretary, banned company newsletters, abolished reserved parking spaces. In a section about monthly reports he said : 'It's a joke because it consumes ten pounds of energy to produce each ounce of misunderstanding.' In the section called 'Mergers, Conglomerations and Joint Failures' he said :

> If you have a good company don't sell out to a con-glomerate. I was sold out once but resigned (see Disobedience and Its Necessity). Conglomerates will promise anything for your people (if your stock sells for a low multiple of earnings and has a faster earnings growth rate than theirs), but once in their fold your company goes through the homogeniser along with their other acquisitions of the week, and all the zeal and most of the good people leave. Two and two may seem to make five when a conglomerate is making its pitch, but from what I have seen they are just playing a numbers game and couldn't care less if they make zombies out of your people.

A lot of people did leave; one of them complained : 'It seemed we spent more time dealing with ITT than we did with the business of renting cars.'[1] Townsend was succeeded by Bud Morrow, a lawyer who had been with Avis for ten years, and who now had the task of fitting the company into

1. *Wall Street Journal,* January 12, 1970.

the hard shafts of the ITT harness. Morrow succeeded, much better than most, in retaining his company's special character, but his monthly letters to Geneen showed the strain; in his fourth letter, for October 1965, he grumbled about the annual business plan : 'This monster project is at least completed and will, I am sure, be of interest and value. I estimate now that the report represents almost a thirteenth month of work for the headquarters staff.' Luckily, as Morrow pointed out (letter No. 39) both Avis' competitors, Hertz and National, had also been taken over, and their managers were likewise engrossed in preparing business plans. 'This is reassuring,' he remarked with dour wit, 'because it tends to equalise the competitive situation in our industry.'

Morrow's letters, too, showed how Avis was trying to get other ITT companies to use their cars—a fact that was to be of special interest to the anti-trust investigators. Morrow now insists that the relationship with ITT, in this matter, was more a liability than an asset. But the letters show the ambition on both sides to make use of the captive market provided by the ITT umbrella.[1]

Townsend watched the bureaucratisation of Avis with unconcealed gloat: 'It didn't take long,' he remarked, 'for the crap to start creeping in.' Avis moved to plush new headquarters, hired a staff of PR men, and began to look like other bits of ITT. Morrow, indignantly disputes Townsend's account of life with Avis : 'You couldn't save a company, or run it, with his methods,' he said to me, 'Townie's not an administrator—he's not consistent enough. He's an artist. He didn't need a secretary, because he used other people's : my secretary typed his book for him. But I'm not ungrateful to Townie. Hell, he made me president.'

Under Morrow, Avis continued to romp ahead—helped by the decline of Hertz, with their own management problems. Morrow installed a master-computer called Wizard of Avis, for world-wide bookings, and expanded rapidly in Europe; the red-uniformed girls popped up in airports all over the continent. Morrow's monthly letters, reveal the difficulties of building up this European empire. In Italy, Avis found themselves confronting Fiat, 'on the wrong side of a monopoly'. In Spain, the telecommunications (though

1. *Conglomerate Report:* pp. 106–124.

made by ITT) were so hopeless that 'our next want ads may be for experienced semaphore signalmen'. In Germany, Hertz sued Avis for misleading advertising, and barred them from using the slogan *Wir Geben Uns Mehr Mühe* ('We try harder'). In France, drivers went shorter distances, only ninety kilometres a day, against the average of a hundred and twenty kilometres. In Britain, the speeding-up of railways damaged their airport business.

But in spite of its troubles Avis in Europe had grown by 1972 to be as big as the whole company when ITT took it over. They had 110,000 vehicles operating from 2,800 bases, from 1,300 airports in ninety-eight countries. It was a triumph of world-wide management, of the ITT virtues of discipline and control: at every airport, the red-coated girls filled in the same forms, and checked them through the same system of accounts. Morrow insisted that ITT had helped him: 'We took off in 1969,' he said to me, 'we wouldn't have gone as far or as fast with anyone else; they had the sophistication to invest in Europe without expecting quick profits.'

In net income Avis rose spectacularly, but in terms of the ratio of income to assets, the performance was much less good. It was later reckoned that between 1964 and 1968, after three years of ITT management, their ratio of income to assets had gone down from 4 per cent to 2.6 per cent.[1]

The acquisition of Avis helped to establish a very close relationship between ITT and Lazards, and particularly with Felix Rohatyn, who arranged the deal, and received (with his wife) shares worth $135,000 for his services. Two years later, he became a member of the ITT board, and possibly its most influential member after Geneen. Lazards were able to find companies for Geneen, to assess them and bargain toughly with them; and on their side, they profited too. Between 1966 and 1969, Lazards received fees from ITT amounting to $3.9 million, of which merger fees comprised $2.1 million.

VIRGIN MARKETS

After Avis, companies came to Geneen thick and fast, not

1. *Conglomerate Report:* p. 124.

only through Lazards, but also through a special new ITT acquisition department. The mid-'sixties were a boom time; there was a merger-mania sweeping through America, and Geneen was on the crest of the wave. The ITT shares were pushing up, encouraged by the expectations of Geneen's management, which made it easier to acquire companies, whose shareholders were paid—nearly always—in ITT stock. Geneen was prepared to buy anything, whatever it made, provided it was growing fast and profitably. He did not want to have contested bids, which would attract hostile publicity; and partly to avoid this, he was prepared to pay well above the market price for the shares.

In five years he built up an astonishing rag-bag of companies, whose only common factor was profits. Some were huge, some were tiny; they included Bramwell Business College, for $40,000 and the Nancy Taylor Secretarial Finishing School of Chicago, for $50,000. Geneen bought insurance companies, mutual funds, pump companies, lampmakers, and as the ITT empire grew, so the interests of the different provinces began to overlap, so that one could help another. In 1966 he bought APCOA, the car-parking company, through Lazards for $27.5, which fitted well with Avis, and the next year he bought Cleveland Motels, for $7.5, which provided somewhere for the cars to go; in 1968 he bought Transportation Displays, which rented advertising hoardings for car-drivers to look at. He bought a sizeable publishing company, Howard Sams, which with its subsidiary Bobbs–Merill brought ITT publishing text-books.

A special opportunity came in 1966, when William Levitt decided to give up his seventy-percent share in the house-building company which his father had founded, which had made 'Levittown' a catch-word for suburban conformity. Levitt approached Lazards; 'Mr. Levitt is apparently a rather mercurial individual,' wrote Rohatyn to Meyer, 'with a highly developed sense of his own importance and requiring a somewhat highly personalised approach.'[1] But Rohatyn was quickly convinced of the value of the company; as he put it in his analysis: 'It has a ready-made virgin market for a complete range of consumer goods and

1. *Conglomerate Hearings:* Vol. III, p. 774.

services. Levitt creates not only new homes but new households that represent continuing purchasing power. Any firm that affiliates with Levitt naturally obtains the best possible entry into this new market.' Levitt was just what ITT needed, to widen their base both in America and abroad.

Geneen was at first not convinced: 'I basically do not believe that this is a business ITT should get into,' he wrote in a curt memo to Hart Perry in March 1966,[1] but he was soon persuaded, and two months later he put the case to the board: 'with a company such as Levitt as part of the ITT system, we would be in a unique position to participate in development projects throughout the world of a highly politically desirable nature while also building a public image by providing one of the most basic service needs. . . .'[2] In a handwritten memo on September 15, Geneen wrote in his spidery hand: 'Twenty-five percent of people working in US directly or indirectly get employment from housing industry . . . L has built 175,000 homes. 350,000 people live there.[3]

There were delays over the Levitt deal, partly because of ITT's troubles in trying to buy the broadcasting company, ABC (see below). But Geneen wooed Bill Levitt with all the 'highly personalised approach' that he could muster, Rohatyn played tennis with him, and eventually the deal was clinched, for $92 million. Lazards' fee (from Levitt) was $250,000.

Levitt was quickly integrated into the ITT system, with the inevitable monthly letters and reports, and with ITT experts swarming over the whole company. A master-manager, Richard Wasserman, was put in charge of it, but Wasserman was an entrepreneur with his own flair, who saw the real-estate business as one which had to be run boldly, using hunches as well as calculations. He jibbed at the controls of the management meetings, and the iron rule of the accountants. Geneen, who respected him, tried to placate him, but failed, and Wasserman soon walked out, to join another conglomerate, Gulf and Western; so that

1. *Conglomerate Hearings:* Vol. III, p. 329.
2. Ibid., p. 331.
3. Ibid., p. 1353.

mercurial old Levitt had to be asked back temporarily to run his old company. The Wasserman episode illustrated an important ITT fact : there was only room for one entrepreneur.

1968 was a wonder-year. Two big mergers brought ITT much further into the field of raw materials, as a hedge against inflation. (Lazards' fees were $850,000 for the two.) Pennsylvania Glass Sand, bought for $112 million, was the biggest producer of silica and clay for glass and ceramics. Rayonier, bought for $293 million, made chemical cellulose, and owned over a million acres of forests in the United States and Canada. The Rayonier estates could also be a great benefit to the 'Land-Bank' of Levitt's—the large reserve of land which Levitt built up for future housing needs; for ITT could use Rayonier as a 'cover' for buying extra land at low prices, avoiding the high prices that would be asked by potential sellers as soon as the name Levitt was mentioned.[1] It was part of a recurring Geneen conjuring trick : one moment he would pretend his companies were quite separate, the next moment they would be cunningly connected.

Another big company which brought ITT into controversy was Continental Baking, which they acquired in 1968 for $279 million. It is the biggest bakery company in America—potato chips in Memphis, candy in Minneapolis, chemicals in Kansas. It has projected its food with far-fetched advertising, prepared by its agency, Ted Bates. Profile Bread claimed to contain fewer calories than ordinary bread, and Wonder Bread had the slogan : 'Helps build strong bodies twelve ways,' claiming to provide special nutrients : its TV commercials showed children growing by leaps and bounds after eating the precious bread. Early in 1971 Ralph Nader investigated these claims—in one of his many assaults on ITT—and protested to the Federal Trade Commission that they were false; as a result, in March 1971, the FTC complained, pointed out that Wonder Bread had the same nutrients as any other bread, and that Profile Bread only contained fewer calories in so far that it was more thinly sliced. ITT and Ted Bates capitulated over Profile Bread,

1. See Geneen's evidence in *Conglomerate Hearings*: Vol. III, p. 134.

and signed a 'consent order' agreeing to devote a quarter of their future advertising to remedy the position—a requirement which infuriated the advertising industry.

Geneen was making rapid progress. But he had one very serious setback, when he tried to acquire the third TV network, the American Broadcasting Companies (ABC). The prolonged battle to obtain ABC became a *cause célèbre*, which deserves special study. For it showed up sharply the ruthlessness and two-facedness of Geneen's methods. It set two government agencies against each other, in a ding-dong fight. And it raised the central issue of whether conglomerates should control media.

The ABC network was specially tempting for ITT, which had always been involved in communications, and had already invested in pay-TV and Cable TV. ABC had, since its beginning in 1941, accumulated 400 theatres in thirty-four states, seventeen local radio stations, and, most important, one of the three major TV networks in the world. It had interests in stations in twenty-five other countries (the 'Worldvision Group') and it distributed ABC films throughout the world. It had been profitable every year since 1953, and its share of the television network revenues had gone up from nine percent to twenty-seven percent. But its president, Leonard Goldenson, a tycoon in the Hollywood tradition, was much worried by the dangers of raiders, and decided it would be safer to merge with Geneen. Eventually at the end of 1965, Geneen offered $85 a share, amounting to $400 million for the whole company. Goldenson accepted, and the merger was approved by stockholders in April 1966. It would be the biggest merger in broadcasting history.

But ITT and ABC had to apply to the Federal Communications Commission (FCC) to transfer the licences, in terms of the Communications Act of 1936—the act which, ironically enough, had been framed with a wary eye on ITT's large foreign interests. (See chapter 2.) The FCC had a special responsibility to ensure the freedom of broadcasting; in fact the ABC company had come into being as a result of their insistence, in 1941, that there should be 'fuller use of the radio as a mechanism of free speech', which forced RCA to sell one of its two networks.

Goldenson and Geneen, supported by lawyers and economists, duly appeared before the seven-man commission in September 1966. Geneen explained eloquently the benefits and technology (including UHF broadcasting) that ITT could provide. He stressed that ABC's operations would 'be performed unaffected by commercial communications, or other similar interests of ITT' : ABC, he said, like other entities within the ITT family, would have its independence assured by 'the ITT management system of substantially autonomous subsidiaries'. He professed deep respect for the independence of journalists : 'The highest ingredient that a newsman has for sale is his professional integrity.' Goldenson explained how ABC urgently needed $140 million to pay for conversion to colour TV, and could not borrow more from the bank.

But Geneen's and Goldenson's accounts were soon flatly contradicted by the Department of Justice, who had also been studying the merger. In December Donald Turner of the anti-trust division reported to the FCC that ITT had estimated that ABC would yield a cash flow of a hundred million dollars in the next five years, 'almost all of which was thought by ITT to be available for reinvestment *outside* the television business'. Far from planning to pour in money to ABC, Geneen would be pulling it out.

The Commission was split about allowing the merger with four for it, and three against. The three-man minority was a formidable one, including the *enfant terrible* of the commission, Nicholas Johnson, the brilliant young lawyer from Iowa, author of *How to talk back to your TV set*. Johnson was inherently suspicious of conglomerates, and he had been urged on behind the scenes by Ralph Nader, who was trying to put backbone into the government agencies. Johnson, in his long dissenting report, complained that ITT's foreign interests conflicted with the free dissemination of news : 'A hint of the involvement of ITT officials in foreign affairs is conveyed by the fact that three of them are members of foreign legislative bodies, two of the British House of Lords and one of the French National Assembly.'

He insisted that ABC's competitive disadvantage was nothing to do with lack of funds or colour programmes, but due to having fewer affiliates. 'Of all the large American corporations,' he summed up, 'there are few whose particular business interests are so clearly of the type which should not be joined with major broadcasting facilities as are those of ITT.'

At this point, just when Geneen thought that the merger was in the bag, the Justice Department complained that the Commission had not fully investigated the issues, and asked them to conduct a full hearing. A battle raged between the two departments, while the shares of ABC and of ITT rushed up and down, according to the expectations. Geneen was exasperated by the delay, and ITT did what they could to swing opinion. With amazing heavy-handedness the public relations chief, Ned Gerrity (of whom we will see more) set about pressurising reporters—just at the time when the company was protesting their concern for newsmen's integrity. One of them, Eileen Shanahan of the *New York Times'* Washington office, a cheerful and much respected reporter, had a succession of encounters with ITT, which she later described in her testimony. An official rang her up to tell her about one ITT report, saying : 'I expect to see that in the paper, high up in the story.' Then Ned Gerrity himself appeared in her office, asking to look at the story she was writing : she refused, and he then badgered her to run the text of an FCC order, in a tone that was 'accusatory and nasty'. Did she not feel, he asked, a responsibility to the shareholders of ABC and ITT, whose shares would be influenced by what she wrote? Was she aware that Commissioner Johnson was advocating legislation to forbid newspapers from owning any broadcasting stations? (A story which turned out to be false.) Gerrity's pressure was followed up by Jack Horner, an ITT PR man in Washington, and long after the case was over, Eileen Shanahan discovered that Jack Horner had been questioning friends about her private life, to build up a dossier about her.

Eventually the Commission were compelled to hold further hearings, in April 1967, lasting sixteen days, making up 3,300 pages of text, with 550 exhibits. More damaging evidence emerged. It became apparent that ITT had no intention of putting money into ABC. It became clear, too, that ITT, far from allowing autonomy to its companies, was a highly centralised corporation, with strict controls over its subsidiaries—which was indeed the essence of Geneen's system. Geneen now quickly changed his tack, and promised that ABC's relationship with ITT would be 'completely unique', with its own board, including outside directors. Once again he was playing the conjuring trick—appearing centralised one moment, separate the next.

But the FCC again approved the merger, with the same three dissenting. The majority decided that there could not be 'any reasonable doubt that ABC would maintain its integrity and independence'; and that there was 'no evidence that ITT or ABC did any more than ask reporters covering the story to be factually accurate in their reporting'. The minority, led by Nicholas Johnson, produced an even longer dissenting report analysing the misrepresentations of ITT's position, and concluding : 'We dissent, more in sorrow than in anger, for it is the public interest in a strong, competitive and free broadcasting and common carrier service which is the real loser from this action.'

The battle was not lost, for the Department of Justice again intervened, this time in the Appeal Court, to challenge the Commission's judgment, in a historic case headed :

United States of America, appellant

v

Federal Communications Commission, appellee International Telephone and Telegraph Corporation and American Broadcasting Companies, Inc, Intervenors.

The Justice Department presented its argument in a hard-hitting brief, attacking both the FCC and ITT. They found that ABC was quite able to finance its own needs without a merger. They refused to believe that ABC could retain its autonomy, in the face of the 'pervasive, centralised control' of ITT : 'It will be inescapable to all directors and officials of ABC that Mr. Geneen and ITT represent the ultimate authority.' They considered that the interference with Eileen Shanahan and others 'can only be regarded as

84

attempts to impose the judgment of an independent news-medium'.

In the most interesting argument they insisted that the integrity of ABC news would be affected because of ITT's foreign interests which 'involve it in close and confidential relation with foreign governments'. They considered that ITT 'could have strong motivation to use a news medium affirmatively to promote certain of its foreign interests, by showing the officials or programs of a foreign government in a favourable light'; and as an indication of this they referred to the 'Deep Freeze' documents (see chapter 3) which had just come to light in ITT's claim for damages, and which had already been noted by Commissioner Johnson. The Justice Department referred to the help that had been given to Admiral Stone, and commented: 'One can imagine the embarrassment to ITT of an unfavourable program concerning the British Defense Minister and Canadian Foreign Minister, persons of newsworthy prominence, who were providing ITT with confidential information relating to approval of the transatlantic cable project.'

Finally the department complained that Geneen and others had, as they tactfully put it, 'not comported with the standard of candor and completeness required in this proceeding'. ITT had lacked candour about ABC's need for extra finance, about its other interests in broadcasting, and about the autonomy within ITT. In other words, ITT had been found out.

In the meantime, Geneen was becoming increasingly exasperated by the delays. The prospects of the merger, even if it did go through, now looked less rosy. Both ITT and Lazards had suffered over the succession of setbacks; Lazards, having been confident that the deal would go through, had speculated through arbitrage, and had lost heavily when ABC shares went down; as the hopes soared and fell over two and a half years, it was said that Wall Street had lost $50 million in arbitrage.[1]

Eventually Geneen held a special board meeting on New Year's Day 1968 — an unprecedented event — to call off the

1. See Felix Rohatyn's evidence: *Conglomerate Hearings:* Vol. III, p. 223.

bid, with unconcealed anger, announcing that the merger was no longer in the shareholders' interests. ABC continued as a separate entity, making record profits with none of the predicted disasters, and Geneen went on to further conquests. But his setback over ABC undoubtedly affected him. He had been frustrated, as he saw it, by the machinations of Washington, which he disliked and despised. From now on he would step up ITT's lobbying in Washington to ensure that ITT's expansion could continue unhindered by governments.

But the issues raised by the ABC case went beyond the doubts about Geneen's methods and ambitions. The deeper question, as presented by Commissioner Johnson and by the Justice Department, was whether any multinational company, however well-meaning, can be relied on to preserve the freedom of news, whose reporting might embarrass their overseas interests. Some of the arguments mounted against ITT might seem nationalistic, assuming as they did that foreign influences must necessarily damage the integrity of reporting. One might hope that in an ideal world news programmes could represent an internationalist outlook. Yet in present conditions, it seems to me, a multinational company will be more tempted to suppress news than to broaden it[1]; and like Behn in the 'thirties, over-zealously to play in with whichever foreign regime is in power. (One dreads to think what kind of picture of the world Colonel Behn would have wanted to portray, had he been given a television network in the 'thirties.) Any large multinational will have its own special interests to play up; and given control of communications, it will be in a position to help to create a foreign policy.

[1]. A small but significant example has occurred in Britain while I write this chapter: a book had been printed about Hastings Banda, President of Malawi, to be published by Penguins, which is now part of Longmans and linked with the *Financial Times*, Lazards etc. In December 1972 Penguins decided not to publish the book, on the grounds that Longman's office in Malawi would seriously suffer. If Penguins had not merged with the larger group, there would have been no such impediment.

For a multinational conglomerate, hotels were an obvious opportunity, and for some time Geneen had been thinking about them. He looked with envy at the phenomenal success of Hilton, whose revenues had gone up from $15 million to $140 million in ten years; and Holiday Inns, up from $2 million to $140 million.[1] But Holiday were much too expensive to bid for, and Hilton was soon swallowed up by TWA. In 1967, however, he saw a chance to buy the second biggest hotel chain, Sheraton, and he sent off a team of experts to examine them.

Sheraton was not obviously tempting; the hotels were rather run-down, many of them in dingy downtown areas. The company had grown up from seedy beginnings; two young Bostonians, Ernest Henderson and Robert Moore, who were room-mates at college, made some money in Germany after the First World War by buying up odd lots, including binoculars, ersatz suits and police dogs, at rock-bottom devalued prices. With their quick profits they bought a bankrupt hotel in Springfield, Massachusetts, as a cheap bit of real estate. They made some money out of it, and bought up more cheap hotels in the depression; one of them in Boston had its name Sheraton (after the cabinet-maker) in huge letters over the building. The partners reckoned it would cost more to remove the sign than the cost of the hotel, so instead they called the whole chain Sheraton.

They went on buying, including some stately old properties, like the Carlton in Washington, or the St. Regis in New York, but they were still more interested in real-estate than hotel management. In the early 'fifties the hotel business began booming, but after 1958 their profits declined, and Sheraton lagged behind Hilton in the more profitable business of building hotels abroad. By the mid-'sixties they had partially recovered, with the help of centralised management and a massive new $4 million computer, the Reservatron II, which could book Sheraton rooms all over the world.

Geneen's experts were conscious of the snags;[2] there was

1. *Conglomerate Hearings:* Vol. III, p. 352.
2. Ibid., p. 345.

no strong 'chain image', many hotels were in the wrong places, and the marketing was poor. But hotels were a growth industry, which could link up with other ITT industries and 'international development', they predicted 'should produce extraordinary results'. Hotels were less vulnerable than telephone companies to nationalisation, ITT could push up room charges further, and make further economies. Most important of all, Sheraton employed very conservative accounting, using their profits to build up assets, rather than to show high earnings.[1] ITT, by changing the accounting, could show a spectacular improvement.

Geneen set about romancing the company with his customary ardour. The president and co-founder, Ernest Henderson, was a paternalist who had felt emotionally involved in his hotels; he composed ballads, and liked Sheraton bands to strike up with them when he came in. But he was now losing interest; he was sixty-seven and had just married a girl of twenty-five. His son Ernest Henderson III had taken over as chief executive, but was not over-interested in management. The senior Sheraton managers were not very well paid, and Geneen, as was his habit, promised them much higher salaries if they agreed to join ITT. One, Richard Boonisar, went up from $56,000 to $105,000, with a $34,000 bonus.[2] Geneen offered a very high price for the chain — $200 million. By the middle of 1968, Sheraton, too, was swallowed up by ITT.

The ITT managers moved in quickly, to pluck profits. They made plans to sell off fifteen hotels in the South and mid-West, and to refurbish twenty-eight others. Young Henderson soon left, to devote himself to a group of convalescent centres called the Henderson Homes. In his place Geneen took on a tough hotelier from Colorado, Bud James, a keen sportsman who had taken a degree in hotel management at Denver University, and had risen to be president of the Sahara-Nevada hotel chain. James and Geneen put into action a five-year plan to triple the number of Sheratons, including motels and Convatels — expensive hotel-hospitals for elderly customers. They linked the existing hotels more closely together, with the help of the Reservatron, and con-

1. *Conglomerate Hearings:* Vol. III, p. 359.
2. Ibid., pp. 719–29.

nected them with the rest of the ITT system; there were ITT telephones in the rooms, and ITT telegraph-forms in the lobbies. On every soap-wrapping, every letter-head, every match-box, every paper napkin, were printed the words 'a world-wide service of ITT'.

Most important, the five-year plan would establish a net-work of Sheratons in thirty-eight countries, to challenge the empires of Hilton and Intercontinental. Sheratons sprouted up all over Europe—tall shining cliffs in the centres of cities, inside which the traveller could forget he was abroad, as detached and protected as a passenger on ship-board. There is no language problem, for all staff speak English; no currency problem, for everything is on credit-cards (Sheraton even has an interest in the Diners' Club); no transport problem, for Avis or Hertz are waiting in the lobby. Usually there is no need to go outside, with shops, airline offices and bookstalls all inside the hotel, and 'dial-a-movie' to show American films in the bedroom. There is really no need to go sightseeing, for Sheratons provide their own local wonders, like the Hans Andersen mermaid in the restaurant of the Copenhagen Sheraton. Sheraton provides its own version of geography, safe, clean and comfortable. Their slogan is 'Sheraton makes it happen'.

The building of the Sheraton empire, like the Avis empire, was a triumph of management—imposing the same smooth routine on so many obstinate and eccentric nationalities—as amazing in its way as the building of British gymkhana clubs through India and Africa. Persians, Swedes, Mexicans or Peruvians, were all trained to provide the same dis-passionate service, to work through computers, credit-cards and accounting machines, to say 'you're welcome' with the same impersonal courtesy.

Sheratons have not in fact been very profitable and nowa-days ITT prefer the franchise system—letting other people build the hotels, while they provide the management and the name. But Geneen has always shown a special interest in Sheratons—even to discussing how they should be adver-tised—and it is appropriate that they play a special part in the story that follows. These self-contained fortresses, rising up with their glass battlements above the old cities of the world, symbolise well enough the new phenomenon of the multinational company—operating in every country, yet separate from them all. They are filled, too, with the new multinational men, the nomadic managers, just arriving or just leaving, rushing with their briefcases and pale raincoats, through the grand lobbies, or waiting forlornly beside the suitcase which is their home.

5

The Moving Finger

> ITT's expansion into multinational, multiproduct operations
> through acquisitions has created a virtually self-contained cor-
> porate structure that exists and acts outside the scope of any
> of the countries in which it provides services.
>
> Conglomerate Report,
> June 1971, p. 95

On the last Monday of every month, a Boeing 707 takes off
from New York to Brussels, with sixty ITT executives
aboard, including Geneen or one of his deputies, with a
special office rigged up for him to work in. They stay in
Brussels for four days, inside their own company capsule,
spending most of their time in one of the marathon ITT
meetings.

A meeting is a weird spectacle, with more than a hint of
Dr. Strangelove. One hundred and twenty people are
assembled in the big fourth-floor room, equipped with cool
air-conditioning, soft lighting and discreet microphones. The
curtains are drawn against the daylight, and a big screen
displays table after table of statistics. Most of the room is
taken up with a huge horse-shoe table, covered in green
baize, with blue rocking armchairs and names in front of
each chair, with a bottle of mineral water and a book of
accounts. On the chairs sit the top men of ITT from all
over Europe, like diplomats at a conference : in the middle
are the senior vice-presidents. Among them, swivelling and
rocking to and fro in his armchair, surveying the faces and
gazing at the statistics, is an owlish figure behind a label
saying Harold S. Geneen.

A low voice, from one of the controllers, intones the

salient facts about each batch of figures; and as the voice talks, a small, sharp arrow appears on the screen, alongside the relevant figure. Some of the figures have brackets round them, indicating a loss, and there the arrow lingers specially long (it seems almost like an extension of Geneen's finger). From time to time, Geneen's voice, also very low, interposes with a question; why has a target not been reached, why is an inventory figure too high? The managing director justifies himself tensely and briefly : 'We're already looking into that, Mr. Geneen.' Geneen nods, or swivels round, or utters some mild reproof. The arrow moves on to the next incriminating figure.

The meetings, whether in Brussels or New York, are the central ordeal of the ITT discipline, the test that its men are attuned to the openness of the system. As Geneen explained to me, it is not enough for him to see the accounts; he must see the expression of the man that gives them, and how he gives them. The words 'I want no surprises' are always there, in the background. If there *is* a surprise, the reaction is immediate; a task force will be immediately appointed, perhaps two or three task forces unaware of each other, to find out the reason, to supply a solution. For a newly-joined manager—and specially from a company newly acquired by ITT—the ordeal can be terrifying; there are stories of one man fainting as he walked in, and of another rushing out to get blind drunk for two days. For the hardened ITT man, it is no more than a routine test of sang-froid; 'You have to be prepared,' said one of them, 'to have your balls screwed off in public, and then joke afterwards as if nothing had happened.'

The most gruelling sessions come each year in September and October, when Geneen and his court come over to Brussels for several weeks, for the annual Business Plan Review. From ten in the morning, sometimes till well after midnight, Geneen or his deputy sits in the swivel chair in the air-conditioned room and watches each managing director come forward with his presentation of his plan. He cross-examines each one in front of his colleagues, who are encouraged to join in the ritual. 'We all said to each other "what a farce!",' said one ex-managing director, 'but you must have this theatrical atmosphere to force you to think.'

The tension of the meetings is not simply the tension of its members, as they face the cross-questioning. It is also the inevitable tension of a group of directors from four thousand miles away, trying to control an empire ranging from dog-food to transistors, from face-cream to telephones. It may be the only way to prevent it breaking apart at the seams. But watching the ordeal it is hard not to wonder : isn't it too big?

In Europe as in America Geneen quickly introduced strict control of the kind that was impossible before jet-planes and computers. When he first moved in, he was appalled by the lack of supervision. As he described it in 1969, in his own special style :

> When we started off, we had 110,000 people in Europe. This is way back at the beginning. We didn't even have an office in Europe. We had one fellow, and he had about five assistants, and he used to travel around on airlines and hold meetings in hotel rooms, for 110,000 people. Today we have a co-ordinated management group in Brussels, which is our headquarters for Europe, which would comprise about 300 executives, and they monitor all of our operations in Europe.[1]

Brussels was an appropriate centre, with its dedication to commerce, its expatriate communities, its sense of placelessness. 'The great thing about Brussels,' Geneen is reported to have said, 'is that there's nothing to do except work.' Belgium is hospitable to American companies, welcoming their investment, and ITT has done good business there, with a very profitable telephone company and many acquisitions, though Geneen had a setback when in 1970 he tried to buy the big food company, General Biscuit. The company fought back, with full-page advertisements saying 'All Big European Companies aren't American', and the shareholders frustrated ITT by voting an increase in the share capital.

The headquarters of ITT Europe will soon move into a twenty-four-storey skyscraper in Brussels, which sticks out above the sedate buildings of the Avenue Louise, casting its shadow over the medieval abbey opposite. It caused a local furore, for the Avenue Louise had strict rules controlling

1. *Conglomerate Hearings:* Vol. III, p. 141.

high building. Belgians assumed it was the fault of ITT in New York; but it was actually organised by the local Belgian managing director, Pepermans, a rugged Flemish tycoon with a strong will of his own. He made a deal with the City fathers (encouraged perhaps by an ex-Premier of Belgium, Paul-Henri Spaak, who was a director of ITT Belgium). In spite of the protest, the steel ribs of the skyscraper began rising up, a tactless monument to ITT's influence.

It is in Brussels that the observer can best watch the habits, colouring and nesting habits of the curious new species, multinational man, of which ITT man is a common subspecies. The initials, they say, really stand for International Travel and Talk, and the European executives are whirled round the limbo of airports and international hotels. Defying geography is an essential condition, and a managing director may even find himself ordered from Europe to New York, just for lunch. Travel is reckoned to cost the company over $4 million a year, and in Brussels alone, ITT occupy 24,000 hotel rooms a year—enough to keep a large hotel going (a Sheraton hotel has just opened in Brussels). A hotel room is the home of an ITT executive for much of the year, and Geneen himself, though he has rooms waiting for him at the Executive Mansions in Brussels, prefers to stay in an ordinary hotel suite in the Westbury. All over Europe, ITT people are bumping into each other in hotel lobbies. In this nomadic existence, telephones become an obsession, not only because ITT makes them, but because they abolish distance and provide a reassuring link with home base. The more uprooted the way of life, the more dependent the multinational managers become on their company, which forms the carapace within which they travel. I overheard one ITT manager in his Brussels hotel room joking on the telephone for twenty minutes with New York.

It is a self-contained world—even more self-contained, people say, than the world of that other omnipresent company, IBM. The contrast between the two is very marked. IBM is much more well-defined, revolving round its one principle product, with a tradition of paternalism and company rules. ITT is much less structured and definable, with its confusions of products and lines of command, but the bewilderment makes ITT men the more anxious to cling together. Within these giant organisms the differences of nationality seem often less important than differences of company.

TELEPHONE TANGLE

While Geneen was hectically buying up companies in America to balance his European business, the European companies were themselves expanding so fast that it was not easy to overtake them. In spite of his gloomy predictions in 1963, none of the European telephone manufacturing companies was nationalised or persecuted, and they were in fact the most profitable part of the ITT empire. In the first five years of Geneen's rule, their earnings more than doubled,[1] and they are now growing by around fifteen percent every year. ITT looms large in Europe. It is the biggest American company in the continent, with nearly 200,000 employees, and ITT Europe by itself ranks seventeenth (in sales) among all companies in Europe.

Geneen remained very worried, almost obsessively worried, by the vulnerability of his telephone companies. As he reminded his shareholders again in his 1972 report : 'The move towards tighter integration among Common Market countries could bring increasing discrimination against U.S.-based multinational companies in favour of European-based multinational companies.' Of course there is some basis for this concern : European companies are not in a position to compete in telecommunications in America, to balance ITT's European invasion; and ITT cannot show, as IBM can, that it is importing the benefits of American technology, for most of their telecommunications research is done in Europe, in their laboratories in Britain, France and Spain. But there is so far little sign of the discrimination that Geneen fears, as this chapter will indicate.

With this worry in mind, Geneen has tried to escape from his dependence on European telecommunications, and as in America, has bought up hundreds of companies, particularly in service industries which were politically safer and easier to manage. Many of the big American companies that Geneen acquired had brought with them a European

1. *Conglomerate Hearings:* Vol. III, p. 747.

bonus, which expanded rapidly in the 'soaring 'sixties'. Avis cars and Sheraton hotels spread through the European capitals, and even Levitt houses, the most American of concepts, sprouted up in a suburb of Paris, of all places; the Ardsleigh house was converted into the Arcy, with only a change in the kitchen; and the houses were laid out without fences or hedges, American-style, in *Les Residences du Chateau*. These new businesses were multinational in a broader sense than the old telephone companies, confined inside their own borders. Hotels, car-hire, insurance, could spread across frontiers; and could be standardised and controlled from New York and Brussels.

But telecommunications remain the largest part of ITT's European business. The telephone, as Sosthenes Behn predicted, continued to multiply on the pattern of America. In France, Holland, Spain and Austria the numbers have more than doubled in the last decade : in Britain they have gone up eighty-one percent. But as ITT often points out, the Europeans are still very un-telephone-minded compared to Americans : these were the telephones per hundred people, in January 1971 :

Austria	19.3
Belgium	20.8
Denmark	34.4
France	17.2
Italy	17.4
Holland	26.0
Norway	29.4
Portugal	7.7
Spain	13.5
Sweden	55.6
U.K.	26.7
W. Germany	22.4
N. America	57.1

ITT's telecommunications business in Europe is not easy to define, for once again it has two aspects. From one side, it appears with a single huge head; from the other with several small heads, like Hydra's, growing out everywhere : and from this double image it derives some advantage. On the one hand, it is by far the biggest telecommunications company in Europe, with a third of the total business, twice as big as its nearest competitor, Siemens. On the other, it is made up of a score of national companies, each with special eccentricities and local traditions; beginning with Bell Telephone in Belgium, set up in 1882, followed by Standard Telephones and Cables (STC) in Britain, founded in 1883, followed by the two French companies Le Matériel Téléphonique (1889) and Compagnie Générale de Constructions Téléphoniques (1892). Each of these companies is locked in a close but awkward embrace with its national post office, the single big customer on which its business depends, and most of them compete in some kind of a 'ring' with three or four rival suppliers. For this reason, if for no other, ITT must appear as 'good citizens' of each country, for telephones, as they have learnt to their cost, are politically highly sensitive instruments.

The backwardness of European telephones are the despair of American visitors, and few industries show more clearly the snags of a fragmented market. Much of the blame must rest on the national governments, each of whom insists on a separate telephone system, and each failing to anticipate the demand, so that they are caught between different stages of development. ITT has to supply seventeen different systems for twenty different governments, with very limited scope for standardisation. It might be thought that this diversity would be very frustrating for ITT, since they would be the best placed company to provide a standardised Europe-wide service, equivalent to their American counterparts, AT&T. But financially ITT does very well out of the fragmentation : by exchanging research and methods, and by rationalising their exports, they make higher profits than most of their nationally-based rivals; in the words of one French analysis 'from the middle of the confusion, ITT achieves the synthesis of the different governments' policies, chooses the best for export, and develops its prosperity.'[1] It gets the benefits, in other words, of being both big and small. But if the systems were unified, ITT would be in a more obviously dominating role, and subject either to discrimination or to effective control – like AT&T in America, which provides a smaller return on capital than ITT.

It is tempting for ITT's critics in each country to ascribe

1. Jean-François Ruges : *Le Téléphone Pour Tous*, Paris, 1970.

their success to sinister advantages. But in fact the lobbying is usually more intense from the national companies, who can plead 'the national interest' to their governments. In France, for instance, the government has tried to encourage national rivals to the two ITT companies with marked lack of success; ITT account for nearly sixty percent of the French exports of telecommunications. In Britain a major row developed in 1972 when the post office chose the ITT system of semi-electronic exchanges, the TXE4; the British rivals, GEC and Plessey, remorselessly lobbied the post office, the politicians and the Treasury, and in the nationalist climate there was great reluctance to grant a huge contract to an American company. But the government had to agree that it was the best system, and consoled the British rivals with other contracts. GEC eventually dropped its opposition, and even decided to collaborate with ITT in developing advanced electronic systems.

As telecommunications become more highly developed, so the nature and scale of the European competition will change. Telephones will become more closely involved with computers, which can store and transfer calls, tot up bills, and supervise the exchanges themselves. ITT will be in a strong position against its smaller rivals, but it will also find itself overlapping with the company that it has always most carefully avoided – the dread IBM. Geneen has taken special pains not to get involved in computers, to avoid experiencing the fiasco that befell RCA: he has even hired a highly-paid man in New York just to stop ITT companies moving into computers. But as telephone exchanges develop, computers must increasingly be at the heart of them, and ITT will find itself confronting its multinational rival across the world. The contest between ITT and IBM, the giants of communications gradually converging, may bring a more intense competition; but the prospect of communications being carved up between two big-brother giants is not an inviting one. And the most obvious third global competitor, AT&T, remains outside the contest, still studiously refraining from competition.

In this multinational scenario, the European governments are unlikely to give up their insistence on national control of their telephone systems; faced with intricate computerised systems, the privacy and security of communications may well become a much more political question. No government will want to forego the benefits of this multinational technology, and the new ease and cheapness of communication that it should bring. But they will need far greater expertise and controls if they are not to be overwhelmed and undermined by the consequences.

VICEROYS AND ENVOYS

For its multinational affairs, ITT have always been deeply involved in industrial diplomacy, recruiting eminent advisers to ease their relations with governments. On their main board in New York they have Eugene Black, the ex-head of the World Bank, and John McCone, the former director of the Central Intelligence Agency—whose relationship will later appear specially significant.[1] In Europe, Admiral Stone —himself no mean negotiator—recruited to local ITT boards Trygve Lie in Norway, Paul-Henri Spaak in Belgium and Lord Caccia in Britain. In Spain and Latin America, ITT has always recruited local politicians and dignitaries. Do these diplomats represent their own country, Britain, or America, or the sovereign state of ITT? It is not easy to answer, perhaps even for themselves : a tough local politician, like Pepermans with his skyscrapers in Brussels, may well get the better of ITT in New York. One ITT man complained : 'It's not as easy to buy people as you might think : after all, they've got their own position to keep up in their own country.' The question about loyalty is increasingly asked from America as much as from Europe, for instance by Professor Mueller, the former chief economist of the Federal Trade Commission :

It is not unfair to ask, are such men on ITT's board because of their business acumen or their prestige in international diplomacy? This raises a corollary question of who is more powerful in international diplomacy, the U.S. State Department or huge international conglomerates like ITT.[2]

In its dealings with European countries (as opposed to

1. see Chapter 11.
2. Willard Mueller : *Conglomerate Mergers,* Quoted in *Conglomerate Report,* p. 95.

Latin American ones) ITT has shown quite sophisticated diplomacy; as Geneen has put it: 'As a bunch of Americans coming over to run a bunch of companies in Europe, all in different countries, all staffed by nationals of their own countries, all speaking different languages, it is entirely different from in the United States, where you can go and order a lot of things done.'[1] ITT are proud of the fact that out of their 200,000 employees in Europe, only a hundred are American. The senior managing directors who sit around the horse-shoe table in Brussels each month, are all nationals of their country, who help to provide the bridge between ITT and their people.

The president of ITT Europe, the chief link between the continents, is a young French-American, only forty, responsible (within limits) for a turnover of $2.7 billion a year. 'Mike' Bergerac, big and bland, with a sleek round face like a seal's provides a kind of identikit picture of a multinational man. He was born in France and earned a Fulbright scholarship to America, where he took a degree in business administration in Los Angeles; in California-style, he worked on ranches, and later joined a West Coast company, Cannon Electric. When ITT bought Cannon, they bought Bergerac with it, and soon realised his usefulness. They moved him to Brussels, and five years later made him president. 'He couldn't have got that kind of break if he hadn't been taken over by ITT,' said one director: 'he may kill himself with work, but in the meantime he'll have a lot of fun.' It is difficult to say where Bergerac belongs. He lives in Brussels as an American citizen, called Mike rather than Michael. He spends half his time travelling, and his hobby is big-game hunting in Africa: he has the horns of a buffalo over his office door. He speaks hearty American with French r's and some intonations, but without French irony or inhibitions. The Europeans regard him as American, and the Americans regard him as European.

The European managing directors lead odd double lives. Outwardly they are powerful and independent men in their own countries, like little Geneens. Many of them, like Geneen, are self-made men who have risen to the top outside the traditional power-structure. They are very highly

1. *Conglomerate Hearings:* Vol. III, p. 142.

paid, entertain grandly. Their local boards of directors, while adding dignity to the company, will not question their authority. But behind the scenes the freedom is severely constricted. Their comptroller reports directly to the comptroller in New York, and as soon as anything goes wrong, teams of accountants will 'swarm over' from New York. Each of the separate groups of products—components, business systems, consumer products etc.—is supervised on a Europe-wide basis by the group general managers in Brussels, who by-pass the national boss. And once a month they come to Brussels to be grilled and cross-examined in front of the moving finger. The duality of their position fits in with the ITT philosophy, that no single man can be trusted; but it takes a special toughness to withstand it.

ITT are careful to adopt local colouring wherever they operate, and they know how to find the right man for the right job. For South Africa, for instance, they deploy a wealthy Texan called Rex Grey, who is based in London with a ranch in Rhodesia and a flat in South Africa; he has a special relationship with Geneen (who often prefers independent men for his really big deals) and he is adept at entertaining visiting South African delegations, with appropriate high-life. South Africa is a big field for expansion, and ITT have been recruiting in London for their South African companies.

In its dealings with countries, as in its dealings with Sheraton or Levitt, ITT takes full advantage of their double character, appearing as convenient either local or centralised : Geneen, like the Cheshire cat, appears and disappears. In my own contacts with their public relations, I became aware of this tendency; at first the national subsidiaries showed themselves proudly autonomous, but when I touched on more sensitive questions, I was abruptly informed by the public relations director in New York that all enquiries should be referred only to him. ITT in New York when necessary can maintain a tight hold over its scattered operations; but in each country they have local politicians and managers to present an independent front, and to connect them to the local political scene.

In Spain the figurehead of their business (the third largest in Europe) is General Barroso, Franco's former minister of war, now eighty: he played an important role in the civil war, when he was attaché in Paris, in stopping French arms to the Republicans. Barroso and his managing director, Marquez Balin, are among the toughest employers. When in April 1971 10,000 ITT workers in Madrid demanded an increase of $22 a month (1,500 pesetas), ITT responded by calling in the police and having key workers arrested; when there were more protests and stoppages, a thousand workers were suspended, and more troublemakers arrested. There were demonstrations by trade unionists in America and Europe, and eventually all but fourteen workers were re-hired.[1] ITT still has the monopoly of manufacture for the Spanish telephones (though Ericssons are hoping to break in) and Standard Electric is the eighth biggest company in Spain, with sales over $200 million a year. But in return Franco's government can drive a hard bargain; and it was their demand for more credit which helped to precipitate ITT's crisis in 1971 (see Chapter 10).

It is in France that ITT encounter the most overtly anti-American reactions, where diplomacy is therefore most important. The *administrateur-général* of their companies is a technocrat, like Bergerac, who can bridge the two cultures: Claude Etchegaray is a graduate of both the Ecole Polytechnique and the Harvard Business School; and to support him he has a *conseil d'administration* which includes General de Bonneval, a former aide of de Gaulle, Pierre Abelin, a centrist deputy, Jean Guyot of Lazard Frères and several other Paris bankers. The ITT business in France has grown rapidly, in spite of political opposition. Their two tele-communications companies, CGCT and LMT, make up the bulk of French exports in that field; and they have expanded into pumps (Salmson), television sets (Oceanic and Sonolor), contractors (Jeanrenaud) and even business schools (Pigier). In 1966 Geneen made an expensive bid for the big lighting company Claude, and was eventually given permission to buy it by de Gaulle's government, who had just chucked out NATO—which provoked wry comment. But Claude was not a good buy: the French and American clashes have been painful, and the case-history has recently been studied at the Harvard Business School as an example of how not to

1. International Metalworkers' Federation: *News*, March, 1972.

do it. Later ITT tried to buy the biggest pump-making company in France, Pompes Guinard, but the government forbade it, and more major acquisitions in France seem unlikely (their latest purchase, the scent company Payot, was bought through Liechtenstein).

In France ITT often have to make do with only a majority of the shares, instead of the outright ownership on which they normally insist; they own only fifty-four per cent of Claude, sixty-seven percent of Oceanic, and sixty-eight percent of LMT. ITT shares are thus quoted on the Bourse, and slightly more is known about ITT companies in France than elsewhere. LMT shares have been a very profitable investment, but for that reason, ITT have been under fire for making too much money out of the French government.

Germany, by contrast, has offered the most satisfactory business environment for ITT, and it is their most important country in Europe, with 65,000 employees. Their chief executive, Dieter Moehring, is an extrovert Americanised German, with broad contacts in German politics. The two pre-war companies, now merged into Standard Elektrik Lorenz (SEL) are still the backbone of the German business, making all kinds of electronics and telecommunications. In the post-war years, re-established in Stuttgart, SEL was one of the wonder-companies, shooting ahead of Britain and France. In the last ten years Geneen has bought up all kinds of other German companies, including insurance (Intercontinental), frozen food (Groenland), and several manufacturers of automotive products. The biggest of them, Alfred Teves, employing 12,000 people, soon showed a spectacular increase in profits. But ITT Germany is no longer the miracle company; telecommunications have become less profitable; Teves is no longer so profitable; and in Germany, too, there are signs of resentment of the American giant.

ITT BRITAIN

Britain, though less openly hostile than France, is probably the most resistant to ITT systems, and has the most stubborn attitudes. It is an ambivalent relationship. Even Geneen, though exasperated by the British attitude of 'expectant pensioners', has a fondness for London, where he feels himself safe and incognito in the streets. The British employees, I noticed, enjoy a very two-sided attitude. They make fun of the regimentation and narrowness of ITT in New York; 'I'm beginning to realise what it was like to be under the Roman Empire,' said one of them. 'It's fatuous, really,' said another; 'this idea of managing telephones one day, cosmetics the next, and insurance the next.' But at the same time the British can be excited and challenged by the stimulus, relieved to escape from the British class system into the ITT money system; while they are more protected against the strain than their American counterparts.

Britain has ITT's second-biggest work-force in Europe, with 35,000 employees, and the rush of acquisitions has produced as elsewhere a hotch-potch of business and products, including Rimmel cosmetics, Sherley dog-foods, Eugene hair-wave, Amplex deodorant, Victor Britain car-hire, on top of the older companies like Commercial Cables, KB television and radio, Creed Teleprinters. Even Sheraton have now opened a hotel at London Airport.

But the main British business remains the original one, Standard Telephones and Cables (STC). It was for a long time one of Geneen's headaches, marked out for the 'red flag' treatment. It was largely run by engineers, not much interested in profits. A succession of managing directors came and went. In the late 'sixties there was a serious proposal to nationalise it under the Labour Minister of Technology, Anthony Wedgwood Benn. The post office wanted to have its own manufacturing company to work with its own research laboratories, and STC seemed the obvious choice, being foreign-owned and with useful technology. There were talks between ITT and the post office, but then came the election, and the end of the Labour Government.

And in the meantime a new managing director, Ken Corfield, arrived, who turned round the company's fortunes. He cut down his work-force, kept the engineers in control, put up prices to the post office, and insisted that ITT would only do research that was profitable. A proud Staffordshire man, he has had the experience, unlike most ITT managers, of having run his own firm (KG Corfield, making cameras and lenses). He joined ITT five years ago, as assistant to the president of ITT Europe in Brussels, and moved up very quickly, taking over STC in 1970. Corfield is detached, right-wing, reflective. Though he looks droopy and soulful, he is very tough, and he can stand up to Geneen : he thinks it is easier for Europeans, who are 4,000 miles away from the centre and can invoke their national mystique : ('that's not how it's done here').

For most of STC's workers there is no hint of American ownership. The factories at Southgate, Newport or Foots Cray are self-contained worlds, full of long-service workers; the official history for the seventy-fifth anniversary hardly mentioned the American connection, and the house magazine is sturdily insular. Since the last war, when STC felt a special need to appear British, there has been a local board of directors, who meet every two months, paid £2,500 a year; they include Lord Penney, the ex-head of the Atomic Energy Authority; Lord Glendevon (formerly Lord John Hope), a Conservative ex-minister of works; and Sir Thomas Spencer, the eighty-four-year-old veteran of the company, who joined Western Electric in 1907 and rose to be managing director for twenty-five years. The chairman of the board is Lord Caccia, the former Ambassador to Washington who is now also Provost of Eton. Caccia talks to the managing director once a week, presides over board meetings once every two months, and is paid £15,000 a year. The local board may sometimes lubricate the relations with government, and reassure the public that STC has British interests at heart, but they are irrelevant to the ITT power-structure; for Corfield, like the other managing directors, is directly responsible, via Brussels, to New York. He has much autonomy in employment, personnel or research—more than many British heads of American companies. But the ultimate decisions about investment, or senior appointments, are all taken in Park Avenue.

When ITT buys a European company there follows a painful reorganisation, to chop it or stretch it into the Procrustean bed of the system; nowadays a 'travelling circus' descends on the new member, to preach the ITT gospel and to explain the meetings, reports, budgets and rules. Sometimes the old managers are offered special incentives to stay.

Sometimes they are quietly eased out. Sometimes they leave as fast as they can.

The acquisition of Abbey Life Assurance in Britain has a revealing case-history. By 1962 Geneen had become interested in selling insurance in Europe, to tap the cash-flow from policy premiums, and since he knew little about it he went into fifty-fifty partnership with a small American company, called Georgia Insurance. They set up a joint company which then acquired for $300,000 a tiny enterprise in London called Abbey Life, which had just been set up by a shrewd young South African, Mark Weinberg, with three salesmen offering policies linked to equities. It did very well: but Geneen was now busily hiring his own insurance experts in New York, and decided he could do without Georgia. Geneen made an offer for Georgia's half, which they refused; each time he upped the offer, they refused again. Geneen became determined: for all his rational system he can be emotional when crossed. He had to hold back his pressure for a time, when ITT was also trying to buy the Hartford insurance company in Connecticut.[1] But once that was in the bag he could press ahead; and since Abbey Life was only a tiny part of ITT's empire, and a large part of Georgia's, he was prepared to damage Abbey Life in the process. So he bought another British insurance company called London and Edinburgh to compete, who even lured a manager away from Abbey Life. Mark Weinberg, fed up with these tactics, decided that if ITT did take over the whole company, he would resign, but they did not believe him. Eventually ITT persuaded Georgia to sell their half for $38 million, and they then offered Weinberg and his team big new contracts. But Weinberg refused and walked out with five others to set up a rival company (now also highly successful) with Hambro's Bank, while Geneen brought in ITT men to run Abbey Life.

ITT were touchy about Weinberg's departure, as reflecting on their image. When the agreement was reached, a team of lawyers and public relations men flew over to London to arrange contracts and a press conference. They had already prepared a sheaf of likely questions and answers for Weinberg, one of which was: 'Do you, like Townsend of

1. see Chapter 7.

Avis, refuse to work a single day for ITT?' The prepared answer pointed out that Townsend, in fact, had worked for several months before he finally left ITT. But the question, of course, was never asked.

Both the ITT British insurance companies have grown spectacularly. London and Edinburgh has a successful new hospital insurance plan, and Abbey Life now also has the biggest property bond business in Britain. Appropriately for an ITT company, the Abbey Property Bonds pioneered investment in Europe, by buying a thirty-three-storey skyscraper in Brussels, the Tour Madou, for $18 million. ITT thus now has two prominent skyscrapers in Brussels, one for investors, one for themselves.

A QUESTION OF IDENTITY

All these European companies appeared to their public as quite separate entities, proudly French, German or Spanish. ITT, like many parent companies, preferred to lie very low. It had good reasons for keeping a low profile: if it began to beat its corporate drum, the local managers argued, it would only stir up anti-American reactions.

But as his empire expanded, Geneen wanted it to be recognised; 'I am disturbed by the fact,' he has said, 'that not one of fifteen people questioned know what or who ITT is.' It would bolster the share-price if investors saw the ITT letters wherever they travelled. It would make advertising more effective—$24 million a year—if it all proclaimed the same company. And ITT could charge more for a product: Geneen looked enviously at some IBM machines, which, he said, cost double the similar ITT ones because of their magic name. ITT was still much less famous than other giants; Americans still muddled it up (as Behn had meant them to) with AT&T. Geneen was not obviously flamboyant or publicity-seeking, but he liked people to note his achievement.

New York thus pressed the viceroys to adopt the name of the central power. There was bitter resistance. The French put up a strong fight; and in London Allister Mackay, one of Corfield's predecessors, stoutly defended the name of Standard. But Geneen's men insisted that the letters ITT should appear in front of each local name; and in December

1968 they announced a massive advertising campaign to proclaim the corporate identity across the globe. By the time of ITT's fiftieth birthday in 1970, they had brought most of their satraps into line; in Britain STC was now ITT-STC. A slogan was coined—'serving people and nations everywhere'—which appeared on advertisements with symbolic paintings commissioned by artists from each country. The 1970 annual report was even preceded by a little poem that developed the sentiment:

> The problems we have now
> Give us a lonely thought:
> Will the future for our children
> Be as bright
> As today has been for us?
> ITT is committed to helping make
> Our world a still better place
> To live in:
> Serving people and nations
> Everywhere.

The timing of the campaign was poignant. For it was in full flood by 1972, when suddenly the corporate identity of ITT was established in a very different way. The viceroys would then have gladly disowned their connection.

COMPANIES AND COUNTRIES

From its beginnings under Colonel Behn, ITT had the ingredients of a modern multinational company, not only trading but manufacturing all over the world, And as it expanded and developed through the 'sixties, with closer controls and communications, it was in the forefront of the new phenomenon. The emerging independent power of multinationals was beginning to transform the ideas of economists and politicians about the nature of world trade and the relationships of business to government.

It is a well-worn fact that giant corporations have a greater revenue than many of the countries in which they operate. General Motors has a bigger income than Belgium or Switzerland: and even ITT, the tenth biggest, collects more than the gross national product of Portugal or (specially apposite) of Chile. The global company overwhelming the small state has become a new ogre for the left. Its menace can easily be exaggerated. The multinationals, after all, have succeeded primarily because they provide the products and jobs that people want; and if there is one thing more alarming to a small country than the presence of multinationals, it is their absence. The serious issue is not whether multinationals should be allowed, but how they should be controlled and counterbalanced; the scale of industrial development has far outstripped the scale of political development, a discrepancy which ruthless companies can easily exploit. ITT has been specially able to exploit it, not only through its size and diversity, but through its tradition of deviousness and many-sidedness, and its mastery of communications.

The comparison of companies to countries can be misleading. Some enthusiasts for the industrial giants regard them as more important than nations : thus Antony Jay, in *Management and Machiavelli*, reports that, 'Future students of the twentieth century will find the history of a firm like General Motors a great deal more important than the history of a nation like Switzerland.' I find this improbable. Every country, even with a weak government, provides benefits to a citizen which no company can rival. It controls his basic rights, his welfare, his security; and it provides a sense of identity and a loyalty which shows no sign of diminishing in the face of common markets and greater mobility. It is governments, not managing directors, who determine the essential background of citizens' lives—not just their working lives, but the lives of their wives and children, their hospitals, schools, cities and countryside.

Yet this is not how it seems to Geneen, behind the battlements of ITT. To him, as to many others, the company is more important than governments because it can make jobs, provide security, incentives and independence. In his speech to shareholders in Memphis in 1972 he quoted Thomas Jefferson, saying that no man can be independent without property, and went on :

> Our contribution is to make as many independent citizens as we can justify on the resources available to us within the framework of our System. At the moment, there are around the world some 400,000 people who have an independence of

judgment and who can, in 90 countries, do what they think is right. And those are only ITT employees. I am not even taking into account the tens of thousands of additional jobs that are created by the purchasing power we give them. They have a place to stand and a place to sit, and a roof over their heads—which might not be there if it were not for ITT...

By contrast with this efficient, life-giving force, governments seem to him puny and negative. Geneen sees his own job as more important than those of prime ministers, presidents, or monarchs. There are many stories told by ITT men about Geneen's disregard for national leaders: how he kept the King of the Belgians waiting, how he postponed a meeting with the Shah. Geneen has ample evidence to suppose himself monarch of a sovereign state. He need rarely step out of the frontiers of ITT-land, and when he travels abroad, he takes his court with him.

There is no doubt that the heads of multinationals have taken over some of the past prerogatives of national rulers. The old theories of free trade being negotiated between nations have been knocked sideways, for the multinationals manufacture inside other countries' frontiers, moving goods from one part of their empire to another, largely independent of national restrictions, tariffs and quotas. Moreover, an increasingly large share of each country's exports consists in exports from one subsidiary of a multinational to another; so that countries are dependent on them for their balance of payments. The multinationals become increasingly oblivious of geography, seeking the cheapest and most efficient place for manufacturing each product. A transistor radio can be made in Hong Kong for selling in Europe, to earn profits in America. For a well-organised multinational a common market like Europe's confers no special advantage. Indeed it may be the reverse; and in Geneen's speeches the words 'common market' have a connotation of threat—the threat of eventual discrimination against non-European companies, and restrictions on new acquisitions. From Geneen's point of view, Europe would be safer without it.

Small countries see their pattern of trade being determined by the strategies of the multinationals, which carve up the national markets for their products, to prevent one subsidiary competing wastefully with another—deciding perhaps that Switzerland will be supplied from Germany instead of France, or that all refrigerators will be made in Italy, and all radios in Germany. Within ITT, there can be angry disputes about these carve-ups; but they are settled inside the empire, between the group general managers, with a final verdict from New York.

Moreover, the multinationals are very independent of movements of currency; they can shift quickly from pounds to marks to yens, speculating on the currency market, sometimes yielding quick profits. They can anticipate devaluations by holding back some payments and pushing forward others. In Britain in 1965, ITT were already expecting a devaluation of ten percent, which they reckoned would reduce British earnings by $1.5 million.[1] When Britain eventually devalued in 1967, ITT announced the next day that they had already anticipated it, and that their annual earnings would not be affected.[2] And in 1971 ITT was suspected of having started the run on sterling which ended in the floating of the pound.[3] What annoys national governments is that the giant companies by anticipating devaluation help to cause it. The British like to blame the gnomes of Zurich for each new run on the pound, but they need look no further than the gnomes of ITT.

The prophets of the multinational companies, like Professor Howard Perlmutter, foresee the time when world industry will be ruled by three hundred global giants competing across continents. If so, ITT is likely—if it holds together—to be a model. For Geneen's system of drive and control can operate across the globe, and the more far-flung the company, the more essential is the controlling machinery at the centre. Only with the new communications—jet-planes, computers, high-speed telex, international telephones —has the modern multinational, dispersed but close-knit, become manageable. Most of them have devised systems which, while giving the viceroys apparent autonomy, watch

1. *Conglomerate Hearings:* Vol. III, p. 748.
2. see John Brooks, *Business Adventures*, Penguin, p. 359.
3. see speech by Gordon Hayman of the British Federation of Insurance Brokers, protesting against ITT's acquisition of Excess Holdings: January 22, 1973.

closely their spending and investment from the nerve-centre. But Geneen's control is both multinational and multi-product. In his system there is no logical reason why one company should not make everything, everywhere.

The big companies compete in portraying themselves as 'more multinational' than each other; A survey in the European business magazine *Vision*, called 'How multinational are the multinationals?' gave points to fifteen major companies in Europe, based on their distribution of turnover, capital, management, subsidiaries and research : and ITT came out fifth in the list, and ahead of the other four American companies (GM, Du Pont, IBM, Kodak).[1] But its polyglot performance cannot disguise the fact that ITT is an American company, owned by American shareholders. (With its present structure, it could not legally be otherwise: for ITT World Communications are regulated by the Federal Communications Commission, and are thus not allowed to have foreign officers or directors.)

Yet to have its base in America is not the same, as we have seen, as following the American government's interest; and ITT is constantly under two-way attack, abroad for being too American, at home for not being American enough; the most serious attack on multinationals is currently (see Chapter 12) being mounted by trade unionists inside America. While it looks to the American government for protection and support, it is free to pursue its own policies, playing one nation against another. And as the ITT whale spouts and submerges in different corners of the world, it becomes always harder to be sure whether it has a real home.

1. *Vision*, June 15, 1972.

6

The Corporate Castle

Increasingly, the larger corporations have become the primary custodians of making our entire system work.

Harold Geneen, 1970

By 1969 Geneen had totally transformed the company that he had taken over ten years before. It was no longer a loosely-knit group of telephone companies operating abroad. It was a highly centralised organisation controlling an unprecedented range of industries, with 331 subsidiary corporations and another 708 subsidiaries of subsidiaries. The name International Telephone and Telegraph was now quite inappropriate. It had factories in twenty-seven countries and operations in seventy countries, but sixty percent of its business was now in North America overtaking the fifty-five percent that Geneen had proposed. In ten years the net income had gone up from $29 million to $234 million, and the sales from $766 million to $5.5 billion. Steadily the corporation had climbed up the *Fortune list* of giant companies from Number 52 in 1959 to Number 9 in 1970, jostling with IBM and Unilever.

Yet behind it all there was still—as much as in the days of Colonel Behn—the personality of only one man. The fashionable theories adumbrated by Professor Galbraith or others, that big business was now in the hands of committees, technicians and a new technostructure, seemed to be flatly contradicted by ITT, as by the other 'conglomerates' that were growing up at the same time. In fact, the more diverse and far-flung the company, the more it seemed to rest on one man. The only comprehensible link between a hotel in Los Angeles and a pump company in Paris, between insurance in London and forests in Canada, was the ambition of the man who put them together. The names ITT and Geneen became inseparable, as ITT and Behn were inseparable thirty years before. But Geneen's domination was very different; as Mrs. Sosthenes Behn II (who married Colonel Behn's nephew) complained in a letter to *Time* magazine (September 22, 1967):

> I am glad Colonel Behn did not live to see his dream become a giant conglomerate, where the personal touch and human values are lost in the balance sheet, drowned in the quest for the almighty dollar.

The personality of Geneen is not obviously powerful; he is not physically rugged or flamboyant. He looks, as he is, the complete accountant, bespectacled, trim. His whole existence revolves round the company accounts: he lives near the office, and works often till midnight, examining the books or questioning his colleagues. He has a country place at Key Biscayne, near Nixon's summer home, and a yacht called *Genie IV,* on which he fishes. But his fishing companions, it emerges, often have commercial significance: what he is really fishing for, one ITT man explained to me, is *on* the yacht. Everywhere Geneen goes, his accounts follow him, and at Key Biscayne he pores over them in his special 'sulking house'. He has no taste for high life or good food; he likes hamburgers and stays in ordinary small hotel suites. He reads little, except accounts. Once a colleague in a plane was amazed to see him looking at a women's magazine, but soon afterwards the reason became clear: ITT had just bought Rimmel cosmetics, and Geneen was studying the advertising.

All companies, like countries, like to make myths of their leaders, to make their employees' lives more comprehensible. But Geneen has been unpromising material. The teams of public relations men do what they can, retelling the same anecdotes again and again. There is the story of how Geneen was taken to a topless restaurant in San Francisco, and peered with fascination at the half-naked waitress, and said: 'You know if I'd had the time I could have been a helluva playboy.' There are stories about how he plays the banjo, collects Dixieland records, loves Vaudeville, enjoys surfing in Hawaii. There was the story about his new-found passion for cricket. The PR men insist that his hobbies include photography, swimming and even astronomy. But everyone knows that the hobby which gives him most fun, night and day, weekdays and weekends, is ITT.

It would be quite wrong to deduce that he is no more than a brilliant accountant, controlling his puppets through money. When Geneen begins to argue or enthuse, with arms flailing and finger jabbing, you can see that glint in his eye that has brought so many men under his spell. He reminded me when I met him of Bernard Cornfeld, the ex-president of Investors Overseas Service, who had the same imp-like ability to inspire and drive others. But Geneen has the ability to control, too, and it is the double capacity, to see big and small, which gives him unique power. In his control, he is reminiscent of Sir Arnold Weinstock, the head of (British) General Electric, which is ITT's main British rival; but Geneen is much more single-minded in his mission to rid the world of inefficiency and incompetence. He sees no confusion in his path and no serious obstacles, like nations or families; and once you accept his goals, as one ex-manager remarked, you are bound to admire him. While he drives his senior men, night and day, at the tasks of control, he still generates the sense of a crusade which is exciting and fun. Those who eventually leave ITT, however exhausted or embittered, still seem to have the bewilderment of people who have abandoned a complete system, like the Catholic Church, the Communist Party, or the army in wartime. For Geneen takes the capitalist system to its logical limits, and for any ambitious businessman, it is an anticlimax to retreat back from those limits.

THE REGIME OF REASON

To rule over his thousand companies, Geneen developed his unique system of controls. From his years as an accountant, studying other men's mistakes, he was determined that *his* organisation should never get out of hand. Geneen's system was to become famous far outside ITT; it became the subject of study in business schools, in magazine articles, and in management courses all over America and Europe. At the time when 'management' was becoming a rallying-cry through Europe, Geneen emerged as the master-manager —even, as the French magazine *Entreprise* described him, as 'The Michelangelo of Management'. Appropriately, he paid himself the largest salary in America, $812,000 a year —though even this, as he explained to *Forbes Magazine,* was not really very much for a man who had contributed $11 billion to his company over 11 years.

He trained a new race of managers, many of whom later left to join, or to run, other companies, so that ITT was dubbed 'Geneen University'. He taught all his executives how to think out all their objectives in terms of profits, to set targets and keep to them, to control details with iron discipline, and many of his techniques have been transplanted elsewhere by the breed of 'little Geneens'. He has taken to its extreme the theory that a good manager can run anything—the final dissociation of profits from things. And because of their wide influence, Geneen's methods have an interest beyond their effect on ITT itself. Geneen was constructing a system of management which, he was confident, would long outlive him; like Alfred Sloan, the founder of General Motors who was one of his heroes (and who, like Geneen, put his company before everything), he was building for posterity.

It sounds, as he describes it, more like a system for ruling the world than for ruling a company. When I met him, I asked him about the question of the bigness of business; wasn't there a point at which companies got too big? He asked what I meant about being big : ITT, when you looked at it, was really a group of companies, many of them quite small, which were held together by a common logic, a system of reason. But wasn't it too big to be controlled by one man? No, he wasn't controlling it, he explained, he was only teaching people how to do it; once they had learnt the system, others could work it just as well; when you've seen it work, he said—with missionary fervour in his voice— you realise it's *the only way*. But didn't the size of a vast corporation, I went on, have a diminishing effect on individuals—particularly young people? No, he said, people in inefficient small companies weren't happy—there's nothing satisfying about inefficiency. ITT can release people's full resources, can show them how to work rationally. As for young people, he went on, what do *they* know about work, and making jobs? They're a problem that he was glad to leave to the next generation.

He insists, again and again, that his system is based on nothing more sinister than logic. It is, as he says, the only way. In his 1971 annual report he restated once again his philosophy:

> More than 200 days a year are devoted to management meetings at various organisational levels throughout the world. In these meetings in New York, Brussels, Hong Kong, Buenos Aires, decisions are made based on logic—the business logic that results in making decisions which are almost inevitable because all the facts on which the decisions must be based are available. The function of the planning and the meetings is to force the logic out into the open where its value and need are seen by all. That logic cannot be legislated or ordered. It comes as a natural process.

He runs the company, he likes to explain, not by giving orders, but by uncovering the facts. 'The real tyrant here,' said one New York executive, 'isn't Geneen; it's the facts and figures. What makes Geneen mad is to discover someone trying to hide his mistakes. What makes him happiest is for someone to come to him and admit his failure; I've seen people fortify their positions that way.' Geneen impresses all his colleagues by his ability to ferret out the true 'unshakeable facts' about a company or a product, uncovering layers of false facts before he reaches the truth; and it is this, perhaps more than anything, which has made ITT more proof against disasters than other conglomerates. In 1965 Geneen produced a short homily for his staff called FACTS: 'Effectively immediately I want every report specifically, directly and bluntly to state at the beginning a summary containing the following facts in this order. . .' He proclaimed that the highest art of professional management requires the literal ability to 'smell' a 'real fact' from all others. All his staff, he insisted, must become connoisseurs of 'unshakeable facts', and warned them: 'You will hear a lot more of this term, "unshakeable facts" as we go forward.'

The very diversity of the ITT empire makes it easier—so

their managers argue—to control it objectively. As one of them put it : 'If you're responsible for only one product, like cars or hotels, you get emotionally involved; you get to like them too much.' ITT executives are taught not to make things, but to make money (engineers, with their hopeless pride in perfection, are their villains).

Lacking this sense of involvement with solid objects, they are forced more single-mindedly back on to their own ambition and ability to make profits. Nor is the organisation of ITT reassuring in psychological terms; 'It's not a good company,' as one of them said, 'for people who like a structured world; you may think you're in charge of something, but you'll soon find out that there are two or three other men working on the same thing.'

It is implicit in Geneen's whole system that no man is given full responsibility for anything; and the more senior the managers, the more they are subject to inspection, checking and cross-checking. The managing director of a huge subsidiary may appear to be his own master; but each department will be supervised by the experts from head office —experts on products, accounting, public relations, quality control or real-estate—who have their own direct lines to the top. Like all despotisms, ITT is based on a system of divide and rule; but the divisions can be justified in the name of profits. In each monthly report and at each monthly meeting, the senior managers have to report the 'red flag items' which indicate a prediction gone wrong, a surprise unforeseen. As soon as the red flag goes up, the experts will move in and 'swarm over him'. Or, to use another ITT phrase, 'Geneen unleashes the pack'.

As the basic safeguard, Geneen has his special band of comptrollers, in each of the companies, reporting directly to the chief comptroller in New York, an accountant of legendary thoroughness called Herb Knortz, one of the few men who dares argue openly with Geneen. From his vantage point, checking all the movements of inventories, profits, receivables, Knortz can detect the first signs of incipient losses, excessive stocks or unprofitable products, and if the local managing director has failed to notice them, he will be in trouble. Knortz is, above all, the secret eye of Geneen; 'If you really saw how Herb Knortz's office works,' one executive said to me, 'you'd realise that being an ITT manager is like living in a room with closed circuit television all round you, and with a bug up your arse.'

Geneen provides his managers with enough incentives to make them tolerate the system. Salaries all the way through ITT are higher than average—Geneen reckons ten percent higher [1]—so that few people can leave without taking a drop: as one employee put it, 'We're all paid just a bit more than we think we're worth.' At the very top, where the demands are greatest, the salaries and share options are sufficient to compensate for the rigours: as someone put it, 'he's got them by their limousines'. In 1971 there were at least six men at the top of ITT who were paid more than the president of the United States ($200,000 a year)[2]; they inhabit a world of company meals, company planes, company parties which gives little opportunity or time to spend it.

Having bound his men to him with chains of gold, Geneen can induce the tension that drives the machine. 'The key to the system,' one of his men explained, 'is the profit forecast; once the forecast has been gone over, revised and agreed, the managing director has a personal commitment to Geneen to carry it out; that's how he produces the tension on which the success depends.' The tension goes through the company, inducing ambition, perhaps exhilaration, but always with some sense of fear: what happens if the target is missed?

The price in human terms is very high. 'Geneen wants us all to be as gung-ho as he is,' as one manager put it, 'but somehow it isn't as much fun for the rest of us.' The sense of strain is very noticeable in the Park Avenue skyscraper, not only the tension of worry and work, but the lack of the satisfactions of personal achievement. It shows itself in heavy drinking, broken families and a dazed, bomb-happy look which seems characteristic of ITT men. The tyranny of facts ruthlessly excludes the indulgence of hunches or gambles which can lend excitement to business, and forbids emotional involvement with a product, as firmly as if it were a bunny girl at a playboy club; There are no tales of

1. *Conglomerate Hearings:* Vol. 3, p. 303.
2. Geneen, Dunleavy, Bennet, Williams, Westfall, Perry.

heroism, of sticking bravely to some ill-starred product, like xerography or zip-fasteners, until faith is rewarded. Not surprisingly, Geneen is sceptical of research, and ITT are weak on product development. There must be no surprises, no surprises. Everything must be tested, analysed, extrapolated, and if the prediction fails, the losses must quickly be cut. ITT are very proud of the speed with which they can change direction, cutting out one line and starting another.

Occasionally there are small kicks against the traces of discipline. Two years ago a spoof film was made, which ITT people enjoy showing, with a grave commentary expatiating on ITT's achievements—its efficient services, advanced technology, smooth communications—while the film shows slapstick disasters, shouting-matches, collapsing furniture and custard pies; the film is improbably attributed to Harold Geneen. Perhaps it was the manifestation of some kind of collective subconscious—a tiny revolt against the tyranny of facts. One reflective ITT man in Park Avenue had on his wall a sad passage from Lord Keynes' 'Economic Possibilities for our Grandchildren', summing up his own attitude to business:

> For at least another hundred years we must pretend to ourselves and to everyone that fair is foul and foul is fair; for foul is useful and fair is not. Avarice and usury and precaution must be our gods for a little longer still. For only they can lead us out of the tunnel of economic necessity into daylight.

'The first requirement for a senior executive,' Geneen has often explained, 'is instant availability.' He must always put his firm above his family; he must be prepared to go anywhere at any time, or simply to wait around in case he is needed. One ex-vice-president told me how he watched three of ITT's senior men waiting the whole evening, having been asked by Geneen to stand by; none of them dared ask permission to go out to dinner, or to ask which of them Geneen would see first. The 'instant availability' means availability to Geneen; for though he sees his method as a universal one, the ITT system rests on the basis that the most valuable resource of the company is Geneen. He likes to keep his colleagues in a state of insecurity; whether as a protection of his own insecurity, or as part of his rational system of control. But it is doubtful whether the technique is efficient. As one ex-ITT manager bitterly remarked, 'He buys them in, sucks them dry, and chucks them out. He treats people like machines. The only way to argue with him is to say that even with a machine, you wouldn't work it night and day without lubrication.' I asked another successful ex-ITT man why he had left : he said : 'I decided to rejoin the human race.'

It would be absurd to suggest that Geneen only attracts and keeps his executives through money. His ideals of efficiency and control, backed by his own 'entrepreneurial zing', have inspired many men to great efforts. The inefficiency of a small company (as Geneen said to me) can be much more frustrating than the loss of identity in a big one. The ITT process of taking over a sleepy company, like Sheraton or Claude, and 'tuning it up', to produce maximum profits, can be exciting and stimulating, to people inside it, releasing energies and ambitions. Geneen's supervision, the ordeal of the moving finger, is a more rational and comprehensible control than the whimsical sanctions of investors : as one European managing director put it to me : 'You can't argue with the stock market; but you can always reason with Geneen.' The sense of a perfectly reasoned world, with unshakeable facts laid bare, can be satisfying intellectually and emotionally.

Yet Geneen's world is never quite as reasoned as it appears. For the old inefficiencies he substitutes new ones— the wastage of centralisation, meetings, and long-distance communications which can be, in one ITT phrase, like 'putting treacle through a spindrier'. Geneen's system may well be the 'only way' profitably to run a vast diversified company; and other conglomerates have copied some of his methods; but it begs the question of whether such size is inherently necessary, or desirable.

Despite the insistence on logic, ITT is nevertheless constructed like a court, where every decision revolves round the monarch. Geneen is surrounded by advisers who may appear as objective experts—by Herb Knortz his finance minister, by Ned Gerrity his foreign minister, by Howard

Aibel his attorney-general—but their main task is to translate his whims into action. The memos that circulate so endlessly round the building may seem like the free exchange of communication; but whenever a memo says 'copy to H. S. Geneen' everyone knows that it is really written for one man on the twelfth floor, and the facts it contains may be far from unshakeable.

Could it hold together without the monarch? The question is insistent, for Geneen, young though he looks, is sixty-two, and the retiring age is sixty-five. He has often been pressed about the succession; and in 1968 he set up a new department called Office of the President, made up of three senior colleagues, so that, according to ITT, the company really now had three presidents. They are all Geneen's protégés, trained by him to think and act in the same way. Richard Bennett, the youngest, is an engineer who joined ITT from a small company, Daystrom, eight years ago as Geneen's assistant; he is a small, tough man who smokes big cigars and excels at company pep-talks, but he lacks Geneen's finesse. Jim Lester, with the look of a grim mandarin, was a former president of ITT Europe; where he could instil dread, but not much enthusiasm. Tim Dunleavy, the glad-handing Irishman, who preceded Lester in Europe, is much tougher than he looks, but he is much more human than Geneen (he made history one day in Brussels when the weather was so hot that he told all the secretaries they could go home). What these three lack is not so much Geneen's toughness, as his imagination, and his ability to give the whole conglomerate a sense of purpose and point.

In December 1972 the board of ITT announced what had long been expected: that Geneen would become chairman of the board, and that Tim Dunleavy would become president and 'chief operating officer'. But Geneen would remain chief executive officer, thus keeping his hands firmly on the controls (as Behn did, twenty-five years before). The announcement emphasised that this action would 'ensure orderly transition of authority', that Dunleavy's promotion was a 'logical culmination' of the top management programme. But Geneen would still be in the building every day; and no-one had much doubt about who would still be boss.

It was essential to the defence of the corporate castle that ITT should have its own intelligence system. From the days of Colonel Behn, it was part of ITT's special advantage that, being a communications company, it had special access to all kinds of information—often more quickly and more effectively than governments. As Geneen's empire grew, so the intelligence system grew too. With ITT telephones and ITT cables and ITT telex, the scattered companies could be quickly and cheaply in touch with each other; and ITT could also monitor its own staff (a copy of every cable that comes into the Park Avenue building, whether it deals with sales figures, or a lunch date with a mistress, goes to top management). Above all, the memos proliferated; for memos were not only essential to keep contact with the world-wide empire; they were the only way that many of the staff could prove to Geneen that they were working. Even more than most companies, ITT was a memo-ridden company.

Internal security became increasingly a worry to ITT, and a whole department of security and safety was set up, under Richard Lavoie, to prevent leaks. A booklet on industrial espionage, written by Lavoie, outlines the constant need for 'indoctrination, education and re-education of employees', and shows pictures of likely dangers : one caption says, 'The distinguished couple standing next to you at intermission enjoying a cigarette, could be recording your entire conversation on a miniaturised wire recorder easily concealed in a coat pocket.' New policy guides in December 1969 outlined in detail the three categories of secret information : SYSTEM CONFIDENTIAL, PERSONAL AND CONFIDENTIAL, LEGAL CONFIDENTIAL; and explained how to safeguard the secrets : '. . . to preclude surreptitious access to the material in the envelopes, they will be sealed by placing a gummed label over the flap of the envelope. . . Proprietary information sent by electrical means (when speed is essential) shall be prepared and transmitted as a CRYPTEL (coded) message. . .[1]'

The precautions seem exhaustive enough. But ITT people

1. *Kleindienst Hearings:* Part 2, pp. 705–710.

have shown (as we will see) an obsession with writing everything down. The Xerox machines could not be stopped from churning out copies: a single disaffected secretary could make a copy of a memo without anyone knowing.

The main link between Geneen and the outside world, is the senior vice-president for public relations Ned Gerrity, who becomes a central character in this story. He is difficult to dislike; he spills out jokes and anecdotes with tireless bonhomie and an almost permanent smile. He looks like an old-fashioned journalist, as if he had walked off the stage of *Front Page*, and he began his career as a reporter on the *Scranton Times* in Pennsylvania. But Gerrity is more important than he looks, and much more than an ordinary PR man. Since Geneen moved into ITT Gerrity has looked after not only public relations, but political contacts, lobbying, and international diplomacy, and Geneen's picture of the world is filtered through Gerrity. He is said to earn $200,000 a year.

Gerrity presides over a huge staff who between them spend around $100 million a year in advertising, promotion and all kinds of public relations. The public relations men — even more than most big companies — are renowned for thick skins : they move through the world like tanks through a field of cavalry. But one or two, at least, are sometimes conscience-stricken. One day I was travelling down in an ITT elevator in Park Avenue, when a melancholy elderly man entered the lift, having just come out from a PR conference. He sighed heavily and turned to me, assuming that I, too, was an ITT man, and quoted a line from Milton's *Paradise Lost*: 'To make the worse appear the better cause.'

For much of the activity the phrase public relations is a misnomer, for the most important relations are covert, and while Geneen insists on uncovering facts inside ITT, outside he is more concerned with concealing them. We have already seen Gerrity's behaviour with Eileen Shanahan and other journalists in the ABC case (page 83); and another interesting example emerged when ITT had been forced by the Federal Trade Commission to provide corrective advertising for their Profile Bread, for which they had made false claims (see page 80). Soon afterwards a fierce attack was made on the FTC by Professor Brozen, a Chicago economist, who talked about 'Salem witch trials' and 'star chamber proceedings'; but later the Professor admitted that he was a paid consultant for a public relations firm, Harshe-Rotman, employed by ITT.[1] Ned Gerrity was questioned afterwards in the Senate hearings which were being held at that time:[2]

SENATOR BAYH: Is it your responsibility to get men like this from the academic community to put the Good Housekeeping seal of approval on the ITT position?
MR. GERRITY: Yes sir.
SENATOR BAYH: And then pay them for this effort?
MR. GERRITY: Yes, sir.

It is a principle of ITT that the less public the relations, the more effective they will be, and a collection of memos which was to come to light from Puerto Rico illustrate their methods. The Puerto Rican telephone company, which ITT have operated since Sosthenes Behn first bought it in 1914, had steadily deteriorated, until in the 'sixties it had become notoriously inefficient. In 1965, we even find the ubiquitous Admiral Stone complaining in a letter to Geneen about its incompetence: he suggested that ITT contact a Puerto Rican senator who was an old friend of his, to try to placate the outcry. Eventually in 1967, when ITT wanted to put up the rates, the Puerto Rican Public Service Commission insisted on public hearings to investigate the complaints; and at this point the ITT staff launched a major public relations offensive to improve their image, outlined in a succession of confidential memos.

One of their problems was an organisation called SOPRECAB (society for the prevention of further abuse to the Puerto Rican telephoning public), set up by an exasperated American businessman, John Hennessey. ITT quickly set about investigating Hennessey, with several reports; but the worst they could find about him was that he had been convicted of a driving offence eighteen years before. An ITT representative called Zoffinger, called on him and later sent a report to ITT in New York, in police-report style:

1. *New York Times*, April 14, 1972.
2. *Kleindienst Hearings:* p. 1176.

HENNESSEY: Approx 45, White, USA, Good physical condition. Intelligent.
Income estimated at $10/20,000 annually
Apartment well furnished, mostly conservative —clean.
Apparently lives alone with poodle—no mention of wife or children.
Outwardly calm and reserved. Became noticeably excited and irritated only once during discussion (billing experience).
Occupation—Sales Representative (Van Haughton). No apparent Telco affiliation (has used ITT equipment in Iran).

The investigator was puzzled by his motivations, but suggested that he might like a job in the communications field.

As the hearings came closer, the PR men prepared an elaborate programme of speeches, advertisements, and nobbling of local worthies; and they did what they could to suppress public criticism. They did so by dealing, not with the public, but with the journalists and politicians. One PR memo boasted that ITT had placed more than forty news stories in the local papers, and was instituting a 'continuing program of increasing social contacts of key newsmen'. Another pointed out that 'The *San Juan Star* did not publish any letters of complaint against Ricotelco during the month of February. . . I believe a key factor for the change has been not only the agreement reached with the managing editor, but the goodwill shown by the company to attend service requests from the *Star* and its staffers.'

They carefully wooed the young Puerto Rican politician who was investigating the telephones, Benny Frankie Cerezo, with lunches and advice, offering to help him contact telephone experts abroad; his attitude was reported to be softening, though they were irritated by his invulnerability. They commissioned special reports on the private lives of relevant politicians, including Cerezo: 'Apparently he does not have marital problems in his marriage to Carmen Consuelo Vargas, another lawyer. Cerezo, who is only 25, comes from a humble home. Perhaps this is why until now he despises membership in Rotary and Lions-type clubs . . .'

When the hearings began in September 1969 ITT secured some favourable news reports by the simple expedient of writing them themselves: Fernando Gomez of ITT described how he had twice reported the hearings through the wires of UPI.

Eventually a rate increase was permitted, and PR men described in their *Recommendations for 1970* the strategy to prepare for it. The report gives a vivid picture of ITT's approach to public relations:

> A full-blown news conference should be called. The Company President, flanked by a panel of respected experts, should regretfully announce the bad news. The 'experts' should be there not only as window dressing but to support with authoritative detail the points made in the President's general statement ... Hopefully, also, a few key newsmen can be quietly briefed in advance so that we will be sure that intelligent and reasonable questions will be asked and the other newsmen will follow the lead of these few ... Ideally, our management people should have a wide range of personal contacts with journalists and politicians ... Gradually, then, the press—the sum of its individual members—will become friendly rather than stand-offish, become our ally rather than our critic. To win the press is a giant step towards winning public opinion ... Let's not forget that public relations should never be public. It should be in the background, out of sight. It is management that should be out in front giving the Company its image, not the so-called image-makers themselves.

But all the careful image-making was abruptly undermined when on December 21, the *San Juan Star* revealed the contents of several of the memos. Benny Frankie Cerezo who was able to read the ITT report on himself, said: 'I think that everyone in Puerto Rico now knows that these people are capable of doing anything just to achieve their economic goals.'

UNACCOUNTABLE ACCOUNTING

The Corporation was no longer primarily a vehicle for conducting business: it had become a machine for compiling an earnings record.

Forbes Magazine, March 1969

Geneen was determined that ITT should present a record of steadily increasing earnings, growing every quarter, to reassure the most sceptical investor that his company, like a liner with stabilisers, was invulnerable to economic storms.

For Geneen, as for others of his generation, the memory of the Great Crash, when he was a page on the stock exchange, had made him determined to resist cyclical movements;[1] and perhaps, too, he had a more private need for reassurance, to build high walls against the world outside, to have no surprises, no surprises. Thus fortified, ITT would be able to show that, being both a conglomerate and a multinational, operating in hundreds of industries in scores of countries it could sail on unaffected by the hurricanes which overwhelmed lesser companies. The steady increase in earnings seems miraculous: in February 1973 ITT reported record earnings for the fifty-third successive quarter. It has been the triumph of Geneen's accounting skills.

The whole massive conglomerate, from Tokyo to Chile, from smoked hams to telephones, rested like a vast upside-down pyramid on a pin-point—the share-price on the New York Stock Exchange. As each new acquisition was paid for in ITT shares, so the share-price determined the scope for expansion. And however substantial and solid the properties, the price rushed up and down in accordance, not with hard facts, but with expectations, appearances and the mysterious factor of confidence. The share-price in turn was intimately linked with the 'price-earnings ratio' or 'multiple', which indicates how far investors have faith in the share in the future, as a growth stock. Geneen was determined to give investors the sense of confidence in ITT's future which would provide a high price-earnings ratio.

But the steady increase in earnings was not quite as remarkable as it looked. As each new acquisition was swallowed up by the ITT whale, so the separate characteristics that had been made clear in its balance sheet went out of sight as completely as Jonah. The separate profits and losses of each industry—whether hotels, car-hire or house-building—were no longer discernible in the consolidated balance sheet, and the breakdown of sales showed only the

1. see his Speech to Stockholders, 1970, p. 6, and the profile of Geneen by Michael Herblay in *L'Expansion* (Paris), October 1972.

most generalised headings : 'Defense and Space Programs' or 'Consumer Services'. In the presentation of the corporate accounts, the profits and losses among companies and countries could be quietly set off against each other without anyone knowing. Sales of Japanese securities, of German factories or of Sheraton hotels can all be jumbled together in the heading of 'miscellaneous income'; and by balancing income from one year, to another, the graph of increased earnings could be kept miraculously steady—growing ten percent, quarter by quarter.

Moreover, the multinationality of ITT made it exceptionally able to defend itself against taxation, like a nomadic millionaire. It was true that it was, at the base, an American company, responsible to American shareholders and subject to inspection and questioning from the Securities and Exchange Commission and the Internal Revenue Service; but that control was diminished by ITT's global scope. Soon after he became president, Geneen held a special conference of his top lawyers and accountants, to discuss how ITT could best make use of the tax havens outside the United States to cut down their American taxes. The experts were doubtful, but Geneen insisted that ways could be found; and ever since then, ITT has surprised other companies' accountants by the smallness of its taxes. In 1969 and 1970, when its earnings once again increased, it actually paid fewer taxes than in the preceding years.[1]

All conglomerates, when they shot up in the 'sixties, benefited greatly from the confusion of accounting methods, and the flexibility of the Generally Accepted Accounting Principles (GAAP). Old-established companies often adopted very conservative accounting systems, concealing much of their real assets and reporting low earnings; so that a potential raider or conglomerator could quickly show exciting profits for shareholders by revealing what had been concealed. By the process of 'pooling of interests' accounting, the conglomerator could absorb the merger company's net assets at their old book value, even though he paid a huge premium on the acquisition. Then the conglomerator could dispose of these acquired assets, and the proceeds, which were compared to the historical cost, could show enormous

1. see Dirks Brothers: *The Manageers*, Newsletter, May 10, 1972.

bookkeeping profits, which could appear on the conglomerates' statements as if they had really been earned. Nearly all Geneen's acquisitions were made through pooling of interests. According to a report of a Congress Committee, ITT suppressed through this process, $744,328,000 in costs incurred on its acquisitions up till 1968.[1] These suppressions, representing the hidden values of the merged companies, could then be surfaced by Geneen whenever they were needed, without anyone outside the inner circle becoming aware of it. It was not so surprising that he could maintain a continuous record of growth. In the words of a report by the Federal Trade Commission on conglomerates in January 1973: 'A company acquired by a conglomerate virtually disappears without trace so far as its real profit performance is concerned.'

The accounting of any conglomerate is obscure: 'a branch of creative writing', as one financial editor put it to me, 'though not entirely fiction'. But accounting for a multinational conglomerate like ITT is even more obscure, for items can cross frontiers inside the whale without anyone knowing. The profits of Sheraton in Germany can appear as profits in Boston. Moreover, overseas subsidiaries are much less vulnerable to inspection by securities analysts or financial journalists; for local experts are inclined to ignore foreign-owned companies—like STC in Britain, for example—which are not quoted on the local stock exchange.

The traditional guardians of the shareholder's interest are, of course, the auditors. When some conglomerates began to crash in the late 'sixties, the American auditors came under increasing pressure to adopt more rigid standards of auditing, and the sudden bankruptcy of the Penn Central company in 1970 brought new storms of protest. But there has been no fundamental change in accounting principles. ITT's auditors, Arthur Andersen & Co., are an international accounting group, who are among the 'Big Eight' both in America and in Britain; they were auditors to Bernard Cornfeld's Investors' Overseas Service, where some critics accused them of being too willing to accept Cornfeld's valuations, for instance, of the oilfields in Alaska; even though it was Andersen's, in the end, who first raised the alarm.

1. *Conglomerate Report*, p. 414.

Andersen's biggest clients in America are ITT, and recently they have been taking over the auditing of substantially all ITT companies abroad. In 1969 ITT wanted to include investment grants, amounting to £844,000 in the income of their London subsidiary, STC—a very unusual practice among British accountants. Their British auditor was then flown over to New York, and the item duly appeared in STC's 1967 profit-and-loss accounts, based on acceptance by STC's auditor. Andersen's have now taken over the British auditing. In 1972 Arthur Andersen issued a new booklet called *Objectives of Financial Statements*. The booklet regretted that the accounting profession had recently shown 'an exaggerated and unrealistic concern for detailed uniformity' (though one of their partners, Leonard Spacek, has frequently written to urge the elimination of alternative principles in accounting for similar transactions), and went on to advocate that the basis of accounting should be current value rather than historic cost : but this would make it still easier (as the *Guardian* pointed out) for conglomerates to overvalue their assets and profits.[1]

The obscurantism of conglomerate accounting has aroused increasing criticism from inside the profession. One of the most outspoken critics is Abraham Briloff, Professor of Accounting at Baruch College, New York, a wiry and enthusiastic man who works from the Gramercy Park Hotel, who has written a witty book about 'Unaccountable Accounting', analysing the tricks that conglomerates can play. He enjoys debunking his fellow accountants with vivid imagery; he sees conglomerate bosses as cowboys who invade the territory of the farmers, sell off the topsoil, and ruin the land; they expand, by raping, reaping, de-dazzling. He complains about 'hot-pants accounting', which reveals the exciting, while concealing the essential. He describes how Geneen can conceal the cost of most of his assets like an iceberg. Briloff is trying to spread an evangelical and proselytising spirit among young accountants, to encourage them to take stands against the corporations; but he sees a long battle ahead.

The inscrutability of the ITT accounts has also increasingly exasperated the experts whose job it is to try to analyse

1. *Guardian*, October 24, 1972.

big companies, the security analysts advising the share-holders (nearly half the shares of ITT are held by the institutions—the banks, insurance companies and pension funds). Most of the stockbrokers are satisfied with the accounts, but a few of the analysts have begun to campaign militantly for further disclosure. And what has made them specially suspicious, ironically enough, has been the very steadiness of ITT's quarterly rises in earnings, through boom and slump, at a time when other conglomerates were foundering. One of them, Ray Dirks, a chubby, long-haired analyst who exposed the equity funding scandal, does detailed detective work to find out what ITT really earns. As one example he has shown how in 1968 ITT showed an increase in income of $56 million, of which $17 million was called 'miscellaneous and non-operating income'. By comparing the prospectus issued by the European subsidiary, International Standard Electric, Dirks showed that $11 million of that miscellaneous income in fact came from 'disposal of miscellaneous properties and investments'—so that a fifth of the increased world income of ITT came from selling off European properties.

Two other thorns in ITT's thick flesh are the analysts Bob Olstein and Thornton O'Glove, who produce what they call a 'Quality of Earnings Report' on big companies, to reveal their true performance. They, too, have uncovered large sales of properties and securities being classified as income. They even wrote to Geneen in 1972, without success, asking for eighteen separate disclosures, and telling him 'this evasiveness on the part of your high ranking officials is not in the best interests of your shareholders. Certainly a corporation with the outstanding growth record of ITT should sell at a price earnings ratio of more than sixteen times the estimated earnings of $3.85 per share for 1972.'

And it was true. Geneen was as aware as anyone that, in spite of all the steady increase in earnings and the rapid growth, the price-earnings ratio of ITT was very disappointing compared for instance to IBM, the company which Geneen so often measured himself against. It was a blow to his pride, a personal affront. 'He looks at the price-earnings ratio every day,' said one of his colleagues, 'as if it were his mirror, to see how he looks to the world.' But the mirror never gave the right answer. What was the explanation? Was it the stock market's fears about Geneen's mortality, and what would happen afterwards, when Dunleavy or others took over? Was it because the profitability of ITT, as a percentage of sales, was not high? Was it, as the analysts suggested, the lack of disclosure? Was it—particularly after the ITT scandal of 1972—a political worry, a 'scandal discount'? Was it, as Geneen himself complained, that ITT was doing *too* well? Or was it an instinctive feeling that there was something unsound about the company : as one investment expert put it 'it looks good, but it doesn't smell good'.[1]

This unaccountability, in the most literal sense, of multinationals, does not only worry shareholders : it also worries the governments of countries where they operate. Huge sums can be shifted in and out of countries, profits can be turned to losses, assets sold off, without anyone being the wiser. Behind all other elements of the corporation's sovereignty is the secrecy of its accounts (as important as the secrecy of the Vatican's or the Queen of England's), and without breaking that down, there is little hope for making it accountable in other ways, too.

1. see *Fortune*, 'Geneen's Moneymaking Machine', September 1972.

7

The Trust-Busters

In this society of ours, we depend on diffusion of power as the best means of achieving political democracy.

Senator Philip Hart, 1968

If we have done anything wrong, send your man up to my man and they can fix it up.

J. P. Morgan to Theodore Roosevelt, 1902

While Geneen was strengthening his records over his European empire, his expansion in America continued; and during 1968 the ITT acquisitions were proceeding at record pace. In October 1968 he announced a merger, through Lazards, with the Canteen Corporation, the leading company in the automated food-vending industry, specialising in providing what is gruesomely called 'in-plant feeding', mass-producing frozen meals. He also proclaimed a merger with the Grinnell fire-protection business, the biggest of its kind in America, which makes eighty-seven per cent of the fire-alarms for American fire stations. At the end of the year, just before Christmas, he announced nothing less than the biggest merger in American history.

THE HARTFORD

For some time Geneen had been watching a stately insurance company, Hartford Fire, which was based on Hartford, Connecticut, the insurance capital of America. It was an ancient company founded in 1810, which had insured Robert E. Lee and Abraham Lincoln. It had kept pace with the times. It was now the fifth biggest property-and-liability insurance company in America, with premiums of $969 million in 1968, and assets of nearly two billion dollars. Insurance companies were specially tempting to conglomerates, for they provided a steady cash-flow from premiums, and they had huge portfolio investments whose capital gains, by changing the accounting system, could be converted from assets into income. Felix Rohatyn of Lazards had persuaded Geneen of the importance of these assets, and of the longterm future prospects of the insurance industry. ITT already had a cluster of life insurance companies, including Hamilton Life, ITT Life and Mid-Western Life in America and Abbey Life in Britain. Hartford Fire would make them one of the world's biggest all-round insurers, and would give them a much-needed respectability. As a later chairman of the Securities and Exchange Commission, Bradford Cook, described it : 'Hartford—she's a blue-blooded lady, ITT— she's a lady of the night.'[1]

The Hartford directors were solid, conservative men led by a chairman, Harry Williams, who had been thirty years in the company. They ran the company very cautiously. Like many other insurance companies, whenever they sold securities at a profit, they put the proceeds into its surplus, to avoid paying tax, instead of declaring it as earnings; in the two years 1968 and 1969 these capital gains had amounted to over $100 million. But the casualty insurance business was not doing well, and in the spring of 1968 Hartford shares had plummeted. The directors realised they were vulnerable to a raid by a conglomerate offering 'Chinese money' (or inflated stock). They consulted their investment banker, Robert Baldwin of Morgan Stanley, about defending themselves. In the summer they had talks with Dow Chemical, whose president Carl Gerstacker was on their board, about providing a possible 'haven'; but in October discussions broke down. Soon afterwards, Rohatyn approached Baldwin suggesting a merger between Hartford and ITT, but Baldwin replied it was not for sale.[2] Then on November 1, one of the Hartford directors, Bill Griffin, received an ominous telephone call. It was from André Meyer of

1. *New York Times*, May 21, 1973.
2. Baldwin deposition, March 16, 1971.

Lazards; his clients, ITT had just taken an option on 1.2 million Hartford shares—six percent of the total—from a mutual fund on the West Coast.

That afternoon, Meyer, Geneen and Rohatyn flew up to Hartford to talk with the rather frightened directors, and over the next months two lunches were arranged for Hartford's key directors to meet Geneen and his men. Geneen was very cordial, and explained how well ITT and Hartford could work together. ('Geneen wanted to romance us,' one of the directors, Raymond Deck, explained later.) ITT produced a secret report called the 'Tobacco Memorandum' (because it referred to the Hartford as 'Tobacco' : Hartford is in the tobacco district of Connecticut). It outlined the glittering prospects for a collaboration. Hartford could provide casualty insurance for ITT's employees, for their shareholders, for their Life Insurance companies in Europe, and for their other customers, including 2.7 millions holding Sheraton and Avis credit-cards. Hartford, too, could invest in Levitt's Land Banks, in the Rayonier land in Florida, and in Sheraton real-estate abroad. Hartford and ITT, in other words, could march together towards a self-contained paradise : their customers and employees could be insured from the cradle to the grave, while they drove their ITT hire-car from their ITT home to their ITT hotel. (It is only fair to say that ITT never achieved widespread reciprocity. But of their ambition, they left little doubt.)

The Hartford directors were not keen to collaborate, and hectically behind the scenes they tried to defend themselves against a raid. Harry Williams asked Baldwin to take charge of a diversification programme, to protect themselves. Baldwin said he would only join them if he became their chief executive officer; the Hartford directors eventually agreed, and the contract was due to be signed on December 26. But Geneen got wind of it. Three days before Baldwin was due to sign, ITT's chief counsel, Howard Aibel, arrived in Hartford with a letter from Geneen complaining that Hartford had not kept their agreement to co-operate with ITT, and announcing that ITT was making a bid for the whole company. They were offering ITT stock valued by Lazards at

$1.5 billion, or double the current value of the Hartford stock.

Faced with this unwelcome Christmas offer, the Hartford board politely replied that it was worthy of study, and quickly commissioned a report on the merger by an independent consultancy, Drexel Harriman Ripley. But Geneen was prepared for opposition. He told his staff to exert 'inexorable pressure' on Hartford and its shareholders. ITT planned for the 'full panoply' of contacts to ensure a favourable frame of mind on the Hartford board; they persuaded an 'insurance friend' to write a letter 'on his own initiative, so to speak', to Drexel, urging the merits of the merger. ITT continued buying stock, in spite of the tax problems (see below). Ned Gerrity was advised to be 'exceptionally alert' for counter-moves in Hartford or Washington, or objections by shareholders.[1] There was now no question of ITT being a flotilla of small ships. It was one big battleship.

The inexorable pressure had its effect, and by May the Hartford directors, under strong pressure from shareholders, agreed to the merger. But there was another hurdle, in the form of the insurance commissioner for Connecticut, William Cotter. The succession of earlier raids on insurance companies had alarmed Connecticut sufficiently for the State to pass a new Public Act, No. 444, to protect companies against conglomerates, giving the commissioner large powers of objection. Commissioner Cotter was an ambitious Democrat politician—the post is a political nomination— and very conscious of local opinion. Most of the insurance grandees of the state were against the merger of Hartford; and although ITT had been trying to reassure them, in December 1969 Cotter ruled against the merger. He complained among other things that the Hartford directors had been granted large stock options by ITT and he judged that the Hartford had better prospects on its own than with ITT. It was a sensational setback.

But Geneen was undeterred, and he quickly stepped up the pressure. He was determined to avoid the fiasco of the ABC setback two years before. As soon as Cotter issued his decision, Howard Aibel of ITT visited him to say that ITT

1. Memo from C. T. Ireland to H. S. Geneen, January 2, 1969; *Kleindienst Hearings:* Vol. III, p. 1217.

would appeal, and produce a new offer, which turned out to be very similar to the first. For the next three months an army of ITT men, including Geneen, descended on Hartford, calling on Cotter and his staff. Just at this time, Cotter decided to stand for Congress, and began to canvas support in Hartford, mounting a campaign whose cost he himself estimated at $100,000.

The second hearings before Cotter were held in Hartford in March 1970. Geneen came up with a bevy of ITT directors. He pledged that he would keep the Hartford headquarters in the city, that he would not cut employment, or interfere with management. As with ABC, he indicated that Hartford needed ITT much more than ITT needed Hartford. 'Our own feeling,' he said, 'is that the insurance field is going to need more capital.' As with ABC, too, he stressed the autonomy within the ITT system, and promised that Hartford would have its own board. Cotter asked some awkward questions about Avis, and why Townsend had not wanted to work a single day for ITT. But Bud Morrow, who was now running Avis, was there to assure Cotter that Townsend was not really being serious. Eugene Black, the ex-head of the World Bank, now director of ITT, testified that: 'I don't know of any company with which I am more favourably impressed than the management of ITT.'

It was just after the second hearing that Cotter happened to meet Ralph Nader. Nader had been brought up (as had Geneen) near Hartford, and through his campaign for auto safety had a special interest in insurance. He had been invited to address a conference of insurance agents at Hartford where Cotter, too, was a speaker. Nader had already been mobilised against ITT, in the ABC case, and he had developed a profound distrust for ITT and its methods, second only to his distrust of General Motors. At the mention of the initials (I noticed) Nader's whole appearance changes; his tall, loose shape stiffens and springs to life instantly; his dark eyes piercing, smiling a discomforting smile. He sees Geneen as a dictator who is interested in power not profit, who wants to build up his own economic nation-state, and who would like, given the chance, to buy the United States. As Nader talks about ITT, one feels that here Geneen has met his match—with an opponent who has his own single-mindedness, the same ability to drive and animate people, not hesitating to disrupt his subordinates' domestic lives. But Nader has one advantage; he can motivate his staff with gods other than profit.

After the conference, Cotter talked to Nader and invited him up to his office. According to Nader, Cotter then explained that he was under pressure to approve the merger, and that ITT had begun to put investigators onto him, and others.[1] Cotter later in court denied this, and said that the pressure was no more than letters and calls from brokers and investors. But indisputably, Cotter asked Nader to provide him with as much information on ITT and Hartford as he could.

Nader thereupon asked one of his 'raiders' to investigate the case—genial young lawyer called Reuben Robertson III, who was to play an important part in the ITT story. Robertson was a much more relaxed character than Nader, without his frenzied involvement, yet with consistent dedication. After Yale he had gone into Covington and Burling, Dean Acheson's old law firm in Washington, which dealt with many of the giant corporations, including ITT. He soon, like other young radical lawyers, felt the limitations of a corporate law practice. He spent a year as an attorney for the Transportation Department, and then joined Nader, with a special interest in the regulated industries. When Nader asked him to take up the case of Hartford and ITT, he put all his energies to it; ever since then, Robertson has become one of the most persistent of all the Geneen-hunters, helped by the network of young Naderites. He works from an informal office above an artist's supply shop in downtown Washington, brooding over a mountain of ITT documents, secret memos and court cases, briefing journalists and politicians, and chasing one case after another, from one court to the next.

After inspecting the evidence, Robertson was convinced that Geneen's real reason for wanting Hartford was the opposite to what he had stated to Cotter; he needed the Hartford's huge assets to give him borrowing power, and he needed the cash-flow. He sent Cotter a number of submissions, including a memorandum spelling out ITT's real

1. Nader v Cotter: Plaintiff's Brief, January 1972.

intentions, and questioning its financial stability. But in the meantime Cotter appeared for some reason to be gradually changing his mind.

ITT intensified their pressure after the public hearings. They had hired a small-time local attorney called Joe Fazzano, without telling their other big firms working on the job. Fazzano was an old friend both of Cotter and of Howard Aibel of ITT, and had been successfully speculating in Hartford shares. He now had long talks with Cotter on ITT's behalf, in restaurants, in his office, on the phone, stressing the advantages of the merger.[1] Then one Saturday morning Geneen came up to Hartford to talk privately with Cotter and an insurance official, Peter Kelly. He chatted about his schooldays at Suffield, about his house at Key Biscayne near President Nixon, and about how useful Canteen frozen-food machines could be in apartments; he assured them that ITT directors were all honourable men who did not wear horns.

Two months after the second hearings, on May 19, Cotter met privately with local Democrats, including the then chairman Michael Kelly and Nicholas Carborne, chairman of a project to build a new civic centre, which was in financial difficulties. They asked Cotter to call ITT for help. Cotter explained, 'As long as I'm going to approve the merger, we might as well do something for the city of Hartford, and ITT has expressed a willingness to make a charitable civic contribution.' Three days after the meeting, Howard Aibel and Ned Gerrity from ITT came up to discuss with Cotter and the others how they could help the civic centre and provide a new Sheraton hotel; the group then toured the site in an ITT car.

The next day Cotter announced that he would permit the acquisition. The biggest merger in history went through.

CONCENTRATION CRISIS

But in the meantime Geneen was coming up against more formidable adversaries in Washington. The hectic expansion of ITT had at last attracted the interest of the trust-busters.

1. For a full account of the ambiguities of the Fazzano-Cotter talks, see *The Hartford Courant*, November 8, 1970 and March 13, 1972.

ITT was an extreme example of the rapid trend towards concentration, both in America and in the whole Western world, and it was rapidly becoming a test case in a major confrontation between government and big business.

ITT was only one, though the biggest, of a group of 'conglomerates' which had swollen up with alarming speed, encouraged by the long stock-exchange boom after 1965, following the stepping-up of the Vietnam war. A handful of shrewd and flamboyant financiers had built up clusters of companies with very diverse interests. They could do so with very little additional capital; they borrowed money to buy another company, and used the profits of the new company to pay interest on the debt. They bought any company which could provide the right profits, and the result was an amazing collection of mixed bags. James Ling of Ling-Temco-Vought built up an obscure defence contractor in 1960 into the fourteenth biggest American industrial company in 1969, including a meat-packing business, an airline, a car-rental firm and a big manufacturer of jetplanes. Charles Bluhdorn, an Austrian immigrant who had made money out of Brazilian coffee, set up Gulf and Western in 1956, when it was making car bumpers in Grand Rapids, and then bought up ninety-two companies, making anything from zinc and sugar to cigars and Paramount films. 'Tex' Thornton bought a small electronics firm, Litton Industries, for a million dollars, and added 103 companies in nine years, with products ranging from ships and calculating machines to text-books and seismic equipment. Saul Steinberg, the 'boy genius' of Leasco Data Processing, increased his assets from $8 million to $402 million in four years, buying into containers, insurance and real-estate, and even swallowing a large (and disastrous) share of Pergamon Press in Britain.

These conglomerates were part of a trend towards diversification followed by many big companies in America and Europe, who did not want to have all their eggs in one basket. In Britain, Imperial Tobacco had bought Yardley perfumes and Ross frozen foods; Unilever, beginning with soap and margarine, had acquired a huge gallimaufry of companies. But most of these older diversifiers were investing their surplus cash; while the new conglomerates had more to do with stock-exchange wizardry. Their success depended on maintaining a high share value, which in turn depended on maintaining their growth by acquiring more companies. The conglomerators insisted that their mergers shook up sleepy industries and made the combination more efficient than the parts. Litton Industries adopted the fancy word 'synergism' from the medical vocabulary, meaning 'working together' and synergism became part of the conglomerates' flim-flam, to prove that 2 + 2 = 5. But as *Fortune* described it at the height of the conglomerate boom in February 1969, there was a 'chain-letter effect, whose terminal stages can be painful. The great conglomerate movement is generating widespread doubt, apprehension and even dismay.'

The conglomerators themselves were a bizarre group of outsiders, and as with ITT, the more complex and diversified a company became, the more it appeared to depend on one man. Most of them came from outside any American Establishment : indeed their arrival helped to give meaning to that concept, as the Establishment companies closed ranks to exclude them. Many of them were first-generation immigrants; like Bluhdorn, 'the mad Austrian', or Meshulam Riklis, the Palestinian who built up the Rapid-American Corporation, or Geneen himself. Many had left school early, with little formal education. Most of them were flamboyant and publicity-seeking : Ling, with his two-million-dollar palace in Dallas, Kerkorian with his walnut-panelled DC-9, Riklis with his Manhattan mansion.

But Geneen was different. Geneen, too, was an outsider, a loner, an immigrant who had started work at fifteen. His ambition, too, was boundless. But he was never flamboyant, never sought the headlines, was never fooled by his own publicity. He kept his stern sense of control, insisted that his business was management-in-depth, and that his growth must be steady rather than spectacular. The Establishment distrusted him too : but they also learnt from him.

The conglomerates were only the dizziest examples of the movement towards mergers in the 'soaring 'sixties', which was making big business still bigger. In 1948 the 200 biggest industrial corporations in America controlled forty-eight percent of the manufacturing assets; in 1969 they controlled fifty-eight percent.[1] Three-quarters of the swelling was due to mergers, and only a quarter was due to internal growth. This massive new concentration was justified by many economists as a necessary price to pay for high technology and long-term planning; witness Professor Galbraith, in his eloquent apologia for the giants, *The New Industrial State*.

The concentration could be justified too by the increasing scope of world competition : giants in one continent provoked rival giants in another. In Europe mergers were progressing even faster, stimulated by the 'American Challenge', and often with the active support of their governments. Renault merged with Peugeot, Montecatini with Edison, Fiat with Citroen, Dunlop with Pirelli. In Britain, the Industrial Reorganisation Corporation, set up by the Labour government during 1967, helped to marry two of the biggest British car companies to create British Leyland, and three electrical companies to create General Electric. In the early 'fifties the hundred biggest companies in Britain had only twenty-two percent of the industrial assets; in 1970 they had fifty percent. The 'sixties, all over the world, was the decade of the giants.

In Europe the wave of mergers continued with very little apparent political worry; the Common Market was more interested in encouraging concentration than in controlling it. But in America by the end of the decade the hectic concentration, and particularly the precariousness of the conglomerates, provoked a worried reaction. It was one of those moods of resistance to big business which have recurred in cycles over the past century, and which have led by degrees to the building up of the apparatus of regulation.

BIG BUSINESS V GOVERNMENT

The machinery of anti-trust looks impressive, particularly to those outside the United States, as an example of American democracy and self-correction; for a country which believes so fervently in business, to dare to jail businessmen compels the admiration of Europeans accustomed to more discreet and doubtful controls. Yet the American anti-trust

1. Speech of the Attorney-General, John Mitchell, at Savannah, June 6, 1969. (2) *Conglomerate Hearings:* p. 4551.

institutions have never been quite as fierce as they look, and the bold confrontations of government with business have a habit of mysteriously petering out. The history of anti-trust in America is a history of evasions and compromises, and repeatedly the biggest corporations have shown themselves stronger than governments.

The last big movement against industrial concentration had been in the late 'forties. At that time, in spite of the curbs of previous legislation, the Sherman and Clayton acts, big companies were still able to buy up other companies' assets, and to connive through their managers. There was a surge of political feeling : as Senator Kefauver said : 'The people are losing their power to direct their own economic welfare.' The Celler-Kefauver Act of 1950 strengthened the controversial section 7 of the Clayton Act, to forbid corporations to acquire assets which would lessen competition, 'in any line of commerce in any section of the country'. It came much closer to limiting concentration as such, rather than simply protecting competition; and the House report insisted that it should apply to horizontal and vertical mergers, and to conglomerate mergers which covered several industries. The Celler-Kefauver Act appeared to mean business, and Kefauver himself, who was chairman of the Senate Anti-Trust Committee, showed his seriousness in his dramatic investigation in 1960 into the 'Electrical Conspiracy' revolving round General Electric, which had cheated the government of a billion dollars. In the subsequent court case, the Judge sentenced seven of the conspiring businessmen to jail, and fined the companies two million dollars. It was the first time in anti-trust history that businessmen had actually been sent to jail.

But the trust-busters were still more notable for their omissions than their commissions. Partly, they suffered from unequal resources. The anti-trust division has grown with each legislation, and its staff looks formidable to an outsider: 316 lawyers, plus thirty-eight economists and statisticians, with a budget of $11.4 million a year.[1] But on any single case these lawyers are far outnumbered by the armies of specialist lawyers hired by the threatened corporation; these corporate lawyers are expert at the techniques of delay,

1. see Mark Green : *The Closed Enterprise System*, 1972.

which may postpone the trial until it is no longer relevant.[1]

The most fundamental weakness of the anti-trust division is that it has never been properly insulated from politics. It exists within the framework of the Department of Justice; all its decisions go through the Attorney-General and his Deputy; and its staff are constantly aware of the political pressures from corporations to which the administration, in one way or another, is indebted. Courageous trust-busters find themselves gradually worn down by the delays, compromises and contradictions that surround them.

Republicans often claim to be more effective trust-busters than the Democrats: much as Conservatives in Britain claim to be better at controlling big business than the Labour party; and for the same reason, that they believe more whole-heartedly in capitalism and therefore in the need to intervene to ensure its free workings: in other words, that business is too important to be left to businessmen. Certainly in America the trust-busting record of the Democrats from 1960 to 1968 was less than magnificent. The Kennedys, both President and Attorney-General, were reluctant to antagonise big business, and Bobby Kennedy was at odds with his anti-trust head, Lee Loevinger (who later became a consultant to ITT). Under President Johnson a promising new anti-trust boss took over, Professor Donald Turner, who had written a radical book called *Anti-Trust Policy,* but he was much less radical in office. He played a part in frustrating ITT's bid for ABC (see page 82), but he also insisted that to move against conglomerates would need special legislation (later he became consultant to ITT in the Hartford case). Only in the last months of the Democrat era, with Ramsey Clark as Attorney-General, were there signs of serious movement, when he mounted the mammoth case against IBM, which is still pending today. It was in the eight Democrat years that the greatest concentration had occurred since the formation of the trusts at the turn of the century.

Nor were the committees on Capitol Hill much more effective. The chairman of the Senate Anti-Trust Committee is one of the most respected men in American politics: Philip Hart, the Democrat Senator for Michigan, a high-

1. see Mark Green: *The Closed Enterprise System,* 1972.

minded Catholic. He is suspicious of the social, as well as the economic consequences of big mergers, draining financial power from the smaller centres to the big ones. In 1964 his committee opened hearings on the problems of economic concentration, and Hart spoke up vigorously. But Hart was severely limited by his own committee, most of whom— including the die-hard Republicans, Roman Hruska, Strom Thurmond and Hiram Fong—were basically not anti-trust, but pro-trust.

In the House of Representatives, the Anti-Trust Committee was headed by a veteran campaigner, the eighty-four-year-old Emmanuel Celler, a rugged war-horse who had been co-author of the Celler-Kefauver Act of 1950. But Celler's own law firm deals with anti-trust cases, and he has been known to intervene politically on his clients' behalf. And in the 'sixties Celler's committee became notably less active—perhaps because he was getting old, or was distracted by civil rights questions.

By 1969 the pace of concentration, and particularly the growth of conglomerates, had become too alarming to ignore; no fewer than six sub-committees, and several agencies, were studying it. The most remarkable outburst came from the Federal Trade Commission, normally a very staid agency; its economic staff under Professor Mueller published a report on corporate mergers which provided ammunition for many other critics. It showed, for instance, that the top 200 corporations in America now owned over three-fifths of all manufacturing assets, or more than the share owned by the 1,000 largest companies in 1941; and that between the years 1953 and 1968, twenty-one percent of corporate manufacturing assets had been acquired through mergers. It indicated links between the centralisation of industry and lessening competition, and commented:

> These interrelated developments pose a serious threat to America's democratic and social institutions by creating a degree of centralised private decision-making that is incompatible with a free enterprise system, a system relying upon market forces to discipline private economic power.

There was much disagreement among economists about what to do about the conglomerates. One report, headed by

Philip Neal, Dean of the University of Chicago, decided that the real problem was not the conglomerates but the old oligopolies, like cars, steels, or computers, which should be broken up by new legislation. Another one, by another Chicago professor, George Stigler, also advised against breaking up the conglomerates, until more was known about their economic effects; Stigler disagreed with Neal's idea of legislation, but advocated a careful scrutiny of the oligopolies and their price-fixing.

The case against conglomerates was not indeed an easy one to make, for by their diversity they cut across the old definitions of monopoly and restriction of trade; and it was partly to avoid anti-trust action that they had become so diversified. Few of them dominated a single industry, and theoretically world industry might be run by a handful of vast conglomerates, each competing with scores of industries, without cutting across anti-trust laws. The fundamental argument against them was not so much economic, as political and social : that they restricted individuality and freedom of choice, that they centralised and concentrated activities which could survive separately, that they were simply, in a word, too big, too ubiquitous and too powerful. But that was a charge that was hard to define in legal terms.

CONGLOMERATE HEARINGS

By early 1969, Emmanuel Celler had at last decided that something must be done—or at least be said—about conglomerates, and in July he began a series of unprecedented hearings. Over the next ten months his committee interviewed seventy-two witnesses, taking evidence which took up seven volumes and 6,300 pages. They singled out six conglomerates for special study, the biggest of which was International Telephone and Telegraph. They obtained a mountain of ITT memos and reports, and on November 20, 1969 they summoned Geneen himself to give evidence.

It was a historic encounter, between Geneen the evangelical entrepreneur and Celler the tough old sceptic, old enough to be his father. Geneen was in his top form; he began by expounding the splendours of his system, and attacking Professor Mueller's FTC report, which hadn't got a good word to say for conglomerates. He explained how the conglomerates, in spite of their size, had not affected market concentration and had actually increased competition and decentralisation, bringing new businesses to small towns; and they were beneficial to the investors, because they insulated them against risks. Celler listened impassively, and said at the end: 'Your statement almost makes me believe that ITT has wings.'

Celler questioned Geneen about his methods: 'I wonder whether the good Lord has given anybody the prowess and the expertise, the ingenuity, to be able to control all those operations.' Geneen described how really the ITT companies were run by two thousand executives, who were very independent. But how, asked Celler, *could* they be independent with the kind of controls that Geneen had described? 'I couldn't begin to run the hundredth of what we have,' replied Geneen, 'and I don't; but I do see that it is run.' Celler asked, 'Which brings more competition? More companies or fewer companies?' Geneen replied that under the ITT system there were not really fewer companies at all, but simply companies with more input and support behind them to be competitive. 'Of course,' replied Celler, 'I must emphatically disagree with you ... Having this great economic concentration in your company, you remind me of what somebody said before this committee some years ago: "Every man for himself, said the elephant as he danced amongst the chickens."'

The committee's counsel, Kenneth Harkins, questioned Geneen about the practice of reciprocity, of 'I-buy-from-you-you-buy-from-me'. He presented a succession of memos showing how ITT pressed its companies to provide services for each other, to cut out competitors, and to use 'leverage' of one company to help another get business. A letter from the head of Rayonier, Russell Erickson, described his plans to sell more paper pulp in Argentina, using the leverage of Continental Baking, which bought large quantities of beef from Argentina. Reports from Levitt, Sheraton and Aetna Finance described plans for providing business for each other. A letter from Geneen to Robert Townsend, discussed how all ITT employees could become salesmen for Avis:

HARKINS: 'You are not only suggesting that he acquire the captive market of ITT's employees, but also to use them as an advertising group?'

GENEEN: 'Well, let me be clear here. I don't see anything wrong with our employees believing in our company and being salesmen for it.'

But, Chairman Celler pointed out, the ITT memos really gave the game away: 'Mr. Geneen, there is an old adage, that is "The Bible says do right. I say don't write". You have written here.'[1]

Geneen's exposition of the ITT system was a brilliant piece of advocacy, of having-it-both-ways. He explained how ITT provided both more independence and more control, both greater rationalisation and greater competition. As Geneen described it, there seemed no reason why ITT should not take over the whole of American business. But Celler interposed: 'You know, if what you say is true, then we wouldn't need any laws at all . . . Everybody would be so good, and so kind, and gentle, and so absent of evil, that there would be no need for any repressive statutes, would there? But the human nature is different. Business nature is different.'

It was not till a year after the Celler hearings were completed that the report came out, in June 1971. It was a provocative document of 700 pages, the most complete study yet compiled of the conglomerates. It debunked several of the conglomerates' claims, including the 'highly touted phenomenon' of synergism: 'In fact, management difficulties with newly acquired companies showed, if anything, that combination frequently had injurious effects on efficiency, productivity and corporate values.'

The section on ITT was very critical. The company, it said had 'created a virtually self-contained corporate structure that exists and acts outside the scope of any countries in which it provides services . . . ITT's relationship to government policies of the countries in which it does business gives one pause.' It accused ITT of using reciprocity and the 'in-house market' to boost its sales, and of conferring, 'desirable heft' in particular markets. It explained that ITT's accounting gimmickry concealed the weaknesses

1. *Conglomerate Hearings:* Vol. III, p. 101.

of newly-acquired companies, and magnified their gains in earnings. ITT was financially less stable than other big corporations; in terms of the ratio of long-term debt to equity, ITT's ratio exceeded that of each of the thirty companies in the Dow Jones industrial average except Alcoa. Perhaps most damaging to Geneen was the suggestion that there were 'indications that efficiency and performance of its constituent units deteriorate after they are taken into ITT's system'.

The report was political dynamite. I. F. Stone wrote a stirring call to arms : 'In the pages of this study, the young can see the morals and mores which mold our economy and threaten to some day remold our politics. For as corporate concentration grows, the threat of a corporate state grows with it.' [1] But in presenting it, Celler showed his embarrassment. He delayed the publication until the Labour Day weekend, when most of Washington was empty, and presented it as the work of the staff of the sub-committee, without the endorsement of the congressmen. It was accompanied by a press release which made it sound much more approving than it was. It had no index, and its lack of notice was an interesting example of the New Secrecy, in which explosive revelations can be concealed by the sheer quantity of evidence, like thieves hiding in the crowd.

ENTER MCLAREN

Soon after it took office in 1969, the Nixon administration had begun to show much more concern with the growth of giant companies than their Democrat predecessors. Nixon's Attorney-General, John Mitchell, made a famous speech in June to the Georgia Bar Association in Savannah; giving the recent figures for the growth of concentration, and commenting :

> The danger that super-concentration poses to our economic, political and social structure cannot be overestimated. Concentration of this magnitude is likely to elimate existing and future competition. It increases the possibility for reciprocity and other forms of unfair buyer-seller leverage. It creates nation-wide marketing, managerial and financing structures whose enormous physical and psychological resources pose

1. I. F. Stone's *Bi-Weekly*, September 20, 1971.

substantial barriers to smaller firms wishing to participate in a competitive market. And, finally, super-concentration creates a 'community of interest' which discourages competition among large firms and establishes a tone in the market-place for more and more mergers.

And he ended his speech with a very specific warning that the Department of Justice might well oppose any merger among the top 200 manufacturing firms, and would probably oppose any merger between them and leading producers.

To show that he meant business, Mitchell found an anti-trust chief who was much respected for his independence. Richard McLaren was a Republican lawyer of fifty-one from a Chicago firm, specialising in representing big corporations against anti-trust cases: he had defended the Sealy Mattress Company and the National Dairy Products. But McLaren was following a familiar path in turning from poaching to gamekeeping, and indeed the anti-trust law is so complex that only its most expert evaders know how to strengthen it. Mitchell and his deputy, Richard Kleindienst, met McLaren in December 1968, before Nixon's inauguration, at the Pierre Hotel in New York, to sound him out. McLaren made three conditions: that there would be a vigorous anti-trust programme, that they would take cases to the Supreme Court, and that cases would be decided on their merits, without political decisions.[1] Mitchell and Kleindienst agreed, and appointed him.

McLaren thought there was a good chance of breaking some of the conglomerates under the existing Clayton Act of 1950 and he preferred to try litigation before asking for legislation. There was much argument among anti-trust lawyers as to whether the controversial Section 7 of the Clayton Act *could* be applied against conglomerates; McLaren's predecessors, Turner and Zimmerman, both thought that they could not, and so did the current Solicitor-General, Erwin Griswold. But McLaren had thought out his policy, and he stuck to it. He was a ruggedly independent man, with a Chicagoan's scepticism of New York and Washington.

He moved very quickly, and made bold speeches. In
1. *Kleindienst Hearings:* Vol. II, p. 117.

March 1969 he told the House Ways and Means Committee that it was urgently necessary to stop the conglomerate mergers, with their 'severe economic and social dislocations'; and later in the month he talked to the American Bar Association about 'the galloping trend towards economic concentration'. In the same month, he backed up words with deeds. The Justice Department filed a suit against the conglomerate Ling-Temco-Vought, to stop them merging with the Jones and Laughlin Steel Corporation.[1]

But McLaren's main target was inevitably the International Telephone and Telegraph Corporation. It was already the biggest conglomerate, and it was still conglomerating. When McLaren moved in, it had just acquired Canteen and Grinnell, and was preparing the merger with Hartford. Of the four cases that McLaren brought in 1969, three were against ITT for these three most recent mergers.

McLaren moved first against Canteen, whose marriage with ITT was due to be consummated on April 10, 1969. He had a formidable case against it, for ITT would be well able to practise the vice of 'reciprocity' with Canteen, by persuading its own companies to use Canteen equipment for staff meals, so that Canteen's rivals would suffer. Three days before the marriage was due, McLaren recommended to Kleindienst, the Deputy Attorney-General, a temporary restraining order to prevent the merger—much easier than breaking it up afterwards. The ITT lawyers agreed to postpone the merger, but came to plead with Kleindienst and McLaren that Canteen was in disarray and urgently needed good management. Soon afterwards the merger was allowed to go ahead, while a new case was prepared to break it up later. It was a mysterious outcome, arousing suspicions of hanky-panky. The Naderites later investigated the case, and gave their version of the story : that ITT had lobbied the White House, who then pressed Kleindienst to drop it; that McLaren was furious, and threatened to resign : the result was the compromise, that the merger would first be allowed, and then contested.[2] McLaren has always denied this story;

1. The merger eventually went ahead, on condition that LTV got rid of two other companies, Braniff Airways and Okonite, largely because of fears that LTV might otherwise go bankrupt : a kind of parallel to the ITT story.

2. Mark Green: *The Closed Enterprise System*, pp. 44–45.

but the suspicions surrounding the Canteen case encouraged the suspicions in the scandal that followed.

McLaren however pursued the other ITT mergers with vigour. In August 1969—four months before Cotter's first hearings had finally approved the Hartford merger—he asked for injunctions to stop the mergers with Grinnell and, much more important, with Hartford. The suit against the Hartford merger claimed that :

> actual and potential competition between the two firms would be diminshed and that the merger will foreclose competitors of Hartford from competing for the insurance purchases of ITT and ITT's customers, increase the power ITT and Hartford to benefit from reciprocity effect in selling insurance, and trigger other mergers by companies seeking to protect themselves from the impact of this acquisition or to obtain similar competitive advantages.

It was the opening of the biggest and most controversial anti-trust case in history. McLaren and Geneen were set on a collision course which would, in the end, wreck both their ambitions.

Geneen, after his victory with the merger, was quite ready for this new obstacle, and he quickly mounted his counter-attack—though it was only much later that the full scope of it became clear (see Chapter 10). ITT had a vast array of lawyers, of all shapes and sizes, to cope with such problems; it was part of Geneen's skill that he knew which man to deploy on which front, which weapon to choose from his armoury. Within ITT's headquarters alone there were 150 lawyers, and there were countless attorneys hired for special tasks, ranging from Joe Fazzano in Hartford to Covington and Burling in Washington. Geneen had earlier taken the precaution of asking the former anti-trust chief, Donald Turner, for his opinion about the Hartford merger, and Turner had deemed it to be safe to proceed. Now, whole armies of attorneys were mobilised to fight the anti-trust decision, backed up by the public relations men. Later in 1970, ITT formally put forward a proposal for settlement; Ephraim Jacobs, of the Washington law firm of Hollabaugh and Jacobs, called on McLaren suggesting that ITT would be prepared to get rid of Canteen, most of Grinnell and

Levitt, provided they could keep Hartford. McLaren stood firm; he would only settle if Hartford went, too.[1]

The two cases, against Grinnell and Hartford, duly came up in the district court in October, and in each case the judge refused to give a preliminary injunction. That was not very surprising to McLaren; he had told Mitchell when he was appointed that he wanted the Supreme Court's ruling, and he promptly appealed in both cases. He went on making speeches, suggesting that the four cases against conglomerates had warned off others, and by January 1970 he could say that, 'Mergers among very large firms, and acquisitions by very large firms of leading firms in other industries seem to have virtually ceased.'

McLaren was indeed emerging as a Republican trust-busting-hero, in the tradition of Teddy Roosevelt, daring to turn against big business as the Democrats had not. Celler praised McLaren for his initiative, and the right-wing attacked him for his anti-business attitude. Congressman Bob Wilson—of whom we will hear more—complained about his 'devotion to tearing down business': James Ling talked about 'legal vivisection', and mounted a personal vendetta against McLaren. Others complained more subtly that McLaren was attacking the new money of the conglomerates, which mostly came from Democrats, foreigners, or Jews, while leaving intact the 'old money' of the established giant corporations—many of which were much more monopolistic than the conglomerates.

The anti-McLaren campaign was even joined in by the British right-wing, for McLaren had at first opposed the merger between British Petroleum and the Sohio oil company, and the *Economist* called him a 'trigger-happy trust-buster'. The British Government, who half-own BP, later brought strong pressure, and the chairman of BP, Sir Eric Drake, went to see Attorney-General Mitchell. McLaren soon gave way, insisting only that BP should get rid of some of the Sohio service stations in Ohio, and its retail outlets in Western Pennsylvania.

While Washington appeared to be worried about big business, the Europeans were still encouraging mergers rather than breaking them up. In Britain the regulating role

1. *Kleindienst Hearings:* Vol. II, p. 102.

of the Monopolies Commission had been eclipsed by the new role of the IRC, under the Labour government, which positively abetted the new mergers. All over Europe, mergers were pressing ahead, many of them blessed by their governments, which regarded them as necessary defences against the massive competition of American or Japanese invaders. In terms of world competition it was true, most of the new European giants were still relatively modest; but in their own country's context, they were towering.

THE SETTLEMENT

McLaren pressed on with his crusade against ITT and all three cases were making their way slowly towards the Supreme Court. In December 1970 the District Court found against him in the Grinnell case; he was, as he said later, 'batting zero, zero, zero'.[1] But he was still hopeful that the Supreme Court would rule in his favour. The highest court had a strong record in enforcing anti-trust cases; and had often taken up a more extreme position than the Justice Department. The lawyers from ITT and the anti-trust department continued to talk to each other (as is customary in anti-trust cases, eighty percent of which are settled out of court). But McLaren still insisted on divesting Hartford.

And then, in June 1971, McLaren abruptly and mysteriously relented. He sent a memo (which only later became public) to Kleindienst, the Deputy Attorney-General. In it, he explained that he had been persuaded that the effects of divesting Hartford would be crippling to the company, because of the high premium they paid. He proposed therefore a settlement which would deprive ITT of Canteen, Levitt, Avis and part of Grinnell, which would prohibit them from acquiring any corporation with assets of $100 million or more, without special approval, but which would allow them to keep the Hartford.[1]

It was a volte-face. For the proposed settlement was very similar to the one that Geneen's lawyer, Ephraim Jacobs, had suggested to McLaren seven months before, with the addition of Avis and the $100 million limit. It went against all McLaren's previous statements. And it prevented any of

1. *Kleindienst Hearings:* Vol. II, p. 171.

the cases going to the Supreme Court for that ultimate ruling which McLaren had been seeking.

The settlement was duly announced on July 31, 1971. It made an immediate sensation. McLaren insisted that it was a great victory, which had stopped the clear leader of the merger movement 'dead in his tracks'. It was the biggest ever divestiture in an anti-trust case. The stock market seemed to agree that it was stringent : the value of ITT stock fell by a billion dollars in the next three days. 'The day of the giant mergers may have ended,' said Gene Smith in the *New York Times*. And whatever the later misgivings, it was indeed a historic settlement : ITT in America would never be quite the same again.

But others were less sure whose victory it was. *Business Week* headed its editorial : 'The Anti-Trusters Cop Out' and complained that McLaren should have pushed the cases through to the Supreme Court, to establish the law beyond question. *Fortune* (September 1971) said, 'Quite clearly Harold Geneen has achieved something of a victory in the negotiations.' The two principal economic advisers to the anti-trust division (though they did not then say so), were against the settlement and were not consulted about it. One of them, Professor Mueller, said later[1] : 'The fact that the decision was made on the eve of the Supreme Court decision, which Mr. McLaren had indicated he wanted very much, suggests that there was a very drastic about-face in policy in this area.' What had made McLaren, who had been so fixed in his purpose, suddenly change his mind? The mystery remained hidden in the bowels of the Justice Department.

Six months later, McLaren was hurriedly nominated and confirmed for a federal judgeship in Chicago, and left the anti-trust department. He had always wanted a judgeship, but the promotion raised new speculation as to whether he was not giving up his anti-trust crusade in despair at the pressures surrounding it—particularly after another merger, between the Warner-Lambert and Parke-Davis pharmaceutical companies, had been permitted against his specific wishes.

1. *Kleindienst Hearings:* Vol. III, p. 1582.

It was true that the conglomerate crisis had—at least for the time being—passed; but that was due to other factors as much as to McLaren's crusade. In the course of 1969 the economic boom turned to slump. From 1969 onwards most of the conglomerates tumbled. Ling-Temco-Vought announced a huge loss of $38 million for 1969; the stock which had been up to 169 in 1967 was down to 27 in January 1970, and James Ling had to step down from his chairmanship. Litton Industries, weakened by the departure of many of its best scientists, saw its stock dropping lower and lower. Gulf and Western's shares also fell, and Bluhdorn made no more mergers : though he still rules over a wide empire from his Manhattan skyscraper, and Paramount Pictures still carry the Gulf and Western label. The conglomerates suffered far more heavily from the slump than the traditional industrial companies, and the Establishment were able to mutter 'I told you so.'

But one conglomerate survived the slump almost intact. All through his vicissitudes Geneen was still able to report, quarter by quarter, a steady increase in the earnings of ITT. His intricate empire had never got out of control, he had never bought a 'big bad company', like Jones and Laughlin. The corporate castle was still well defended, and though the trust-busters were taking away some of his companies, he had kept the latest and biggest acquisition, which he had most wanted. He could not acquire companies in America worth more than $100 million, but he could still buy in Europe—the base from which he had first started—where the anti-trust laws were much weaker.

Moreover Geneen could take hope from some signs that the whole anti-trust movement might be losing its momentum. For, as the American trading position began to look more perilous, and the competition was intensifying from Europe and (much more) from Japan, so the whole philosophy of anti-trust was being called in question. The commerce secretary, Maurice Stans, testified to the Joint Economic Committee in June 1971 that the present anti-trust philosophy might no longer be appropriate for companies competing against foreign producers. And by 1972 Geneen was specially encouraged by the views of John Connally, then Secretary of the Treasury—who advocated 'turning anti-trust policy inside out, so that in many cases the government would encourage mergers instead of discouraging them ... Washington must become less of an antagonist for U.S. industry and much more of a co-operative partner.'[1]

Perhaps Japan was beginning to force its rivals into its own mould—of a close, centralised nexus of government and industry, going out together into the world to fight other nations. Why should Washington, argued Geneen, be wasting time trying to break up his conglomerate, when it was just this kind of weapon that America most needed, to hold its own against the Mitsubishis and Sonys? Why couldn't they realise that ITT was the God-given instrument for America's fight-back—with its strong American base and international industries, bringing home valuable currency for the balance of payments? While McLaren was skirmishing with the out-of-date law, Geneen could reflect, the financial powers in America were at last beginning to see the true light.

THE GOLD-MINE

ITT duly went ahead with its divestitures. The Canteen company, which had not been doing well, proved difficult to sell, and the first prospectus was withdrawn. But Avis was successfully offered to the public; and it had expanded so fast that twenty-three percent of the company sold for more than ITT had paid for the whole company seven years before. The Avis president, Bud Morrow, did not conceal his pleasure at going it alone : 'When Geneen called to tell me we were being divested,' he said, 'I was able to control my disappointment manfully.' He was glad, he told me, to have had the education of working under Geneen : but he preferred to fly with his own wings. For Geneen, the restriction on buying more large companies was a severe one; but he went on buying smaller ones. In the nine months after the settlement ITT bought twenty American companies and twelve foreign companies, with total sales of around $300 million; there was no restriction on the size of companies that ITT bought abroad.

1. see Geneen's address to stockholders, May 1972.

And the Hartford, as Geneen and Rohatyn had predicted, proved to be a gold-mine for ITT. Already in 1970 it accounted for a quarter of ITT's earnings—more than the whole ITT telecommunications business—and in the next two years the Hartford earnings showed spectacular increases; sales went up by thirty-six percent to $1.5 billion, and profits by fifty-seven percent, to $70 million. The Hartford went up from fifth to third place among casualty and property insurers, and laid plans for expansion in Europe; in December 1972 it gained a foothold in Britain by bidding for a troubled British insurance company, Excess Holdings. ITT thus had a general insurance company in Britain to work alongside Abbey Life Insurance.

Part of the extra earnings of the Hartford came from a general upturn in underwriting earnings, which affected most insurance companies, and part came from applying mass-marketing techniques and excluding less profitable policies. But a great increase also came from realising the capital gains on selling investments, which amounted to $33.8 million in 1970; this could appear as extra income on the ITT consolidated balance sheet, accounting for nearly ten percent of the total ITT income. The acquisition of the Hartford, with its huge equity investments, made the ITT balance sheet, with its inheritance of heavy debts, look much more healthy : ITT could show extra assets of about $500 million, so that the ratio of long-term debt to the total capitalisation could go down from thirty-four percent to thirty per cent.[1] The concealed profits within the Hartford investments were just what Geneen wanted to ensure his continuous upward trend in earnings; as Professor Briloff put it : 'ITT picked up a suppressed pool of profits in the Hartford securities portfolio of, I believe, at least $250 million. ITT will be able to surface these dollars whenever it suits their accounting practice.'[2]

In Hartford itself, local opinion appeared to have been mollified; the directors continued to serve under ITT, with higher salaries and bonuses. In terms of the agreement with Cotter, ITT promised that for ten years it would not reduce

1. see the Ramsden Report: *Kleindienst Hearings:* Vol. II, p. 103 ff.
2. Interview in *Dun's Review*, October, 1971.

its employment in the city, or change the Hartford lines of business, or take in dividends from Hartford more than their annual earnings. The civic centre scheme collapsed, but ITT began building a Sheraton hotel which would incorporate a new civic centre complex.

The giant merger had transformed ITT, and perhaps saved it from a major financial crisis. But in the process Geneen had also acquired a train of enemies determined to catch up with him. Ralph Nader and Reuben Robertson were in the forefront. They first asked Commissioner Cotter for a re-hearing, which was refused, and then brought an appeal against the Commissioner, in the case of Nader v. Cotter in the Hartford Superior Court. In their brief they complained about ITT's pressure tactics with Cotter and accused ITT of concealing and misrepresenting their true intentions regarding the Hartford, as they had done three years before in the ABC case. They submitted that the actions of the Commissioner were 'illegal, arbitrary and an abuse of discretion'. The appeal failed, but the depositions and evidence that emerged from the case threw some further light on Geneen's operations. When Geneen gave a deposition in Hartford in April 1971, to Nader's lawyer Dwight Schweitzer, he was asked whether, if he were to have difficulties with ITT's foreign operations, he might 'at least be tempted' to withdraw funds from Hartford. Geneen firmly replied :

> Well, if I'm clear in my thinking, I don't think what happens to our foreign operations would have any effect on our ability to meet our domestic obligations . . . I think the theories you're talking about are so highly hypothetical they haven't happened in fifty years of our company . . .

It sounded convincing enough. But at almost exactly the same time, as emerged later, ITT was arguing the opposite case in Washington : that if ITT were not allowed to keep Hartford, they would have a serious liquidity crisis with respect to their foreign companies. It was in the old tradition of the company, to say one thing in one place, another in another, to present themselves as so big and indispensable that in the end no one could touch them.

The Hartford merger had also raised suspicions of the Securities and Exchange Commission, and the Internal Revenue Service, the tax authorities. The question was technical, but important. When Geneen had first bid for the Hartford, he had had to buy six percent of their shares for cash, to establish his foothold; but it was a ruling of the IRS that the Hartford shareholders could only avoid paying tax on their capital gains if ITT acquired all their Hartford shares through an exchange of stock, not in cash. So ITT had to sell its 1.7 million Hartford shares as quickly as possible, and the sale, according to the IRS rules, had to be unconditional. They did so through Lazards, who found an Italian bank, Mediobanca—connected with Fiat, themselves connected with Lazards—who bought the whole block, earning $1.3 million in fees. To show that the sale was 'unconditional', Lazards offered Mediobanca three options on the pricing of the shares; but only the first option involved any risk to Mediobanca, and that option was ruled out before the sale. When the merger went through, Mediobanca duly exchanged its Hartford shares for ITT shares, and then sold the ITT shares. The merger thus went through without Hartford shareholders having to pay tax—a saving of about $200 million. But could ITT's sale of its Hartford shares to Mediobanca be described as unconditional? Was it really a genuine sale at all—since ITT virtually undertook to protect Mediobanca against gain or loss? The IRS permitted the deal to go through without being taxed, having apparently accepted the options as genuine ones; but the Securities and Exchange Commission, who were also watching the deal, later complained that Lazards 'exercised a degree of control' over the Hartford shares; in other words the sale *had* been conditional.[1] The SEC complaint was settled by a consent decree, and the IRS appeared to be taking no further action. But the Mediobanca deal like other ITT operations was laying up trouble for the future : three years after the deal, in April 1973, the IRS reopened the question of tax exemption, causing a drop in the ITT share price of $4\frac{1}{2}$ points in two days. And in the meantime the SEC continued to investigate other aspects of the Hartford merger, with the

1. SEC v. ITT, Mediobanca, Lazards etc. Complaint June 16, 1972.

help of thirty-four boxes of ITT correspondence which they had subpoenaed. They were concerned with reports of 'Insider trading' (share-dealing on inside information) with Hartford and ITT shares; not only by small operators, but by senior ITT officials, who had sold their ITT shares just before the settlement was announced. The thirty-four boxes soon proved to contain all kinds of explosive material.

But it was the nature and timing of the anti-trust settlement itself which had the most explosive time-fuse. For it soon turned out that there was much more behind it than met the eye.

8

The Convention

Conventions all over America are bought all the time by
business communities, and everyone in this room knows it.
                              Senator Roman Hruska, at the
                              Kleindienst hearings.

San Diego is a city where the future still looks bright. It sits
in the south-west corner of California, facing the Pacific in a
climate of unbroken sun, and the troubles of the rest of
America seem hardly to have reached it : even Los Angeles,
a hundred miles north, with its smog and rebels, seems a
world away. San Diego occupies one of the most beautiful
sites in the world, between a huge natural harbour and a high
range of hills leading over to the desert. The San Diegans
have defiled and desecrated the landscape. They have sliced
off the hilltops to build housing estates, dredged the harbours
to make artificial islands and marinas, bridged the island with
a high swooping bridge like a roller-coaster, dwarfing the
natural outlines. The city sprawls shapelessly along the coast,
all the way to Mexico in the south, and halfway to Los
Angeles in the north. The freeways cut through the hills and
the filigree coastline is littered with drive-in eateries, gas
stations and car parks. The airport roars in the centre of the
city, with the planes flying low over the old downtown
buildings and the Santa Fé station.

And the city still grows. Unlike northern California, it
still has the labour, the space and ambition for new industries. Its motto is the 'City in Motion', and it is now the third
biggest city in California. Its first patron, the navy, has been
followed by aerospace, electronics, oceanography, and now

more and more tourism. Hotels have shot up like concertinas —palatial hotels along the coastline, seedy motels along the highways, skyscraper hotels gazing out at each other along Hotel Circle. With its semi-tropical climate, its long beaches, marinas and cheap Mexican labour, San Diego is still a fantasy-land for refugees from the cold East. In spite of its industrial expansion, it still seems like a lotusland; the San Diegans walk and talk like somnambulists, their eyes bleary with the sun and the sea.

It is deeply conservative. The suburbs are full of retired people, especially naval and military officers, who have saved to relax in the sun. The younger generation are too busy with sports, skin-diving or sailing to feel very rebellious: only a mild movement of protest has arisen against the wrecking of the coastline. The city itself, in spite of its size, is dominated by a handful of local tycoons as if it were a small town. It is a place where money and political power are assumed to go hand-in-hand, and where journalism is very close to public relations. Both local papers, morning and evening, are owned by a rich Republican, James Copley, a passionate admirer of Nixon, who purveys unswervingly Republican views. The uncrowned Republican king of San Diego for the last twenty years has been the legendary C. Arnholt Smith, who has dominated the city through his bank, the U.S. National, and his conglomerate, Westgate-California; his extravagant monument is his luxury hotel, the Westgate Plaza, a glittering skyscraper filled with Louis XIV decor—tapestries, escritoires, chandeliers—furnished by his wife's decorating company. Arnholt Smith has been one of the munificent benefactors of the Republicans, credited with raising a million dollars for Nixon in 1968, and often entertained by the President.

San Diego is Nixon territory; in the 1968 election it had provided a solid Republican turn-out, and Nixon called it 'my lucky city'. It was in the President's home state, only a hundred miles from his home town, Whittier. It was only twenty minutes by helicopter from the 'Western White House'—the retreat which Nixon had bought at San Clemente, where he enjoyed staying. And Nixon's aides had close connections with San Diego—Bob Finch was a former Lieutenant-Governor of California, and Herb Klein, his communications aide, had edited the *San Diego Union,* and had loyally supported him in his earlier campaigns.

The key Republican in the practical politics of San Diego is the local Congressman, Bob Wilson, who for the last twenty years has represented the district in Congress. Wilson is popular in San Diego; he represents, well enough, the simple optimism of the place, the spirit of 'go along and get along'. He has the look of dazed innocence, with a round cosy face like a puppy, and a shy, worried smile. His career outside politics has not been spectacular; he dropped out of school, became an art student, then a salesman for a dairy; he went into advertising with Norman Tolle, who built up the prosperous Tolle Agency, of which Wilson now owns six percent of the shares, and which handles local Republican campaigns. He was drafted to the army, and hated it so much that he got Tolle to get him out.[1] But he gets on well, nevertheless, with the military men of San Diego. He works hard in Washington to get defence contracts for the city, and sits on the Armed Services Committee in Washington. He has been a hawk over Vietnam. And for ten years he has been chairman of the Republican National Congressional Committee (RNCC), where he has shown amazing ability to collect money for the Republicans. For San Diegans, he has been the man who brought money and jobs back from Washington. And he was close to the President—seeing him not only at the fortnightly 'Leadership' breakfasts, but for private talks in which fund-raising was clearly relevant.

Since the early 'sixties, Bob Wilson had been very friendly with Harold Geneen. They had met when Wilson had been asked to address a seminar of ITT executives. They both enjoyed fishing; Wilson took Geneen fishing for albacore off Mexico, and Geneen took Wilson trout fishing in Maine. While fishing, they talked business. ITT had several plants in California but nothing in San Diego except a few offshoots like Avis and Wonder Bread. Wilson was always pressing, to everyone, the benefits of San Diego. In 1969 Geneen wanted to build a new cable plant to supply undersea cables for the Pacific, as the ITT factory in London supplies the Atlantic. Wilson soon found a site of forty acres on Southern San

1. see Joseph John Trento: 'Voice of San Diego', *The Nation,* August 7, 1972.

Diego bay; and talked to his friends on the Port Commission, who rented the site to ITT on generous terms. (Later, when ITT complained about faults on the reclaimed land, they got a $400,000 rent rebate.)

Bob Wilson also told Geneen in 1969 about a garden hotel in San Diego called the Half Moon Inn; it was a row of small chalets in Californian-Polynesian style; complete with a thatched Volkswagen bus, built round a swimming-pool alongside the Marina—a delightful place, with palm trees and birds of paradise round the pool. The owners were in difficulties, Wilson said, and Sheraton could get it for $3 million; it would be full the whole year round; 'It's a steal'. Geneen was excited, and to Wilson's amazement picked up the telephone there and then, and told Bud James, the president of Sheraton, to buy it—which he did (so much for the autonomy of ITT subsidiaries). The Half Moon Inn was not, it turned out, quite the money-spinner that Wilson had said, in spite of its charms: it was far from full, and Sheraton had a heavy touch. They bought a French restaurant next door, called L'Escale, and converted it into Ye ol' Port Royal, with a pirates' cove, serving grog and Captain Ahab's special, with yo-ho-ho decor; the pirate waiters surveyed empty tables, and the cove didn't catch on.

But the Half Moon Inn was an important beachhead for ITT's landing in San Diego. Soon afterwards Wilson reported that another hotel was available—the Ramada Inn near the airport, on Harbor Island looking over the bay. Geneen bought that too; and it was quickly renamed the Sheraton Inn-Airport, with a big S put up on top of it. And next door to it, another prime site was put up for bidding by the Port Commissioners, Geneen wanted that, too, and got it. The new Harbor Island hotel was soon designed as a showpiece of the Sheraton empire, one of the few new hotels both owned and managed by the company: it cost $20 million, with 700 rooms. Very soon a great honeycomb structure, like a folded screen, began rising up from the bare island, dominating the view from the airport. Here, too, there were delays and difficulties with the site, and ITT, through Bob Wilson, drove a hard bargain; collecting a rent rebate of $50,000.

In the course of three years, ITT had now become a major

factor in San Diego, with a cable plant and three hotels with a thousand rooms. There was even talk of Sheraton moving their headquarters from Boston to San Diego. Geneen was now very close to Bob Wilson, in a cosy alliance. The Tolle advertising agency, in which Wilson held shares, represented ITT companies, and it represented the Port Commission too, until one commissioner had protested about the conflict of interest with Sheraton. Wilson was the ideal fixer and contact man, and to most San Diegans there was nothing wrong with that.

But to the small band of San Diegan Democrats, the friendship between Geneen and Wilson was deeply suspicious; Geneen had contributed to both parties in the past, but since 1968 he had given only to the Republicans, up to $10,000 in a year.[1] The alliance seemed specially sinister to the Southern California chairman of the Democrat party, Larry Lawrence; for he was both a Democrat and a hotelier. Lawrence is a mysterious financier who looks like a film star: he bought the oldest and grandest hotel in San Diego, the Hotel del Coronado—a fantastic turreted pile, in Victorian-tropical style, with spacious splendour (it has a Prince of Wales bar which proclaims its special place in British history; for it is in this hotel that the young Prince of Wales first met Wallis Simpson). Lawrence looked on the Sheraton invasion, and Geneen's visits to San Diego, as a threat both to his hotel and to the Democrats; he saw ITT as reinforcing still closer the links between Republicans and big money. And other Democrats, too, suspected that Geneen was concerned with much more than hotels : as one of them put it to me : 'Geneen could see which way politics were shifting. Bob Wilson was the bagman for the whole Republican Party! He was just what Geneen needed, to provide the secret of happiness. He could set Geneen free!'

THE CONVENTION

While the newest ITT hotel was going up, in the beginning of 1971, the Republican National Committee was trying to choose a city for their convention in the following summer, before the Presidential election. They had invited several

1. *Kleindienst Hearings:* Vol. II, p. 671.

cities to bid, including familiar centres like Chicago and Miami, and also, rather surprisingly, San Diego. But the city had not shown much excitement at the prospect, and had not put forward a bid. It was not obviously an ideal site for a convention. Its facilities had not caught up with its expansion, and in spite of the great hotel boom it was still short of rooms. A party convention needs to accommodate 2,692 delegates and alternates, and an army of camp followers : the Republican committee was insisting on having 18,000 first-class hotel rooms, including 1,000 suites— equivalent to thirty-six hotels, the size of the London Savoy. A convention also needs enough taxis, restaurants, policemen to cope with this sudden invasion, and a huge convention hall.

San Diego was not in the same league as Miami or Chicago. It had only about 13,000 hotel rooms in the city itself, and the hotels were not close together, as in Miami, but scattered along the coast. To provide for 18,000 would mean delegates staying as far away as Oceanside, thirty miles north, or even in the dubious city of Tijuana over in Mexico. Moreover San Diego (unlike Miami) has its high season in August, when hotels are ninety percent full. The convention would not serve to fill rooms that would otherwise be empty: it would push the tourists away. San Diego did not have enough taxis, and would have to import them. And the only building big enough to house the convention itself was the Sports Arena, a grim grey concrete block, like a bunker, miles away from most of the hotels. It was owned by an eccentric Canadian millionaire, Peter Graham, who commuted from Vancouver and was notoriously difficult to deal with.

Worst of all, the businessmen and hotel-keepers of San Diego did not seem to *want* a political convention. Since the hippies and yippies had descended on Chicago in 1968, turning it into an armed camp, other cities had been noticeably less keen on having the conventions. The Mayor of San Diego, Frank Curran, who was a Democrat, described convention delegates 'a bunch of brown baggers', recalling the experience of San Francisco in 1964, where many delegates brought their own food with them in brown bags; they spent too much time meeting, talking and watching television in the evening, and not enough time in serious eating and drinking which would be good for business. By the time the city had paid for extra police and extra services, it might well make a loss. There was also more extreme opposition from a group called Lesser San Diego, who were afraid that a convention would attract more residents, ruin the environment, and raise taxes.

And the convention would cost money. Both parties were asking for a cash guarantee of $800,000, in exchange for bringing their business and publicity to a city. The business of 'buying' conventions has frequently been attacked, as a form of political corruption. The Federal Corrupt Practices Act emphatically states that, 'It is unlawful for any national bank or any corporation organised by authority of any law of Congress to make a contribution or expenditure in connection with any election to any political office, or in connection with any primary election, or any political convention . . .' But both parties still look to their convention cities as a useful source of party funds. They get round the Act by asking companies to subscribe, not to their party, but to a special convention fund; and local companies can justify their subscriptions on the grounds that the convention is good for local business.

But San Diegans were not at all convinced that the convention *would* be good for local business, or that it was worth 800,000 dollars.

Why should the Republicans be so intent on San Diego, in the face of all this apathy? The answer could only be one word : Nixon. It was a place where he felt safe, among friends. He could fly down easily from the peace of San Clemente. His local patriotism could well help him win the important forty-five electoral votes in California. And if Nixon wanted San Diego, it was hard for the party to say no.

By the beginning of May 1971 it looked as if San Diego was out of the running. The official closing date for bids had passed, and the Republicans were reported to be considering San Francisco, Miami, Chicago and Houston. But by the middle of May there were signs of mysterious new pressure for the city to put in a last-minute bid. Several White House men, including Bob Finch, Dwight Chapin and William Timmons, had been seen in the city, and the vice-chairman of the Republican State Committee, Gordon Luce, who was close to Nixon, suddenly urged San Diego to press her claims. On June 3 it was reported that the Republican site committee, headed by the party chairman, Bob Dole, would be inspecting San Diego as a possible site. The Lieutenant-Governor of California, Ed Reinecke, revealed that he had been talking to the White House and to Bob Dole about San Diego, and the city manager, Walter Hahn, explained that the city council would put in a bid as a kind of 'command performance'. The Republicans were now said to be more flexible in their requirements, and to be able to make do with 12,500 hotel rooms.

And over the last four months, the staff at the Half Moon Inn noticed a rather mysterious new guest, who brought an atmosphere of unwonted bustle into the South-Seas setting: a large convivial woman with a loud voice, a rich repertory of slang and four-letter words. She came to stay several times, sometimes with her daughter, and often gave parties in her room; sometimes Bob Wilson was there, sometimes other local politicians. There was a lot of late-night drinking and one night, very late, she was actually seen in the swimming pool. It did not take the staff long to realise that Dita Beard, as she was called, was not only from ITT, but a rather special representative from the company. In spite of her unusual habits she was clearly very well-connected, and she had a commanding manner which was more like a man's. The words soon got around that she was in fact the chief lobbyist for the giant corporation. Not everyone was aware of the fact, and there was an embarrassing moment when she was arrested one evening for driving under the influence of drink; her daughter came back to the hotel with a cheque signed by her, for bail; but the girl at the desk refused to cash it, not knowing who she was.

Officially, Mrs. Beard was concerned with arranging defence contracts for the new cable factory, which called for a good deal of lobbying; as she described it in a memo (revealed a year later), 'Our new division requires constant touch with the Department of Defence on contracting for cable in a top secret program, plus contact with the Congressmen of that area, plus the Governor and his staff.' Certainly she was resourceful in her contact with Congressmen.

She was not only very close to Bob Wilson : she had also be-friended the other representative of San Diego District, the Democrat Lionel Van Deerlin. It so happened that Van Deerlin was planning his first-ever family holiday in Europe, with his six children and his daughter-in-law : he mentioned it to Dita Beard, who quickly arranged for him to rent a Fiat camper in Europe, through an Avis credit-card. When Van Deerlin got back from the holiday, Mrs. Beard simply re-fused to let him pay the six hundred dollars it cost, and Van Deerlin eventually surrendered. As he later described it to the *San Diego Union* : 'It was one of those cases where it's a matter of : how far do you press? Looking back, it was a mistake. I certainly am not going to say I exercised the greatest judgment in not insisting to pay.'[1]

It was only later that the full scale of Mrs. Beard's acti-vities was to come to light. But there were some San Diegans who already suspected that Mrs. Beard's hospitality had a motive deeper than cables; and was connected with the prospects of the convention.

ITT's interest in San Diego soon became more evident. In May 1971 — while the ITT lawyers in Washington were arguing about the anti-trust settlement, and while McLaren was still firmly disallowing the Hartford merger — Geneen and his directors descended in force for their annual general meeting. It had become the company's custom to hold their meetings in a different state each year, partly perhaps to escape from hecklers, but also to advertise themselves to different communities. This year they met in San Diego, under a chandelier, in Arnholt Smith's Louis XIV hotel, the Westgate Plaza. Geneen paid tribute to the Golden State, 'which has been a good home for ITT', described ITT's achievements, and criticised the government's anti-trust policy in the context of international competition : 'We are going to have a difficult enough contest on our hands without being penalised by the referee for alleged violations of rules which exist only for ourselves.'

On the same evening, Dita Beard had arranged an open-air dinner party on the lawn of the Half Moon Inn, between the palm-trees and the Polynesian chalets. There were about seventy people there, including the ITT directors, Bud

1. *San Diego Union*, April 28, 1972.

James, the president of Sheraton, Bob Wilson and, of course, Dita Beard. Bob Wilson was talking to Geneen about the hotel business, and then mentioned to him that he had been talking to the President's aide, Bob Finch, that morning in San Diego; Finch had said that there was still a chance of San Diego getting the convention, if they could put up $800,000. Geneen said, 'Well why don't you do it?', and talked about it with Bud James: then he said, according to Wilson, 'Look, if you'll check and get some local support, I'll guarantee you up to 400,000 dollars of that 800,000 commitment.'[1] There was much argument later as to the exact sum that was promised, and the nature of the guarantee; Geneen insisted that he only promised $100,000, or $200,000 if others raised an equal amount. But Bob Wilson was consistent that $400,000 was a firm backing. He was confident he would not need it, and could raise the money from other hotels; but it was a bait for the rest: 'It was like the story about someone who asked J. P. Morgan if he would loan him $100,000 and he said, "No, but I will put my arm around you and walk across the floor of the Stock Exchange."'[2]

The sum of $400,000 seems piffling enough, in the context of ITT's world turnover, or the $50 million spent by the Republicans on the election; why should there be such a fuss about it? But in the context of the convention and the limitations of the law, it was not a sum that was easy to come by, and most corporations were wary of such gifts. ITT were able, once again, to take advantage of the two-sided character of a conglomerate; now they showed themselves, not as huge and centralised, but as small and local. Sheraton, they insisted, had little to do with ITT: why shouldn't local hotels put up money for a local convention? But whether it was Sheraton or ITT, a backing, a pledge or a guarantee, did not basically affect the significance of Geneen's offer. At the same time that his lawyers were

1. *Kleindienst Hearings:* (interview with Robert Cox) Vol. III, p. 876. Elsewhere (Vol. II, p. 756). Dita Beard also claimed credit for telling Geneen about the possibility of the Convention. According to her testimony Geneen said to Bud James: 'This sounds like a natural, Bud, with this new property. We should certainly do something with the Convention Bureau'.
2. Ibid., p. 890.

trying to negotiate an anti-trust settlement 'at arm's length' in Washington, he was providing the Republican party, and Nixon in particular, with what they most wanted—the underwriting of their convention at San Diego. What actually went on in Geneen's mind on that warm evening at the Half Moon Inn will probably never be known. Did he think that it was a purely business investment to advertise Sheraton, without political repercussions? Did he see it as just part of the 'inexorable pressure' to keep the Hartford company, backing up his campaigns in Connecticut and Washington? Was he, as his speech that morning might suggest, so preoccupied by the anti-trust question that he was using every weapon he had? Did he think it best to go straight to the top, to the President, as J. P. Morgan would have done, to fix it up? Was there far more than that casual talk with Bob Wilson; was there a cut-and-dried deal preceding the offer? The full answers may never emerge. But what seems clear is that Geneen, with his political naivety, never understood then and later the explosive potential of his offer; that he did not realise, or did not mind, that he was offering to Nixon what in the context and timing might be seen as a bribe.

SHERATON MAKES IT HAPPEN AGAIN

After the Half Moon dinner party, Geneen's promise was kept very secret; but Bob Wilson rushed round other hoteliers and businessmen, helped by Lieutenant-Governor Reinecke and Gordon Luce, the local Republican chairman, trying to make sure of the rest of the money. Two weeks later, on June 3, he told the *San Diego Union* that he had received a pledge of $400,000, and that there would be no problem about the other $400,000, so that the city could bid for the convention; but he kept quiet about the source of the pledge. The city council were still not keen on having the convention; Mayor Curran complained that he had been left out of the discussions, and Councilman Landt said that everyone knew more about the discussions than the council. But eventually on June 30 they agreed to contribute $600,000 to the bid, paid out of room taxes, and two days later a formal bid promising $1.5 million was submitted to the Republican committee. Most of the money would be in the form of services; but out of the $600,000 promised in cash, $400,000 came from Bob Wilson's mysterious source.

In the next six weeks, the civic committee in charge of the convention managed to rustle up pledges from local business people, so that Bob Wilson could call up Bud James of Sheraton to tell him that the Convention Bureau would only need $200,000 underwriting from Sheraton, though they would like a formal commitment for $100,000. So Bud James sent a careful telegram to the San Diego Convention Bureau, care of Bob Wilson in Washington, explaining in very deliberate language Sheraton's interest in San Diego hotels, and committing $200,000 to the Convention Bureau, 'in consideration of the naming of the Sheraton Harbor Island Hotel as Presidential headquarters hotel'. It now appeared, in fact, to be a straightforward deal; we deliver the money, if you deliver the President.

Two days after the telegram on July 23, the Republican National Committee finally met at Denver to decide on the site of the convention; among those present were Dita Beard, in a state of some excitement, and Bob Wilson, armed with the telegram. Miami was still fighting for the convention; the chairman of the Florida Republicans, L. E. Thomas, warned the committee that there were more two-legged nuts in California per square inch than anywhere else in the world. But the White House was making its preference for San Diego very clear: Herb Klein was even wearing a San Diego button, and at the last minute President Nixon put a call through to Bob Dole, the party chairman, in Denver. Eventually the committee voted 119 to 12 in favour of San Diego. It was a remarkable victory for Presidential prerogative.

There was still plenty of apathy in San Diego: 'Everybody seems excited about it except the people,' commented the Democrats. Young radicals made plans for a massive invasion, and one resident complained: 'The City in Motion will soon be a City in Shambles.' But the preparations went ahead. A special air-conditioned building was planned to house the newsmen, adjoining the Sports Arena; there was talk of a luxury liner with 450 rooms being docked across from the headquarters hotel. There was a plan for hundreds of volunteers to meet delegates at the airport, in a 'massive host programme'; and the shortage of cabs would be overcome with the help of Arnholt Smith, who would import some of his Yellow Cabs from Los Angeles and San Francisco.

The source of the original underwriting of $400,000 dollars remained a mystery; but there were growing rumours in San Diego that connected it with ITT, and with the new Sheraton hotel that was rising up on the waterfront. At last, on August 5, Bob Wilson came clean. The whole of the original guarantee of $400,000, he said, had come from ITT-Sheraton. He had kept it secret before, he explained, because Sheraton also owns hotels in Miami, which might have been offended if Sheraton had sided with San Diego. Anyway, he said, the $400,000 was only a temporary underwriting, until the local businessmen came forward. On the same day, the Harbor Island Hotel made out a cheque for $100,000 to the Convention Bureau, which was endorsed and deposited the next day.[1]

It was quite possible to argue, as Bob Wilson and Geneen later persistently argued, that the money was a shrewd local investment, which had nothing to do with politics. It was emphasised that the pledge came from Sheraton, not from ITT : Wilson insisted that he had worked out the deal with Bud James of Sheraton, not with Geneen, and he even denied that he had discussed it with Geneen, though (as it turned out) he had met him in May, June and July.[2] Sheraton always allowed large sums for launching their new hotels: for the Sheraton Waikiki, which had recently been opened in Honolulu, they had spent $250,000, and for the Sheratons at Copenhagen and Stockholm they had spent $100,000 each. The President's presence at the new hotel, which Wilson had negotiated, would provide 'unbuyable publicity' through the coverage of the TV networks, promoting the Sheraton name on the screens from coast to coast. (Geneen later reckoned that it might be worth a million dollars.)[3]

The fact that there was some kind of deal between the

1. A photocopy of the cheque was released by ITT on March 19, 1972.
2. *Kennedy Report*, p. 87.
3. *Kleindienst Hearings:* Vol. I, p. 657.

White House and ITT became known to a few San Diegans. One local advertising man, Jack Canaan, who had been working with the construction company, was talking one day with a manager on the site of the hotel, when he said: 'Where you're standing—that's going to be the helipad for the President.' 'What President?' 'President Nixon. He's going to stay here. It's all been fixed by that PR babe from Washington!' Canaan was struck by the boldness of the bargain : as he put it : 'It wouldn't need Klieg lights, public relations, press parties; they'd rent the President instead!'

The deal was clearly good business for Sheraton. But in terms of the Federal Corrupt Practices Act, if literally enforced, it was sailing very close to the wind. Eight years ago the Democrats had been under heavy fire for soliciting advertisements for their convention programme at $15,000 a page, as an indirect way of allowing corporations to curry favour with the ruling party. The ITT pledge was more obtrusive than that; it was thought to be the biggest sum ever promised by a corporation to a convention; and it was twenty times as much as anyone else in San Diego had pledged. Bob Wilson and Leon Parma, the chairman of the convention committee, insisted that an underwriting was quite different, and ITT (as they revealed later) had taken legal advice. 'There's no way they can put up that kind of money.' Parma explained in an interview : 'the law is very specific'; but in the same interview he said : 'If we asked, we could have a cheque for that amount from them any time we wanted it.'

But what was more remarkable was the timing; for on July 30, 1971, nine days after Bud James had sent the telegram to Bob Wilson, the settlement of ITT's anti-trust suit was announced.

9

The Lobbyists

I don't put anything in writing. If it's important enough, you
shouldn't, and if it is not important enough, why bother?
                                                    Dita Beard, 1972

It did not take journalists long to become suspicious of the
coincidence between ITT's anti-trust settlement and the
pledge to the San Diego convention; for their previous encounters with ITT, over ABC and Hartford, had already
sown the seeds of distrust. The first clues in the trail were
found just before the settlement was announced. Richard
Dudman, chief Washington correspondent of the *St. Louis
Post-Dispatch*, had contacts in the Justice Department and
the SEC who were suspicious of the settlement; and he had
happened to overhear a remark by an ITT man at Jean-
Pierre's restaurant in Washington, suggesting that something
was cooking. He had also had a chance encounter with a
near neighbour, Henry Sailer, ITT's counsel from Covington and Burling; Dudman had asked casually, 'Is it true that
ITT is going to settle?' Sailer had glowered and replied:
'Not a word of truth in it.' As Dudman said afterwards : 'I
didn't realise how much I knew'. He wrote an article putting
together various clues, suggesting that both Bob Wilson and
Felix Rohatyn had been involved in the settlement.

The first formal allegations came two months later, from
Reuben Robertson, who was ferreting away at the facts
behind the Hartford merger. On September 21 Robertson
wrote to Kleindienst, the Deputy Attorney-General, object-
ing in detail to the settlement, complaining about the sec-

recy, and ending with the question: What was the relationship between the settlement and ITT's support for the Republican Convention? Robertson received a short prompt reply, not from Kleindienst but from McLaren, answering his last question with the words: 'There is no relationship whatsoever between the settlement of the ITT-Hartford litigation and any financial support which ITT may have offered to the City of San Diego.'

Two months later, on November 28, a serious-minded young correspondent from the *Washington Evening Star*, Bob Walters, who had been in touch with Robertson, was on holiday in San Diego. He met Larry Lawrence of the Hotel del Coronado, who told him of his suspicions that the settlement was linked with the convention; and Walters, quoting Lawrence's suspicions, wrote a long article describing the strange history of the $400,000 pledge.

In December Larry O'Brien, the national chairman of the Democratic party, took it up. He wrote to the Attorney-General, John Mitchell, asking whether he could allay any suspicion that there was a connection 'between ITT's sudden largesse to the Republican Party and the nearly simultaneous out-of-court settlement of one of the biggest merger cases in corporate history'. O'Brien received a reply the same day, not from Mitchell but from his deputy, Kleindienst, explaining that Mitchell had removed himself from all ITT cases, because his former law firm had done work for ITT. Kleindienst went on to say emphatically that he had no knowledge of an ITT pledge, and stating: 'The settlement between the Department of Justice and ITT was handled and negotiated exclusively by Assistant Attorney-General Richard McLaren.'

It was not till this point that the ITT pledge was known to a wider public, including directors of ITT: and among those who were surprised by it was Felix Rohatyn, who had been involved in the settlement and who was embarrassed by the discovery, not least because on that same day he was organising a fund-raising evening for Senator Muskie, with guests including Harold Geneen. Rohatyn asked Geneen why the company had made the pledge; and Geneen assured him that it was not linked with the settlement, and was just a 'normal substitute' for advertising the San Diego Sheraton hotel.[1]

Why Kleindienst felt compelled to make his statement, which was both unnecessary and, as it turned out, untrue, remained a mystery. But for the time being, the matter rested there. The critics all lacked a piece of the jigsaw to complete the puzzle—the evidence from inside ITT itself. It was not till two months later that a single eccentric document escalated the suspicions into a national scandal.

In February 1972 the document arrived, like other incriminating documents, at the Washington office of the columnist Jack Anderson, and thus immediately became highly explosive. For Anderson was the king of the muckrakers; he had only recently published the *Anderson Papers* revealing Nixon's support for Pakistan in the Indo-Pakistan war. He is a big thundering man, half demagogue, half preacher. He was brought up in Salt Lake City, and for a time was a Mormon missionary; at his house in Maryland, where he lives with his wife and nine children, the only books on display are the Bible and *The Mormon Story*. But he combines his evangelical zeal with political shrewdness. He worked for years with the late Drew Pearson, the veteran exposer, and with Pearson he wrote the book *The Case Against Congress: A Compelling Indictment of Corruption on Capitol Hill*. He took over Pearson's daily syndicated column, the 'Washington Merry-Go-Round', setting up as the spokesman for the small man (his column appears on the comics page of the *Washington Post*, where he thinks it is more widely read). He is as dedicated to disclosures as the big bureaucracies are to secrecy, and his office files, full of confidential memos and pamphlets, are open to visitors to inspect and copy. Sometimes he has overreached himself, as in his charges of drunkenness against Senator Eagleton (McGovern's first choice for Vice-President in the Presidential elections, 1972), when he had to apologise. But through its disclosures, Anderson's column has become an informal, if erratic, part of the American constitution.

It was Nader who put Anderson on the trail of ITT, asking him to find out more about the Hartford negotiations. Anderson was naturally interested in the 'carnivorous cor-

1. *Kleindienst Hearings:* Vol. II, p. 165.

porate monster', as he calls it; and he had his contacts within ITT. He 'sowed some seeds, and cast some bread upon the waters', and his assistant, Brit Hume, who used to work for the *Hartford Times,* was in touch with Reuben Robertson. Eventually the seeds came to fruit, and there came mysteriously into his hands the extraordinary document that came to be known as the Beard Memorandum. This is it:

PERSONAL AND CONFIDENTIAL

ITT

Washington Office
1707 L Street, N.W.
Washington, D.C. 20036
Tel. (202) 296–6000
Date: June 25, 1971

To: W. R. Merriam,
From: D. D. Beard.
Subject: San Diego Convention.

I just had a long talk with EJG. I'm so sorry that we got that call from the White House. I thought you and I had agreed very thoroughly that under no circumstances would anyone in this office discuss with anyone our participation in the Convention, including me. Other than permitting John Mitchell, Ed Reinecke, Bob Haldeman and Nixon (besides Wilson, of course) *no one* has known from whom that 400 thousand commitment had come. You can't imagine how many queries I've had from 'friends' about this situation and I have in each and every case denied knowledge of any kind. It would be wise for all of us here to continue to do that, regardless of from whom any questions come; White House or whoever. John Mitchell has certainly kept it on the higher level only, we should be able to do the same.

I was afraid the discussion about the three hundred/four hundred thousand commitment would come up soon. If you remember, I suggested that we all stay out of that, other than the fact that I told you I had heard Hal up the original amount.

Now I understand from Ned that both he and you are upset about the decision to make it four hundred in *services.* Believe me, this is not what Hal said. Just after I talked with

Ned, Wilson called me, to report on his meeting with Hal. Hal at no time told Wilson that our donation would be in services ONLY. In fact, quite contrary. There would be very little cash involved, but certainly some. I am convinced, because of several conversations with Louie re Mitchell, that our noble commitment has gone a long way toward our negotiations on the mergers eventually coming out as Hal wants them. Certainly the President has told Mitchell to see that things are worked out fairly. It is still only McLaren's mickey-mouse we are suffering.

We all know Hal and his big mouth! But this is one time he cannot tell you and Ned one thing and Wilson (and me) another!

I hope, dear Bill, that all of this can be reconciled— between Hal and Wilson—if all of us in this office remain totally ignorant of any commitment ITT has made to any-one. If it gets too much publicity, you can believe our negotiations with Justice will wind up shot down. Mitchell is definitely helping us, but cannot let it be known. Please destroy this, huh?

The document was so apparently incriminating that it seemed to justify all the most conspiratorial theories about the power elite. It connected in four hundred words the President, the Attorney-General, Harold Geneen, Bob Wilson and Ed Reinecke; and its allusiveness made it sound even more incriminating. It was addressed by ITT's only registered lobbyist, Mrs. Dita Beard, to the head of the ITT Washington office, Bill Merriam. It was written on June 25, 1971 (eight months before it reached Anderson) at a crucial time, when the San Diego bid was being organised, and just before the final ITT settlement. Mrs. Beard said that she had just had a long talk with Ned Gerrity (EJG), who was upset because ITT had decided to restrict their $400,000 offer to services only; but Mrs. Beard insisted that Geneen (Hal) had offered cash as well as services; and Bob Wilson had just rung up to confirm this.

The chief message of the memo was that the $400,000 must be kept secret. Only Bob Wilson, John Mitchell, Ed Reinecke, and Nixon, together with the White House ad-viser, Bob Haldeman, knew that the money had come from

ITT. Merriam had evidently been indiscreet about it, to someone in the White House who had just called, and no-one should reveal the ITT pledge because publicity could wreck the anti-trust settlement. Mrs. Beard was convinced, after talks with the Governor of Kentucky, Louie Nunn, that ITT's 'noble commitment' to San Diego had gone a long way towards helping the anti-trust negotiations to come out 'as Hal wants them'. President Nixon himself had told the Attorney-General, Mitchell, to see that things were worked out fairly, and Mitchell 'is definitely helping us, but cannot let it be known'. And the memo concluded with poignant irony with the words that were to become a Washington catchphrase : 'Please destroy this, huh?'

The memo, if it was genuine, provided the missing piece of the jigsaw. Emerging eight months before the election, it could hardly be more inflammatory.

THE LOBBYISTS

The apparent originator, Dita Beard, was one of the most colourful of the tribe of Washington lobbyists, and a free-booting figure within the ITT organisation — as she appeared in San Diego. She was a well-known character on Capitol Hill, where she popped up everywhere, larger than life, as if she had stepped out of a musical — a tough, hard-drinking dreadnought of a woman. 'Mother Beard', as she liked to be called, had already seen a good deal of life, and was now fifty-three; she was a colonel's daughter, brought up in the army, where she picked up a repertoire of four-letter words. She had married twice, with five children, and when her last marriage broke up she came to Washington with her children to make her living. She got a job as a secretary with ITT, who had just opened an office in Washington, in the early Geneen period. She soon showed she had useful contacts, and Geneen promoted her to become a lobbyist and general trouble-shooter. As she described it later : 'Within a very short time I realised none of them knew the name of the game in Washington. They had no political representation. They were babes in arms. They didn't realise that you have to know what is going on in Washington or you can't run a company.'[1] By 1966 she was featured in *Fortune,* looking very soignée, as one of the top lobbyists in Washington, with 'a reputation for picturesque language and knowing what makes Congressmen tick'.

She was important to Geneen, and quite close to him—a professional relationship. She had the same unstoppable energy as her master, and could translate his zeal into politics. She rushed around the country, to Governors' conferences, conventions and meetings, talking to any Congressmen and Senators in sight. She was a heavy drinker, but ITT are accustomed to drinkers, and she had remarkable powers of recuperation. As Bob Wilson put it : 'She has heart attacks every once in a while but a little bit of nitroglycerine and a shot of Scotch will really bring her out, see?' Her job, as she described it, was 'to find out what's going on, why, and to whom—and when it is going to happen to us'. She was a lifelong Republican, and her friendships sounded spectacular; she had known Mel Laird 'since he was a baby, it seems like'; Ed Reinecke 'since he was in candidates' school'; Bob Wilson and his wife had been friends for 'years and years and years'; and she knew most of the Governors 'extremely well'.[2] Nor was this necessarily boasting, and many politicians returned the compliment : Bob Wilson said, 'She's got a heart as big as good, and she comes from a very good family'; 'there's not a more effective lobbyist for any company,' he told Geneen, 'than Dita Beard is.'

Dita Beard was the only registered ITT lobbyist but she was only one of a large Washington staff which had grown up since Geneen took over ITT, which constituted a formidable industrial embassy, representing the company both to politicians and to foreign diplomats. There were lobbyists for every purpose, as can be seen from a remarkable series of memos written by the staff in June 1971 (at the same time as the Beard Memorandum) which came to light with so many other memos a year later.[3] They were written in response to a request for 'job description' from the head of the office, Bill Merriam. Merriam sub-edited the memos into

1. *Kleindienst Hearings:* Vol. I, p. 745.
2. Ibid., Vol. II, p. 746.
3. Ibid., pp. 1312–29, see also Robert Walters in the *Washington Evening Star*, May 1, 1972.

ITT

To: W. R. Merriam   *Date:* June 23, 1971

From: R. V. O'Brien

Subject:

I spend the early part of my day in the office planning the
rest of the day and determining what is involved in the future affecting ITT. I read through the Congressional Record each
morning to determine what developments occurred the previous
day that would be of interest and importance to ITT. These
include bills introduced, reports filed, speeches given and positions taken by Members of Congress. I can determine what
activity took place in a committee and in the Chambers and what
will be coming in the future.

The rest of my day is spent on the Hill monitoring committee hearings, visiting Congressional offices and developing
new contacts and maintaining old ones. I present company positions on legislation to Members of Congress and their staffs and
advise them of our business activities in their states and Congressional districts.

In addition to the Congress, I keep in touch with friends
in various Executive departments and agencies including the FTC,
HEW and GSA.

I also try to assist Government personnel when they have
inquiries from constituents or ask for help in securing hotel ac-
commodations, an Avis car, etc.

An increasing part of my time is now devoted to problems
at the State level -- checking on a tax bill in Pennsylvania or a
parking contract in Rhode Island.

Lobbying, ITT-style. A Washington lobbyist, Raymond O'Brien,
describes his contacts and duties to the head of the office, Bill Merriam, who then sub-edits the memo, crossing out indiscretions, for
forwarding to New York.

ITT-ese, to send them on to New York—presumably to impress Geneen—translating them into stiff prose in the passive tense, and crossing out indiscreet references; it is the crossed out lines which are the most revealing. These lobbyists' self-justifications not only show the extent of ITT's pressure-machine; they show too, the lobbyists' fatal itch to write it down, contrary to the whole undercover nature of their profession.

Raymond O'Brien, for instance, described how he spent his day monitoring Congress committees, and then added (crossed out by Merriam) 'I also try to assist Government personnel when they have enquiries from constituents or ask for help in securing hotel accommodation, an Avis car, etc.' Thomas Joyce boasted how every day he knew the situation of every bill affecting ITT on Capitol Hill, how he spends two nights a week with government personnel, and how (crossed out) 'almost every day I have lunch with a Member or staffer'. L. J. Stone described his lobbying for defence and international projects, and added (crossed out) 'I am contacting, socially and business-wise, Embassy, Governmental and Industry sources of information.' Bertram Willis described how he 'provided input' for Congressional activities, helped members of Congress, and mobilised other companies to defend multinational interests. Jack Neal, the Latin-American expert (see chapter 11) described how in the last two weeks he had been invited to ten Embassy functions, and how the trend of economic nationalism required increased ITT activity with government agencies and banks. Bob Schmidt, who looked after the Democrats in Congress, provided ITT with early warnings of investigations that might be embarrassing, such as (crossed out) bread price-fixing. Bernard Goodrich, the manager of press relations, described how he got to know the idiosyncrasies of the Washington press, 'through private entertainment at home and at public functions' (crossed out). Ken Vigue, specialising in international projects, described how his staff handled three hundred foreign VIPs in 1970, and covered six to nine Embassy functions a week: C. R. Bergwin, in charge of export and import licences, described the need for 'effective personal relationship with licensing officers'. Jack Horner, the director of news services, described how he went every day to one of the press clubs; he was also responsible for the ITT monthly newsletter, *Report from Washington*, which provided gossip and inside information for the New York office, in suitable jargon : ('we are down to the nitty gritty of politics à la Washington', said the newsletter in October 1969).

Much of ITT's lobbying has to do with defence, which accounts for $300 million a year in ITT sales. Bob Wilson, in the Armed Services Committee, was a useful contact, and so no doubt were the extraordinary numbers of former serving officers within ITT : in 1969 they included three rear-admirals (including Ellery Stone), two brigadier-generals, 22 colonels and eight captains.[1] Two lobbyists were specially assigned to defence : T. J. Gallagher maintained 'constant surveillance' of the defence department, and had direct relationships with the Armed Services and Appropriations Committees : T. H. Casey had social contacts 'on the highest level' with the defence department. But all the lobbyists were involved in defence; Bob Schmidt was very active, and in 1972 he was reported to have paid $500 to a senior congressman's office to try to ease the progress of an ITT contract for electronic airfield equipment for Vietnam (though they did not get it).[2]

But Dita Beard was the most active lobbyist of them all, constantly helping out Congressmen and Senators. Mostly she concentrated on Republicans but she was not above rescuing a Democrat, like Congressman Van Deerlin in San Diego, with his Avis camper. She was well-known for her generosity. 'The thing that shocked me,' said her secretary at the time of the memo, Susan Lichtman, 'was that members of Congress would sometimes call Mrs. Beard for favours on a big scale' : Senator Hartke, for instance, would use ITT as 'a sort of personal taxicab company'. Dita Beard was always glad to provide free services, ready-made speeches, or free trips on ITT planes. ('How in the world can you expect a Congressman or a Senator to stay on Capitol Hill and do his job and still run out and make speeches and do his campaigning? There are times you can't depend on

1. *Conglomerate Hearings:* Part 3, p. 1105.
2. Jack Anderson's 'Washington Merry-Go-Round': April 11, 1972.

commercial airlines because of the time involved.')[1] She helped, she explained, with anything from recommending a dentist to advising on campaigns. She was always available : 'I'm just the old Mother.'

Her position in the ITT hierarchy was unique; on the company chart, as she explained, 'Beard is sitting way up near the top of the page in a little box by herself.' She was very much the personal emissary of Geneen, and many senior people in ITT knew nothing of her existence until the scandal broke. She operated outside the confines of the corporate castle, away from the controls of Herb Knortz : and she was the only senior woman in this intensely male company (there are only three women among 3,000 ITT executives). Her special relationship clearly aroused the resentment of her two nominal bosses, Ned Gerrity and Bill Merriam : Bob Wilson said that they both 'have an intense hatred for Dita just because Dita was able to get to Hal Geneen'. Her relations were specially strained with Bill Merriam, a sociable aristocrat of sixty who had once been a friend of the Jack Kennedys, but who was much less adept at politics than she. Not surprisingly Mrs. Beard felt her position insecure, or as Gerrity put it : 'She had a severe ego problem.' Once, when she was convinced she was going to be sacked, Wilson intervened with Geneen and (according to Wilson) Geneen then told Gerrity to keep her on. But Dita Beard insisted that her relations with the ITT Washington office were on the whole very good :

> They all put up with me. I don't know why. We really had a wonderful group, but when the staff meetings got a little dull . . . my normal procedure was to stop that nonsense right quick with the filthiest story I could think of and shock them back in their own offices and shorten the meetings a little. It worked.

There was so much comic melodrama in Dita Beard's story that it was easy to forget that she was, in fact, a high-powered operator. She was well paid, with a salary of $30,000, an annual bonus of $15,000 and an expense account of $3,000 a month; but more important, she had the resources of a vast corporation behind her. Behind her

1. Interview with Mike Wallace, *Kleindienst Hearings:* Vol. II, p. 1642.

drinking and joking, she never lost sight of her mission—to press the case for ITT wherever she saw it. She was unswervingly loyal to Geneen, 'the man I think more of than anything in the world'.

It is the fashion among sophisticated businessmen to maintain that lobbyists are nowadays redundant, even counter-productive, in the subtle interdependence between business and government. If so, a great deal of money is wasted, for there are reckoned to be around 5,000 lobbyists in Washington—half of them unregistered—making an average of ten lobbyists to each senator or congressman. It is true that lobbyists, by the nature of their job, cannot prove what they have achieved. It is their occupational disease to claim credit for events that would have happened anyway, and to exaggerate to impress their head office. Inside ITT, with its complexities and dependence on memos, this tendency was likely to be magnified. But a persistent lobbyist can be more effective than he realises. He is always generating a sense of goodwill and community of interest, between the company and the politicians, so that almost imperceptibly they move in the same direction.

His chief weapon, he insists, is nothing more sinister than friendship. There is not much danger of overdoing it, for the lobbyist knows that politicians, though they may complain, really *like* to be lobbied. It is not only the free lunches and plane trips; it is the simple reassurance that they are people that *matter*. As one recipient has put it: 'I am lobbied, therefore I am.' A skilful lobbyist can create an atmosphere in which the whole conflict between government and business seems unnecessary, and where strict enforcers of laws seem merely carping pedants.

Geneen, who was so often up against government, armed with his missionary fervour, understood better than most the importance of lobbying. He has often said that the right to lobby is a basic democratic right. Representing the livelihoods of 400,000 employees, he maintains it is his duty to press the company's claims, and he can quote the First Amendment, which guarantees the right of the public 'to petition the government for a redress of grievances'.

But the rest of this story shows how easily the doors of government open to the big money lobbies, and how closed they are to anyone else. Moreover ITT, like other conglomerates, had a special advantage in the lobbying business : unlike the old industrial giants, the car or steel companies, with employment concentrated in one or two states, ITT have factories in forty states. They could, when they needed, mobilise Congressmen and Senators all over the Union.

THE SCOOP

As soon as Jack Anderson received the Dita Beard memo in February 1972, he passed it to one of his reporters, Brit Hume, without telling him the source of it. Hume is a young and dedicated investigative reporter, with a slow voice and a soulful look, but dogged in pursuit of a scandal. He had started in journalism six years before on the *Hartford Times* (which gave him an extra interest in ITT), and he had joined Anderson's staff two years before. It did not take him long to realise that it 'was the single most incriminating piece of paper that I had ever seen'. He quickly took it round to his friend Reuben Robertson, who was as excited as he was, and who could explain more of the background. They decided that Hume should confront Dita Beard as soon as possible, and the next day Hume rang her up and explained that he had a document from her files that he wanted to discuss with her. She invited him straight round, and he went to the ITT offices two blocks away, armed with the original of the memo—having made a copy which he hid in his desk. He was met first by the ITT's press relations man, Bernie Goodrich, and then by another PR man, Jack Horner. Finally Dita Beard bustled in; as Brit Hume vividly described her :

> She was an astonishing sight. A large woman in her mid-fifties, she had grey hair that showed traces of having once been red or blonde, or dyed one of those colours. Her skin was leathery and puffy and she wore no makeup. A paper clip held her horn rimmed eyeglasses together where one of the hinges had broken. She had on a chartreuse, short-sleeve sweatshirt, and a pair of soiled yellow cotton slacks. Her flat, slip-on shoes were battered and dirty. Her voice had an edge of raspiness that might have been the result of the Chesterfield Kings she chain-smoked. The impression she gave, though,

was not of a broken-down woman but of a middle-aged tomboy. She moved and spoke with self-assurance, and it occurred to me as we shook hands that she must have considerable influence in that office to get away with being dressed as she was in the middle of the week. She reminded me of Tugboat Annie. I liked her.[1]

Hume, with his heart thumping, tried to sound calm as he took the memo out of his pocket and put it in front of Mrs. Beard. She read it in silence. Then she began shaking her head. She said (according to Hume's account), 'We weren't involved at all. We aren't involved at all . . . I had nothing to do with the settlement . . . All we ever did was offer to help raise that money.' But she did not deny that she wrote the memo. They went through it together, and she gave ITT's official line about the San Diego convention, while Goodrich (as she later told Hume) periodically kicked her under the table. Eventually Hume left them with a copy of the memo, saying that they would have plenty of time to discuss it and check their files. He wanted to prevent ITT from quickly issuing their own statement in a panic.

The next day Dita Beard called Hume, to ask him to come straight out to her house in Virginia. Hume was let in by her teenage son, Bull Beard; and inside he found a very different Mrs. Beard, without the brassiness, and with red swollen eyes. They sat together on stools in the kitchen, while she talked about the memo between tears and four-letter words. 'I know you got it from Jack Gleason,' she said, but Brit Hume did not then know who Gleason was.[2] Later she said : 'I wrote it, of course I wrote it,' and then explained that Bill Merriam, her Washington boss, was politically naive, and that she wrote it to 'put some sense into the head of that stupid shit Merriam'. It was he, she explained, who had the idea of ITT helping to bring the convention to San Diego, after talking with the Lieutenant-Governor, Ed Reinecke. Geneen had enthusiastically agreed, and Reinecke had told John Mitchell about it on a visit to Washington.

Finally and most sensationally, she admitted that there had been an agreement behind the settlement, which she herself

1. Brit Hume: 'Checking Out Dita Beard's Memo', *Harper's*, August, 1972.
2. *Kleindienst Hearings:* Vol. II, p. 454.

had negotiated. She described how she had discussed it with the Attorney-General, John Mitchell, when they were both guests at a buffet luncheon given by the Governor of Kentucky, Louie Nunn, at the Kentucky Derby in May 1971. Mitchell had scolded her for an hour for her relentless lobbying, and had then said that even the President had told him to make a reasonable settlement. Eventually Mitchell had asked her, 'What do you want?'—meaning what companies did ITT want to keep in the anti-trust settlement. Dita Beard had replied that ITT must keep the Hartford, 'because of the economy', and also part of Grinnell. Eventually they reached an agreement together, as they went through the buffet line and sat down to eat: it was exactly the settlement that ITT actually got. But (Dita Beard insisted) Geneen knew nothing about this agreement, and she reiterated again and again, in spite of what the memo had said, that there was no connection between the settlement and the convention pledge. After two hours of outpourings, Brit Hume got up to leave, and Dita Beard, to his surprise, embraced him, as if expecting him to kiss her goodbye like a son. He went back home to write his notes from memory.[1]

The next day, Hume rang the Attorney-General's office, to try to get Mitchell's side of the strange story of the meeting at the Kentucky Derby. Mitchell's press officer, Jack Hushen, admitted that Mitchell *had* met Dita Beard there, but only 'like hello-goodbye'. He insisted that Mitchell could prove that the memo was false.

On the Friday, Hume wrote up his scoop for Jack Anderson's 'Merry-Go-Round', giving extracts from the memo and his conversations with Dita Beard, and concluding with Mitchell's denial. He carefully refrained from saying that there had been a bargain over the convention. Anderson made a few changes and approved it. The column began with the sensational words:

> We now have evidence that the settlement of the Nixon administration's biggest anti-trust case was privately arranged between Attorney-General John Mitchell and the top lobbyist for the company involved. We have this on the word of the lobbyist herself, crusty capable Dita Beard of the International

1. The notes were later handed in as evidence to the Judiciary subcommittee (*Kleindienst Hearings:* Vol. II, p. 491).

Telephone and Telegraph Company. She acknowledged the secret deal after we obtained a highly incriminating memo, written by her, from ITT's files.

The memo still left many questions unanswered. So Hume quickly tried to follow up this first column, before it was published the following Tuesday. He managed to talk to a former ITT director, who cannot be named, who had been involved in the Hartford merger, who tipped him off that ITT's pressure had been on a very broad front; 'The overall theory of ITT management', he accurately explained, 'is that if one approach can do it, seven approaches can do it seven times better.' He suggested that a key man in the antitrust negotiations was the banker Felix Rohatyn: 'I'm labouring under the general impression that out of one or two more talks between Rohatyn and Kleindienst, things began to move.'

Hume quickly rang Rohatyn, and caught him at Kennedy Airport. He told him about the memo, and started to read it out. Rohatyn interrupted with, 'That's absolute bull-shit.' He ought to know, he went on, because he had been assigned by Geneen to make the ITT case to the government on the economic side; he had had about six meetings with Kleindienst, at the same time that the ITT lawyers had been meeting McLaren. It was not till later, that Hume realised the full significance of what Rohatyn had said. For Robertson reminded him of that letter that Kleindienst had written two months before to the Democratic National Chairman, Larry O'Brien, insisting that the settlement was 'handled and negotiated exclusively' by McLaren and his staff. This was now flatly contradicted by Rohatyn's account of his talks with Kleindienst.

Hume also traced Jack Gleason, the man whom Dita Beard suspected of leaking the memo; he turned out to be a public relations consultant who had worked in the White House, and who now did work for ITT. Gleason said that at the time of the memo, Bill Merriam had asked him to find out what the White House was expecting from ITT at San Diego, and that he had rung up his friend, William Timmons, at the White House.[1] It seemed to confirm the first part of the memo.

1. *Kleindienst Hearings:* Vol. II, p. 455.

There were still many missing links to the story; but there was enough to suggest secret dealings between ITT and the government. For his next column Hume began with the words :

> We have now established that Attorney-General-designate Richard Kleindienst, told an outright lie about the Justice Department's sudden out-of-court settlement of the Nixon administration's biggest anti-trust case.

The timing of this attack on Kleindienst was specially poignant; for on the very next day, he was due to take over the Department of Justice as Acting Attorney-General in succession to Mitchell, who was leaving to run Nixon's election campaign. Only the previous week the Senate Judiciary Committee, with some misgivings among its members, had confirmed Kleindienst's nomination by Nixon to the Attorney-Generalship.

Anderson and Hume were thus aiming their blows at the very heart of the Nixon administration—attacking the integrity of two Attorney-Generals. Both Mitchell and Kleindienst were headstrong political animals. Mitchell, from Nixon's old law firm, had been Nixon's campaign manager. Kleindienst had first come to prominence in Arizona as the leader of the 'Goldwater Mafia' in 1964; he had become a key organiser for Nixon in 1968, rewarded with the Deputy Attorney-Generalship. In that job he had become a hero to the right and a villain to the left, a thick-set, broad-shouldered 'Mr. Tough', priding himself on plain speaking : when the police arrested 10,000 protesters against Vietnam, and herded them into detention centres, Kleindienst talked about the 'vicious mob', and its 'international threat'. The more fundamental charge against Kleindienst was that he could not withstand the pressures of money or politics; and two scandals in 1970, the Harry Steward affair and the Carson affair, had raised serious doubts about his probity. In the first, Kleindienst had surprisingly exonerated a United States attorney, Harry Steward, who had been charged with obstructing investigations into corruption in San Diego; in the second, Kleindienst had been approached with an offer of money by a Senate aide, Robert Carson (later sentenced for perjury and bribery) and had only reported it a week later, when he heard that Carson was under FBI surveillance. When Kleindienst had come up to the Senators for his confirmation as Attorney-General in February 1972, three of the committee (Senators Hart, Kennedy and Tunney) voiced their worries about his judgment in view of the past scandals. But they reluctantly agreed to confirm him.

When Anderson's columns broke, in seven hundred papers across the United States, the repercussions were immediate. ITT, as soon as they saw the first column, rushed in with a denial of remarkable rashness, in view of what Rohatyn had already said; they said that 'neither Mrs. Beard nor anyone else except counsel was authorised to carry on such negotiations'. Mitchell, too, denied that he had been involved in any way with the negotiations for the San Diego convention; and said that he 'had no knowledge of anyone from the [convention] committee or elsewhere dealing with ITT'. But Brit Hume managed to get a contradiction of this in a telephone conversation with Edgar Gillenwaters, the Californian Director of Commerce, who had worked to bring the convention to San Diego. Gillenwaters told Hume that he and Ed Reinecke, the Lieutenant-Governor, had told Mitchell about the ITT offer as early as mid-May, nearly three months before it had been made public; Mitchell had said : 'If you can do it, more power to you.'

And then, on the Tuesday evening, Kleindienst took a precipitate step. He did not, he said, want his confirmation as Attorney-General to take place with a cloud over his head; so he asked that the Senate should resume the hearings as to his fitness for the job. It was a surprising move, because there was not at that time any pressure to reopen the hearings; and because, in the light of what Kleindienst himself must have known, the Senate were likely to uncover embarrassing facts. Kleindienst evidently thought that the hearings would be short and sweet, redounding to his credit. But Anderson had no worries; he told Hume : 'This is the stupidest thing he could have done.'

10

The Senators

We are just one more chapter in this loaded story of why
people lack faith in the system.

                                      Senator Philip Hart [1]

On Thursday March 2, only two days after Jack Anderson's
first revelations appeared, the Judiciary Sub-Committee of
the Senate assembled on the semi-circular dais of room 2228
of the New Senate Office building, to re-examine Kleindienst's nomination. The small high-ceilinged room was
packed, with reporters standing along the wall. In election
year, the political atmosphere was electric, and the Dita
Beard affair had overnight become the symbol of corruption
in government. Mayor Lindsay called it 'a marriage between a giant corporation and the Justice Department'.

Ostensibly, the procedure seemed straightforward enough:
the Judiciary Committee, as the watchdog of the Justice
Department, had to assure itself of the Attorney-General's
integrity, to keep check on the power of the executive; and
since the committee was predominantly Democrat, its check
might be expected to be the more effective. But nothing in
the Senate is quite what it seems; and the chairman, 'Big
Jim' Eastland of Mississippi, provided, as one participant
described it, a specially Kafkaesque element. A tough old
attorney of sixty-eight, rolling a huge cigar round his mouth,
he stage-managed the hearings, as chairmen can, with evident relish — producing surprise witnesses, suddenly adjourn-
ing and reopening the hearings, applying the ten-minute
limit on each Senator's questions with whimsical variations.

1. *Kleindienst Hearings:* Vol. II, p. 121.

Though a Democrat, he was of the most conservative kind, and in the subsequent election campaign he was actually endorsed by President Nixon : he was very friendly with Kleindienst, who stayed with him later in Mississippi during the campaign. Eastland clearly expected that the hearings would be over in two or three days, clearing Kleindienst's name; and Kleindienst had taken the precaution of talking to each of the sub-committee before the hearings began.

Most of the committees were conservative and predictable, including such die-hards as Hiram Fong from Hawaii, Roman Hruska from Nebraska, Strom Thurmond from South Carolina and Marlow Cook, the closest to Nixon. But the committee also included Philip Hart, the much-respected Senator from Michigan, who had been so critical of industrial mergers on the Senate Anti-Trust Sub-committee. And there was a group of three young liberal Democrats who were determined to make the most of the hearings. They were John Tunney, the boxer's son, Birch Bayh, the rumbustious Senator from Indiana (who left for Africa in the middle of the hearings); and their leader, the Senator from Massachussets, Edward Kennedy. These three saw the hearings as a chance not only to bash the Republicans in a vulnerable spot, but in a populist election to champion the small man against big business, as symbolised by ITT.

Jack Anderson, too, was determined to beat Chairman Eastland at his own game, and to mobilise the full power of the press. 'Eastland didn't reckon with my power,' as he put it : 'My column gets into the backyards of all those Senators.' Usually, Anderson explained to me, he sees his role as simply that of a journalist, to throw light on a subject and let others take over; but this time he felt personally challenged. Anderson called up the Senators, and made it clear that he wanted to testify, and that he was throwing his weight into the case. When Eastland banned the television cameras from the hearing room, the cameras appeared instead in the corridor outside, and Anderson made the most of it, giving his own version of the story to reporters and interviewers, so that television could steal the show from the Senators.

Jack Anderson, Brit Hume, Reuben Robertson and other ITT-watchers all weighed in to provide a constant flow of new tit-bits for the press, to keep the story alive. They worked closely with Kennedy and his allies, and Kennedy deployed his whole staff—five attorneys and three assistants —to assemble the massive documentation. The Kennedy team pursued every trail and clue, in a paperchase through the labyrinth of power, and the nomination (as Tunney put it) became 'the focal point for a new look at what is wrong with the whole system'. It was to be the longest nomination hearings in the history of the Senate—twenty-four days of questioning, spread over two months, covering 1,700 pages of text in two fat green volumes.

The hearings became increasingly inconsequential and surrealist—with eccentric digressions, comic witnesses, ir-relevant arguments. It was less and less clear who was ac-cused of what; and though all fourteen Senators were attorneys, they were like attorneys on holiday without a judge, allowed any amount of hearsay, gossip and 'fishing expeditions' to catch odd clues. Like so many scandals, the investigation left large areas of darkness in the middle; but it lit up, like a roving searchlight, all kinds of incidental murky corners. The first question, of whether Kleindienst was fit to be Attorney-General, soon became overlaid by all kinds of others—about the White House, Dita Beard, John Mitchell, and above all about ITT and Geneen. By the mid-dle of the hearings, it was really the giant corporation that had become the main subject of study: 'Welcome to our ITT-Dita Beard hearings,' said Senator Gurney to Ed Reinecke. And it was as a study of the pressure of big busi-ness on government that the real fascination lay.

THE ENEMY IS US

But in theory at least the first question before the sub-committee was: did Kleindienst lie when he said that the anti-trust settlement 'was handled and negotiated ex-clusively' by McLaren? And on the first day, sitting at the witness table, were Richard Kleindienst, Richard McLaren the former anti-trust chief, and Felix Rohatyn, the director of ITT and partner of Lazards.

Kleindienst began by thanking the Senators for giving him a chance to clear his name, and then read a prepared statement. He admitted that he had met several times with Rohatyn; Rohatyn had telephoned him out of the blue, on April 16, 1971, three months before the actual settlement, asking to discuss the consequences of the divestiture of Hartford. Rohatyn made his case, and Kleindienst then set up a further meeting for Rohatyn to meet McLaren and other anti-trust staff on April 29. Rohatyn talked to him several times later, about the 'punitive' terms. But none of this was 'negotiation'; and Kleindienst insisted he knew nothing about ITT's contribution to San Diego.

McLaren and Rohatyn then followed, corroborating Kleindienst, insisting that the arguments for the settlement had been straightforwardly financial. But soon the plot thickened. Why had Kleindienst been so prepared to see Rohatyn in the first place? At first he went on insisting to Kennedy that Rohatyn called him out of the blue. But soon afterwards Kleindienst was observed talking anxiously to Rohatyn and Kleindienst explained: 'I have had my memory refreshed as to why he called me in the first place.' He then explained that a neighbour of his in Washington, Mr. Ryan, who worked in ITT's Washington office, had talked to him at a neighbourhood party about ITT's difficulties, and had asked Kleindienst whether he would be willing to see someone from ITT about it. Kleindienst had agreed.

And why, Kennedy asked Kleindienst, had the Justice Department asked at the last minute on April 19 (the day after Rohatyn had first called Kleindienst) to delay an appeal to the Supreme Court in one of the ITT anti-trust cases, the case against Grinnell? Kleindienst could not recollect, nor could McLaren. But four days later Kleindienst had again refreshed his memory; he now said that he had received a letter from Lawrence Walsh, a former Deputy Attorney-General, who was now acting for ITT, asking for more time on the Grinnell Case; Kleindienst discussed it with McLaren, and agreed.

Rohatyn, too, denied that he was negotiating. 'What did you think you were doing?' replied Senator Hart; 'giving an economics course?' 'I was trying to make an economic case, sir, of hardship.' Kleindienst insisted to Senator Bayh that all he did was to listen: he had a duty, he said, to listen to people with grievances: 'we serve ITT as well as anybody else in this nation.' He could not cut himself off from political influences: as he characteristically put it later, 'I am not in a prophylactic sack with respect to the White House.' But Kleindienst eventually admitted that it was he who had 'set in motion a series of events' that had led to a settlement. Could this be squared with his statement that 'the negotiations were handled exclusively by McLaren'? Why had he felt it necessary to make that statement in the first place? There was no reason why, as Deputy Attorney-General, he should not have been involved in discussing the case. The evasions and lapses of memory suggested that other facts, too were being concealed.

Had John Mitchell, too, discussed the settlement with ITT people, as Jack Anderson's column suggested? Mitchell was called to give evidence and again denied any involvement. He described how Dita Beard had accosted him at the Kentucky Derby, but denied that he agreed anything with her, and his account was backed up by a surprise witness, Louie Nunn, the Governor of Kentucky. Mitchell did say that he had met Felix Rohatyn four times in the course of 1971 — but that was, he insisted, strictly about stock-exchange matters. Geneen, too, had come to see him in July 1970, to discuss anti-trust policy, but he had not mentioned, said Mitchell, specific ITT cases; yet it was hard to believe that the discussion was not relevant to ITT. Mitchell said he had supported settling the ITT cases, and that he often talked with Peter Flanigan of the White House about anti-trust cases, and about an inter-agency group studying whether the anti-trust laws should be revised. Clearly Mitchell had *some* interest in the ITT question; and he had come a long way from that militant speech at Savannah in 1969.

As for Mitchell's involvement in San Diego, the evidence became increasingly incredible. The two Californians, Reinecke and Gillenwaters, eventually gave evidence, but they were so devious that Birch Bayh burst out to Gillenwaters, 'Your credibility has gone from a hundred to damn near zero.' It became harder to believe that Mitchell did not know, by May 1971, about both the pending settlement and the ITT pledge to San Diego.

McLaren, now a federal judge, was in the most moving

situation of any of the characters under attack; for he, having been the heroic trust-buster, was now accused of having caved-in. He was hurt and angry at the charges: 'I pinch myself sometimes, Senator,' he said to Birch Bayh: 'we carried out a billion-dollar divestiture, the biggest in history. We stopped this juggernaut from making acquisitions that we feel are anti-competitive. We stopped this and now I am up here defending it.' Later he lost his temper with Tunney: 'I think it is an absolute outrage the way this committee is inquiring into this matter.' Yet as the new evidence emerged, it seemed clear that McLaren had been under intense political pressure to change his mind about the Hartford; and that, however much he thought he was immune to pressure, he had—like so many anti-trust chiefs before him—been gradually worn down.

Underlying the whole hearings was the fundamental question of whether the power of big business was now so overwhelming that no anti-trust chief could withstand it. Philip Hart, always the most interesting speaker in the committee, asked the question of Erwin Griswold, the Solicitor-General, who had been tangentially involved in the case, when he enabled the case against Grinnell to be delayed: 'Have we now reached a point in our society,' asked Hart, 'where there has been permitted to develop a private concentration of power which, because of the enormity of their reach, make impossible the application of public policy to them? We had better get an answer,' he went on, 'or the day will come when there will be private power—and there needn't be anybody with a black hat involved with its creation—beyond reach.'

Griswold replied that it was a very interesting and puzzling question, but he ducked it, and said merely that Congress should strengthen the law with respect to conglomerate mergers. Marlow Cook took it up, and said: 'I couldn't agree more with the philosophical approach of Senator Hart. But it is kind of like saying, we have met the enemy, and it is us. It is Congress that wrote Section 7 of the Clayton Act, and it is Congress if it wants to do something about it, which should do it.'

Jack Anderson in the meantime had been sitting in the front row with Brit Hume impatiently waiting to be called.

At last, on the sixth day, Chairman Eastland summoned him and he quickly fired a full salvo : 'The public record on this episode is blotted with falsehood. The aura of scandal hangs over the whole matter.' He accused Kleindienst of 'dancing a semantic tango' round the word negotiate. He warned the committee that Ned Gerrity of ITT was masterminding an effort to discredit Dita Beard as a crackpot and a drunk. He concluded with a final blast : 'Mr. Kleindienst is a man who has trouble recognising a crime when he sees one. Now, let us make no mistake about it. The contribution of $400,000 by a corporation to support a political convention is a crime. . . .'

Senator Gurney asked how Anderson got hold of the memo, and he refused to say : 'Senator, if a newspaperman's sources can be identified and hauled before the Government every time we write a story, then the first amendment is absolutely meaningless.' Brit Hume at first refused to disclose the notes of his crucial interview with Dita Beard; but when he eventually did so they corroborated the columns and provided basic evidence throughout the hearings. The Republican Senators tried to discredit Anderson and Hume by quoting previous stories which had been found to be false. Anderson apologised for one of them, but defended his record for accuracy. Anderson came back to the question of contributions to political parties—'a far more paramount issue than whether or not Richard Kleindienst is confirmed' —a question which came close to the bone of the Senators. Philip Hart again examined his conscience ; 'I like to think that I have never been influenced by a campaign contribution in any action I have ever taken. The truth is that we do not even understand our own motives. We can just hope that we were not influenced. But the public, inevitably, wonders, and dramatically so in this case.'

Senator Hruska agreed : 'I think you are right, all of us think we are free and clear of any obligation to those who subscribe to our campaign funds. I do not know that it is always true, whether it is conscious or subconscious.' Senator Scott said, 'Let us let everybody on this committee tell what they got from whom, and we would cut this hypocrisy out.'

In the meantime the one crucial witness, Dita Beard herself, had vanished. The case acquired a surrealist dimension, the more so as it coincided with the Howard Hughes affair. Chairman Eastland issued a subpoena but still there was no trace of her. The FBI were asked to find her, and eventually it was learnt that a woman answering her description had become ill on the flight to Denver on March 2, and had been given oxygen, but refused to identify herself, saying, 'I don't need a damned doctor.' J. Edgar Hoover at last reported that she had been discovered in the Rocky Mountain Osteopathic Hospital in Denver, Colorado. The FBI agents were first refused admission until her personal doctor, Dr. Liszka had examined her heart : then, after they served the subpoena, the doctors stated that she was too ill to give evidence, suffering from impending coronary thrombosis.

Dr. Liszka himself appeared to give evidence to the committee in mysterious circumstances; he had presented himself to the Justice Department the previous Friday, to give his version of the events. He testified in disjointed Hungarian English about Mrs. Beard's coronary ischemia and said that she was periodically 'disturbed and irrational'. He said that Mrs. Beard had given him the impression that she had written the famous memo, but had said, 'I was mad and disturbed when I wrote it.' But the doctor's reliability soon came under some doubt when it transpired that he and his wife had both been under investigation for medicare fraud; and that he had previously done some work for an ITT subsidiary, Hamilton Life Insurance.

Mrs. Beard's medical advisors looked increasingly odd. Her osteopathic cardiologist, Dr. Radetsky, who decided when she could give evidence, also turned out to have been investigated for medicare fraud. There was a good deal of doubt, in fact, as to whether there was anything wrong with Dita Beard at all : and two other Denver doctors, Ray Pryor and Joseph Snyder, who had first supported the diagnosis of angina pectoris, later stated that there were no objective findings, and that it was based entirely on her personal history of chest pains 'which is subjective information'.

It was not till March 10 that Dita Beard made a public statement about the memorandum, just after Jack Anderson and Brit Hume had given evidence; it was issued by an attorney, David Fleming, who had been hired by ITT to represent her with regard to the hearings (for which he sent a bill for $15,000). Mrs. Beard categorically denied 'that there was ever an arangement between ITT and the Administration involving a favourable settlement of the anti-trust action'; but she did not suggest that she had not written the memo. A week later, however, she dictated a further statement from her hospital bed, saying that the memo published by Anderson was a hoax, with forged initials. Jack Anderson roughly retorted that she had not denied the memorandum earlier, and that her statement was absolutely incredible. 'The only explanation I can give is that she is fifty-three, divorced, has five children and hospital bills to pay. She is at ITT's economic mercy.'

At last, three weeks after the beginning of the hearings, a few Senators were allowed to question Dita Beard. A special sub-committee, with Hart as chairman and including Kennedy and Tunney, flew to Denver to take her testimony in hospital, accompanied by one reporter and one photographer. They recorded an astonishing scene. Dita Beard was sitting up in her hospital bed, strapped to an electro-cardiograph, with her two doctors, Radetsky and Garland, standing by the oxygen equipment : any change in the rhythm of the heartbeat, the doctors announced, would bring the questioning to an end. Her attorneys, David Fleming and Harold White, stood by. The seven Senators, embarrassed by the melodramatic setting, sat round the bed-side : 'It makes you feel like some sort of ghoul,' said Tunney.

David Fleming read out Mrs. Beard's statement. She denied again that she wrote the memorandum, and gave her version of her meetings with Brit Hume, claiming that he was determined to show a connection between San Diego and the settlement, whatever she said. But under questioning from Kennedy she admitted that many bits of the memo *did* seem familiar, and she even explained why she had written them. She recognised the first two paragraphs, except for the bit about Mitchell. She was familiar too with the subject matter of most of the third paragraph; but after that, she said, she was confused—particularly by the reference to talks with Governor Nunn, and 'our noble commitment'. She couldn't understand how she could have said that 'the President has told Mitchell to see that things are worked out', but she agreed that 'this last paragraph does sound very familiar'.

After two hours of hearings Senator Gurney had just begun questioning Mrs. Beard about the time she met Kleindienst in Tulsa, Oklahoma. She gave a gasp and a start of pain. Dr. Radetsky moved forward: 'Let's recess for about five minutes, please.' The Senators waited while the doctors examined her. She was suffering chest pains. She would not be well enough to answer any further questions.

Kennedy, who had hoped for nine hours of hearings in the hospital, was suspicious—the more so after the facts emerged about Dr. Radetsky. His suspicions deepened when, only a week after her mysterious relapse, she was well enough to come out of hospital and to appear on television with the gruelling interviewer Mike Wallace, to whom she revealed rather more than she had to the Senators. But her doctors insisted that she could not give evidence again for six months, and her attorney David Fleming protested against the 'ruthless and obsessive disregard' shown by Jack Anderson and Senator Kennedy: 'That a sick and distraught woman responsible for upbringing five children has been driven to the point that she would risk her very life that the truth be made public, is a sad and disgusting commentary on the almost untrammelled power of Jack Anderson, an arrogant and brazen journalist and his pathetic muck-raking investigator, Brit Hume.'

THE MEMORANDUM

The authenticity of the memo had become increasingly confused. It had already become a battleground for the typewriter experts, without whom no big American scandal would be complete. Chairman Eastland had sent it to J. Edgar Hoover at the FBI, and a reply came back, stating that the alleged memorandum was written on an IBM model C machine, with 'documentary' type with 1/32 inch pitch, on paper watermarked Gilbert Bond 25 percent cotton; and that these characteristics, together with the ribbon and indentations, were identical with those of other ITT documents written at the same time. 'Nothing was found from such examinations to suggest preparations at a time other than around June 25, 1971.'

But ITT had also managed to get hold of the original memo, and sent it to *their* experts, Mr. and Mrs. Tytell, of Fulton Street, New York. They examined it for days and discovered that under ultra-violet light the fluorescence of the questioned document was *not* the same as that of other documents written in June 1971, and that the 'write' was very similar to that of a letter written in January 1972. Armed with the Tytell's report, an ITT lawyer with the appropriate name of De Forest Billyou, took the memo to another husband-and-wife team, Walter and Lucy McCrone in Chicago, experts on paper chromatography and 'microprobe analysis'. They discovered a small amount of barium sulphate in the paper coating, which they said suggested that it was written in 1972. ITT presented their experts' evidence to the Senators, but they were not inclined to take it too seriously, against the FBI's report. The Tytells, it turned out, were paid $8,000 for eight days; and the McCrones were paid $7,000.

ITT also issued a press statement on March 20 saying that they had recently discovered what they now called the 'Genuine Beard Memorandum'; which was written on the same date as the alleged 'Anderson-Beard Memorandum' and which proved there could have been no deal involving Mrs. Beard. But the 'Genuine Beard Memorandum' turned out to be one of the 'job description' notes written by the Washington lobbyist to Bill Merriam, explaining her work in San Diego but proving nothing. ITT also came up with an affidavit from Susan Lichtman, who had been Dita Beard's secretary at the time of the memo, who testified that she remembered typing parts of it, but not the incriminating bits. But five days later Mrs. Lichtman gave another affidavit, this time at the behest of one of Mrs. Beard's attorney's, saying that she did not recall typing the ITT 'genuine' Beard Memorandum, either.

There were thus now three alleged memoranda, all dated June 25, including this modified Anderson-Beard Memorandum, with the incriminations missing, as now recalled by Dita Beard and her secretary. But this last one never really became convincing; for though Dita Beard said that she had delivered it to Merriam, neither Merriam nor Ned Gerrity, when they appeared to give evidence, could remember anything about it.

Why, if the Anderson-Beard Memorandum was a forgery, was Dita Beard three weeks late in denying it? Bob Wilson, to whom Dita Beard talked soon after Brit Hume showed her the memo, did not gather from her that it was a fake; he explained in an interview how Merriam had come to see him on February 28, and had said that he did get the memo, but had given it back to Dita: 'ITT puts out the story that nobody ever saw it. Well that's Gerrity saying nobody ever saw the memo. The hell they didn't. Merriam personally told me last Monday that he got the memo—he said Dita insisted that she write the memo. . . .'[1]

In any case, most of the subject-matter of the memo was graually confirmed by the evidence. Successive witnesses helped to decode the cryptic language, and Merriam even said that she was in the habit of using the phrases 'Hal and his big mouth' and 'Please destroy this, huh?'. Dita Beard herself explained the references to the call from the White House, and the need to keep the $400,000 secret: and the confusion as to whether the money would be in services or in cash was corroborated by Gerrity and Merriam.

What was never corroborated was the implication that Nixon and Mitchell were both helping ITT, and the assumption of a deal ('our noble commitment has gone a long way toward our negotiations coming out as Hal wants them'). But Anderson and Hume had themselves carefully avoided making this charge; and if there *had* been a deal it was unlikely that anyone would admit it. As Kleindienst himself put it, in his testimony: 'If Mr. Flanigan bribed me or set up a bribe, I doubt if he would come down here under oath and tell you, "Yeah, I set up a big fix with Kleindienst by

1. Interview with Robert Cox: *Kleindienst Hearings*: Vol. III, p. 880.

which we were going to get bought for 100,000 bucks to settle a one-billion-dollar anti-trust case." '

Why, if the memo was genuine, had Mrs. Beard written it? The explanation offered by Bob Wilson seemed the most convincing; that the Washington office was riddled with internal politics; that Gerrity and Merriam resented Mrs. Beard's special relationships, both with Geneen and with key Republicans; and that she was fed up with Merriam's misunderstandings, and wanted to put on record her own considerable achievement. Her belief that the pledge to San Diego had helped the anti-trust settlement could have been due to the lobbyist's occupational hubris; but it could have at least an element of truth.

Why and how the memo reached Jack Anderson's office remains a secret. ITT people now suggest that she herself leaked it, as a misguided manoeuvre to safeguard her position. But this is impossible to square with her reaction to Brit Hume. She herself said that Jack Gleason must have leaked it; it does seem likely that someone within the ITT orbit must have passed on the memo, perhaps half-jokingly, without realising the earthquake it would cause.

THE SHREDDER

ITT's credibility sank further with the discovery that on the day after the Anderson memo was revealed, they had ordered a mass-shredding of documents in their Washington office. The shredder—a machine which eats up documents and leaves them in thin strips—became a new comic element. The Senators called for a special report on the shredding from ITT, which was duly presented by their senior counsel, Howard Aibel. It told how, after Brit Hume had paid his first call, Merriam told his staff to remove all documents which could be misused and misconstrued by Jack Anderson. In the afternoon an ITT security officer, Russell Tagliareni, arrived from New York to supervise the shredding, 'in accordance with ITT's standard practice'. ITT, of course, insisted that none of the destroyed documents linked the anti-trust settlement with the convention; but as Kennedy said afterwards: 'Even the nominee's supporters have stopped saying "There's not a shred of evidence" . . .

because they realise that *all* there was, as far as ITT's Washington office was concerned, was shreds of evidence.'[1]

The luckless Bill Merriam, when he came to give evidence, made matters worse. He explained that he received hundreds of memos over his desk every week, and Senator Tunney said : 'Not alleging such matters as are contained in the Anderson-Beard memorandum, I hope,' Merriam replied : 'Well, you would be surprised.' (Laughter.) Later Senator Ervin questioned him :

ERVIN :   Who issued the order to the Washington office of ITT for the Washington office to destroy any records which might be embarrassing to the company or to any individuals concerned with the company?
MERRIAM : I did, sir.
ERVIN :   Is that a policy of the ITT?
MERRIAM : It is when you have a memo like this one we are talking about that has escaped your files and had been distributed to the press.
ERVIN :   Well, you could not destroy that memo because you did not have it.
MERRIAM : No. That is right, but there might have been a lot of others in there like that. (Laughter.)

(Merriam explained later to Senator Gurney, who came to his rescue : 'I mean a lot of other memos that would embarrass the company if they had got out.')

The shredder became a new by-word, and the ITT report conjured up a whole network of secret company intelligence. The manufacturers of shredders, or 'Dita Beard Machines' as they were now called, reported record sales in the following months, as other corporations took fright. Geneen later said that he thought that the shredding was ITT's biggest mistake[2]; but there was a poetic justice in the corporation being caught out by its own memo-mania. The proliferation of memos was an inevitable result of the ITT system of control; but for a company so deeply involved in undercover politics, the dangers should have been obvious. As Senator

1. *Kennedy Report:* p. 24.
2. Speech to shareholders at Memphis, May 1972.

Ervin said, talkings about the shredding—echoing Celler in his anti-trust hearings—'I've always heard it said, do right and fear no man, and don't write and fear no woman : so I can understand why this was done.' However busy the ITT shredder had been, plenty of documents were lurking to embarrass ITT still further.

CORPORATE SIEGE

In the face of this public battering, Geneen and the ITT officials scuttled behind the walls of the corporate castle, protected by an army of lawyers, occasionally opening a narrow slit or letting down the drawbridge to issue a denial or an affidavit. The ranks closed, and the corporation appeared as never before as a one-man-band, which could say and do nothing without Geneen. Only Lazards showed open unease about the company's tactics; for Lazards were clearly embarrassed by the cavortings of Dita Beard and the Washington lobbyists. Felix Rohatyn said he was worried about ITT's involvement with 'anything that looks political', and about the effect of the Washington office on the company's image.

Geneen himself, when he appeared to give evidence, sounded as usual confident, evangelical, far more convincing than his underlings. He denied any connection between the settlement and the contribution to San Diego, which he said was quite legal : he had obtained counsel's opinion. He described unrepentantly his crusade against McLaren's policy, how he had sought to bring his views to the attention of all who would listen. He outlined the heroic history of ITT : how its growth was not a question of mere aggrandisement, but a means of balancing foreign risks; how they were being unfairly sued, in an attack on bigness per se. The anti-trust laws were quite out of date in the context of America's current economic predicament, competing against the Common Market and Japan.

His tone was hurt and amazed; 'I am surprised to find a company such as ours put in a category of a non-constructive and fearsome force within our society.' He sounded assured enough, but underneath he was, his colleagues observed, bitter and disillusioned—not so much by the assaults from the Democrats and the press, as by the lack of reinforcements from the business community. He was, indeed, in an unenviable position; for ITT had been cast in the role of the ritual sacrifice on the altar of big business—the chosen victim who would serve to purify the tribe. Other tycoons from Establishment companies made it clear that Geneen had always been an outsider and an adventurer.

The press were having an anti-ITT festival. At the height of the scandal, Jack Anderson disclosed *another* big batch of ITT memos, this time about Chile (see next chapter), in many ways more damaging than the Beard memo. The newspapers took up the charges about insider trading, and reported that several senior ITT men had sold ITT stock just before the settlement became public. (Later, in June, the SEC formally charged ITT and Lazards with insider trading, and a consent decree was hurriedly made, in which the officials, while denying they had done it, promised not to do it again.) Senator Kennedy accused ITT of having paid no federal income tax during the year 1971, and Senator McGovern took up the charge in his election campaign. Stories proliferated about ITT's lobbying methods and pressures. The corporation that had striven so hard to display its 'corporate identity' to the world, to distinguish itself from AT&T and other more famous rivals, now found itself suddenly notorious as the chief symbol of the power of big business over government.

Faced with this bombardment, Ned Gerrity's public relations machine and Bill Merriam's lobbying machine could do little to restore the image : they had to resort to mid-Western newspapers with obscure names to find words of praise. They issued a succession of statements, and a huge blue folder of *Allegations v Facts*, but their explanations were contradictory and confusing. The only man who seemed to know what had really happened was Harold Geneen, and he was incommunicado, with his lawyers insisting that he say nothing, which was not reassuring for his employees. When Mike Wallace interviewed Dita Beard on television, she complained that no-one from ITT had been in touch with her :

WALLACE : But you told me on the way over here that you still love ITT.

BEARD: Well, I do, as a company, it's a tremendous
           organisation. Harold Geneen is without doubt the
           most brilliant man, the most loyal man. . . .
WALLACE: He's loyal? You've not heard from him.
BEARD: Well, I would assume there are 42,000 lawyers
           suggesting that he not get in touch with me until
           all this testimony is over.

With its captain thus silenced, the ship seemed in total
disarray. The whole great pyramid of logic and control,
the management in depth, the rule of reason, dissolved into
a group of worried and contradictory witnesses. It was hard
to say which came worst out of the hearings, the company
or the administration: as one ITT director commented:
'It reminds me of the couple of whom it was said, "they
married beneath each other."' But the collapse of the ITT
image was the more spectacular. As Senator Ervin described it:

> The ITT officials descended on Washington like locusts, like
> a swarm of locusts, and apparently they wanted to talk about
> anti-trust policy to anybody who would listen to them. Then
> when they came on in testimony in this case, in the whole
> procedure, if they had gotten a committee of the wisest men
> in the universe and asked them to study some way they could
> perpetrate boneheads, they could not have come up with a
> better program than they did out of their own heads and
> imaginations.[1]

THE WHITE HOUSE

That is where the buck stops, and that is where the bucks
should have stopped.

Senator Kennedy [2]

The Liberal Democrats, led by Kennedy, relentlessly
cross-examined witness after witness but still the ultimate
truth evaded them. For Kennedy, it was an ironic reversal
of roles, three years after Chappaquidick. As one ITT witness
complained: 'when Kennedy said to me: "Don't you remember? Don't you remember?" I nearly replied; wasn't
there a time when you couldn't remember something?

1. *Kleindienst Hearings:* Vol. III, p. 1637.
2. *Kennedy Report,* p. 21.

Luckily my lawyer was sitting beside me and stopped me.'
As the Senators followed the trails through the maze, they
seemed to lead closer and closer to the White House, as the
likely source of any link between the convention and the
settlement. Kennedy was no doubt disingenuous in his apparent outrage, for he knew as well as anyone how Presidents
become indebted to big companies. But in election year the
pursuit into Nixon's backyard added special excitement.

Nixon himself lay very low, angry at the scandal which
had (as his aide Bob Finch complained) dimmed the glow of
his triumphant return from China. There were signs that the
White House was intervening to damp down the investigation. Ken Clawson, the deputy communications director,
complained to editors about their coverage, and Marlow
Cook, Nixon's closest ally on the Judiciary Committee, did
what he could to discredit the critics. Jack Anderson even
alleged (March 23) that, 'Dozens of government gumshoes,
Presidential aides and political flunkies have been assigned to
investigate us, to prepare attacks on us and to plant stories
in the press against us.' ITT, he said, were working with
the White House and with Intertel, the international detec-
tives, to show that Anderson had conspired with Dita Beard
to concoct the memo. (Eventually he confronted Intertel, he
told me, and warned them off.)

It was clear, from the events early in 1971, that the White
House, more than anyone else, wanted the convention; and
it was Bob Wilson—a close ally of Nixon's—who fixed up
the ITT pledge. Was there a deeper understanding? Was
the White House also involved in arranging the settlement,
as the Beard Memorandum said? ('Certainly the President
has told Mitchell to see that things are worked out fairly.')

Early in the hearings, McLaren explained that the document which made him change his mind was the Ramsden
Report, which analysed the financial consequences of divesting the Hartford company. It was prepared by an independent young investment analyst, Richard Ramsden, who gave
very credible evidence. His report was a conscientious analysis stating that the divestiture would be damaging to ITT,
largely because of the premium that ITT had paid for the
Hartford. But there were suspicious facts surrounding the
use made of it. Firstly, McLaren asked for it in great haste,

after all his months of preparing the ITT case: it was written by Ramsden in two days, for a fee of $242. Secondly, it did not support the theory that the Hartford divestiture would have a 'ripple effect' on the rest of the stock exchange —a theory which Rohatyn had urged to McLaren and Kleindienst, and which McLaren had accepted. Thirdly the request to Ramsden, as McLaren belatedly admitted, came not directly from McLaren but via the President's business adviser, Peter Flanigan.

As soon as McLaren first mentioned Flanigan's name there was a murmur of laughter in the hearing-room; for Peter Flanigan in his three years in the White House had become labelled as the 'Mr. Fixit' to the President. Ralph Nader, who had been frustrated by Flanigan in his campaign for airbags for automoblies, had attacked him as a 'mini-president', and Flanigan, a rich aristocratic banker-politician, seemed to enjoy the title. There were a series of stories about Flanigan's support for industrialists—for Anaconda Copper against the environmental protection agency, for American and Western Airlines against the anti-trust case, for Henry Ford against compulsory airbags. It was likely that Flanigan knew a good deal about the ITT anti-trust case (he had met Geneen in February 1971), and it would be surprising if he were not told about the ITT pledge to San Diego, which interested so many of his White House colleagues.

The Senators determined to question Flanigan, but he soon made it clear that he would invoke the principle of 'executive privilege', which protects the President's personal staff from revealing confidential information. The principle stems from the doctrine of Separation of Powers, but its application is supposed to be limited to communications between the President and his aides, or between the executive officials specifically assisting the President as Chief Executive. And Nixon had insisted soon after he took office that he would open up the White House, in a memorandum saying that, 'Executive privilege will not be used without specific Presidential approval.' Flanigan nevertheless refused to give evidence, presumably with Nixon's approval.

Flanigan now became an even more sinister bogey for the Democrats, and on the floor of the Senate Thomas Eagleton laid into 'The Flanigan Factor'. Mrs. Beard, he said, was not the only missing witness:

> There is one other, a man who works in the shadows—but only at the highest levels, only with the fattest cats. That man is Peter Flanigan . . . there is reason to believe that he is the mastermind, the possesor of the scuttling feet that are heard, faintly, retreating into the distance in the wake of a White House-ordered cave-in to some giant corporation.

Flanigan was unruffled. 'I've gotten, as my wife says, a little leathery,' he said to the *Washington Post*; 'It's an election year, and I note who's making these charges.'

The young Senators' suspicions of the White House connection increased when, as they came closer, the obstructions became greater. Jack Gleason, the ITT consultant who had worked in the White House, arrived to give evidence with his attorney, Edward Taptich; and Reuben Robertson, who was sitting nearby, noticed that Taptich received a message to call the White House. Senator Tunney asked Taptich whether he had talked to anyone in the White House, and Taptich reluctantly agreed that he had been talking to the President's counsel, John Dean.

It was becoming clear that behind the scenes the ITT lawyers and White House lawyers, with the help of their allies on the Judiciary Committee, were working closely together to protect their clients. When one of Kennedy's staff wandered into the room behind the hearing-room, which was normally reserved for the Judiciary Committee staff, he was told that it was now reserved for them *and* for ITT.

On April 6 the Senators formally invited Flanigan to give evidence, but after four days John Dean replied stiffly, referring to the separation of powers, and concluding that, 'By reason of this long-established and fundamental principle of our federal system, Mr. Flanigan cannot accept the Committee's invitation to appear.' At this point Sam Ervin, the seventy-five-year-old Senator from North Carolina who was the leading expert on constitutional law, burst out with an ultimatum. 'I have reached a deliberate and unalterable conclusion that I am not going to support any nomination made by the White House by any administration when the White House says to the Senate, 'We refuse to allow you to hear evidence within our power which is relevant to the question you are called upon to decide.'

There was now an open clash between the executive and the legislature; Sam Ervin wanted to have Flanigan sub-poenaed, to test his claim to executive privilege, while other Senators pressed him privately to give way. Eventually Flanigan relented, and wrote to Chairman Eastland saying that he would welcome the opportunity to appear, provided his testimony was limited to narrow questions. The Senators had a stormy session to thrash out what limitations they would accept : Kennedy rejected the limitations, but was outvoted twelve to one.

On the morning of April 20 Flanigan at last appeared, suave and unworried — a historic confrontation between the Senate and the White House. It looked like a victory for the Senators but it soon turned sour. Flanigan began by insisting that he was only a 'conduit' for obtaining the Ramsden Report; but as soon as Senator Hart asked him whether Rohatyn had complained to him about the divesti-ture of Hartford he said that was outside the limitations. The Senators wrangled and recriminated between them-selves; 'We are going to come out of here looking like the biggest snow job in the history of this country,' complained Senator Bayh (who was now back from Africa). When Bayh asked Flanigan the obvious question, whether he had ever talked to Kleindienst about ITT, he was again ruled out of order, and Bayh burst out : 'If we cannot even ask him whether he talked to the man we are supposed to confirm, if we cannot even ask him about this alleged deal, what sort of sense does that make?'

The Senators, realising the absurdity of their position, decided to put two extra questions in writing to Flanigan, about his contacts with ITT, and about any contacts he had made following the Ramsden Report. Three days later, on April 24, Flanigan replied with important new clues; a month before the final ITT settlements he *did* see Rohatyn in his office, primarily to discuss the securities markets; Rohatyn, just before he left, *did* complain to him about the anti-trust proposals, as being so tough as to be unacceptable to the company; two days later Flanigan *did* mention to Kleindienst what Rohatyn had said. He also revealed that when he delivered the Ramsden Report to McLaren, Kleindienst was with him; but that there were only 'perfunctory remarks' between them. It had taken the Senators seven weeks to extract those clues.

In the meantime, after nearly two months of fitful sessions, the Senators had decided at last to bring the hearings to an end, with much protest from the Kennedy group. They called back Kleindienst, now more confident and more persuasive, but still suspiciously forgetful—for his memory seemed both most faulty and most emphatic, about just those meetings which were most important. He had previously said that he had no conversation with Flanigan; yet Flanigan was sure that he had. And what emerged after eight weeks was that the decisive document, the Ramsden Report, had been delivered to McLaren by Flanigan, in the presence of Kleindienst. Kleindienst couldn't remember why he was there : he was a very close friend of Flanigan's, he explained, and bumped into him often. But this mysterious conjunction of three top people, after all the previous denials, made it still more difficult to believe that 'the negotiations were exclusively handled by McLaren'. As Kennedy remarked in his own report : 'It might be marvelled that three top Administration officials could meet and pass from one to another a key document relating to three important cases with the only conversation being "Thanks, Pete"; "Don't mention it, Dick".'

WHAT HAPPENED?

The most illuminating evidence was not about the White House, Kleindienst or McLaren, it was about the relentless machinery of lobbying that a giant corporation can bring to bear on government; so that the question could be put another way; how could anyone withstand such a barrage? In spite of ITT's apparatus of secrecy and document-shredding, and in spite of the non-appearance of key witnesses, the Kleindienst hearings provide a unique case-history of prolonged lobbying tactics, on the frontiers of business and politics. As Kennedy puts it :

The sustained and sophisticated ITT anti-trust lobbying effort from 1967 to 1971 is a tribute to the advanced state of the lobbying art. Any cabinet member or White House aide who was contacted by ITT must now be suffering from a feeling of second-class citizenship. It is probably a status symbol in official circles to have been lobbied by Harold Geneen personally, and an embarrassment to have been visited only by Ned Gerrity or Bill Merriam.[1]

At the centre of the ITT web lay always the watchful spider, Harold Geneen : the threads converged on him, and him only. Without him, the story behind the hearings makes no sense, but when the reader sees the story from his vantage point, all the intricate sub-plots, secondary characters and casual encounters begin to fall into place as part of a grand strategy. The master-plot was not Kleindienst's, or Mitchell's, or Nixon's, but Geneen's. Even Geneen no doubt was unaware of the full extent of the machinery he had set in motion : but he knew far more than anyone else. Trying to see inside Geneen's mind, as he worked his puppets from Park Avenue, the story begins to make sense.

Of all Geneen's lobbyists, the most effective by far was himself; no-one else had the same drive, the advocacy, and the mastery of figures. In politics, he was still something of an outsider, but this was often an advantage : 'I felt like Paul Revere,' he explained, 'trying to wake people up to what had happened.' He expressed ITT's case to anyone who might be involved. He talked twice to Maurice Stans, then Secretary for commerce. He talked to the Secretary of the Treasury, David Kennedy and his successor, John Connally. He talked to four members of the White House staff, Arthur Burns, Charles Colson, John Ehrlichmann and Peter Flanigan. He talked to Paul McCracken, as chairman of the Council of Economic Advisers, and Peter Peterson, as White House economic adviser. He lobbied countless Senators and Congressmen, including Philip Hart and Vance Hartke, Emmannuel Celler and Bob Wilson.[2]

Bob Wilson was active not only in San Diego, but in speech-making in Congress. On February 2, 1971 he attacked McLaren's anti-trust policies, and his 'devotion to tearing down big business'; and a week later he put into the record a

1. *Kennedy Report:* p. 12.
2. Geneen's letter to Chairman Eastland : *Kleindienst Hearings:* Vol. II, pp. 779–780.

speech by Lee Loevinger, McLaren's predecessor as anti-trust boss (who later became legal adviser to ITT) attacking the current anti-merger policy, including the ITT cases. At the same time there was a mysterious surge of interest in ITT by other Congressmen; one of them, Michael Harrington of Massachusetts, later admitted that he had been lobbied by Merriam, and that he felt that perhaps 'all was not as it was presented to be'.[1] The bills never had much chance, but the Congressmen were probably asked to put them forward, to try to soften-up the bureaucrats; by April, when ITT moved its pressure to the Justice Department, the campaign in the House dissolved.

Of Geneen's many meetings with Cabinet ministers, it is not known which bore fruit; but certainly his encounter with John Mitchell, an August 4, 1970, when McLaren was first asking for an injunction against the Hartford merger, looked significant. Mitchell had disqualified himself from dealing with the ITT cases, and both he and Geneen claimed that they only discussed anti-trust policy in the most general terms; but since three of the five anti-trust cases were ITT cases, it would have been hard *not* to refer to them, and the picture of these two hard-nosed men discussing philosophical theory is hardly convincing. Geneen was always well able to confuse ITT's interest with the national interest, to argue that a multinational company like his relieved the balance of payments, that strong competition abroad needed a strong base at home, that in fact what was bad for ITT was bad for the country. Geneen's Paul Revere tactics were beginning to take effect, and the Japanese threat was beginning to induce a change of thinking among many Republicans.

While Geneen was personally campaigning, he had also sent 'Gerrity's troops' into action. Gerrity himself had been to see McLaren, to explain that ITT was a fine company which should not be harassed, though McLaren had not been encouraging. But Gerrity's chief job was to influence public opinion. As he explained it to Birch Bayh, 'The idea was, Senator, to tell anyone who would listen that we thought the anti-trust policy being pushed by the administration was not in the national interest. . . .' The public relations army

1. Robert Walters in the *Washington Evening Star*, April 24, 1972.

in New York and Washington pursued Congressmen, journalists and editors with all their resources. And on top of
that (as Gerrity told Bayh):

> We sent our outside public relations agency across the
> country city by city. We picked out the leading cities in the
> United States and sent men into every one of those cities
> as we had them call essentially on the business editors,
> editorial writers, radio and television stations. We just sent
> them out with the gospel and tried to acquaint everyone as
> widely as possible with our position.[1]

But what mattered most were the big guns which could
reach the key emplacements in Washington. A formidable
piece of weaponry was Judge Lawrence Walsh, the partner
in Davis, Polk, a veteran attorney who was expert in the
bridges between government and business; he had been
Deputy Attorney-General—the same job as Kleindienst's—
twelve years before, and was now chairman of the judiciary
committee of the American Bar Association, which has to
approve appointments to federal judgeships; and he was a
close friend of Kleindienst's.

So Geneen approached Walsh, even though he was no
expert on anti-trust law, and saw him for three hours in the
spring of 1971 with two of his partners, Frederick Schwartz
and Guy Struve, and with ITT's legal director, Howard
Aibel. Geneen delivered his usual spiel and persuaded Walsh
—who was at first discouraging—to try to obtain a high-level
review of the Administration's anti-trust policy. Geneen
wanted to approach the President, but Walsh dissuaded him,
and they agreed to press for an interdepartmental review,
through the Department of Justice. Walsh prepared a brief,
and sent it on April 16 with a letter to his friend Kleindienst
(Dear Dick . . .). The letter asked for a delay in the Grinnell
case, then pending, to allow a full presentation; the brief
covered Geneen's familiar arguments, asking for 'a comprehensive, Government-wide review of the national interest
implications of diversification by merger'.

Walsh's intervention was very effective. Kleindienst asked
him to discuss it with himself, McLaren and the Solicitor-

1. *Kleindienst Hearings:* Vol. III, p. 1174.

General, Erwin Griswold. None of the three, by their own evidence, seemed to want a delay in the Grinnel case but a delay was agreed, despite the fact that none of the government lawyers cared for an extension.

In the meantime Gerrity's troops advanced to the front line. On March 18 there was a meeting in the New York office of ITT, with a whole army of lawyers: Sailer and Schaeffer from Covington and Burling; William Gentes from Kirkland Ellis; Howard Aibel, Scott Bohon and others from ITT itself. Bill Merriam was also invited, with his deputy John Ryan, the 'listening post'.

About this time John Ryan hit lucky. His job, as he explained it, was to talk to 'anybody who would hold still about any company problem, that is what I am paid to do'. He happened to live a few doors away from Kleindienst in Virginia and gave a neighbourhood party at his house for twenty to forty people, including Kleindienst (there were also a couple called Fitz, a fellow named Don Carpenter, a physicist, Dr. Micky Davis, who had just changed jobs, and a family named Dupuis). Ryan accosted Kleindienst and was, as Kleindienst described it, 'very very sharp in his statement to me that Mr. McLaren and myself were highly unreasonable in the ITT anti-trust matters . . .' Kleindienst evidently did not mind the lobbyist being sharp: Ryan asked Kleindienst whether he would be willing to talk to someone from ITT, Kleindienst said yes, he would.

Ryan quickly passed the message back to Geneen, and Geneen chose Felix Rohatyn as his next weapon. Rohatyn was the ideal broker on the economic front, as Walsh had been on the legal front. Although he had worked for the Democrat candidate, Senator Muskie, he had good Republican connections (in May 1971 he became trustee for Peter Peterson). And he was also at the time chairman of the New York Stock Exchange Surveillance Committee, which had been so important to the government in the stock market crisis of 1970 in preventing the collapse of Wall Street firms; he thus represented the very spirit of the consensus between business and government. Early in April, Geneen asked Rohatyn to go and see Kleindienst, with a report on the consequences of divesting the Hartford. Rohatyn described how ITT, as a truly multinational corporation, was the third largest contributor to the U.S. balance of payments, and how they needed the Hartford to help finance cash-short foreign customers; the divestiture would cause a 'major financial hardship' to ITT shareholders. Rohatyn then made an appointment to see Kleindienst—his way prepared by John Ryan—on the same day that Judge Walsh had delivered his brief. The twin prongs (apparently unknown to each other) were converging on the same target.

Rohatyn outlined the case to Kleindienst, and asked whether he could give a presentation of the ITT case to the anti-trust staff; Kleindienst agreed. This first meeting went so well that Geneen told Judge Walsh that he would not be needed. Nine days later, on April 29, Rohatyn went to a full meeting of the anti-trust officials, headed by Kleindienst and McLaren. It was a remarkable day for Rohatyn, for both before and after this anti-trust meeting he was discussing the stock-exchange crisis in the same building, with John Mitchell, Peter Flanigan and Ross Perot, the Texan financier who was negotiating to rescue the bankrupt brokerage firm of Du Pont. Immersed in this crisis, Rohatyn kept the anti-trust meeting waiting for almost an hour, and appeared with the special prestige of having been with the boss.

Rohatyn then gave his presentation, assisted by Howard Aibel from ITT, Henry Sailer from Covington and Burling, Raymond Saulnier, professor at Columbia, and Willis Winn, the Dean of the Wharton School. Kleindienst wrote notes in his meticulous hand, with a doodle at the top, mis-spelling the name of his visitor : Rayaton. Rohatyn now spelt out not only the general problem of ITT's lack of liquidity for its foreign companies, if it got rid of the Hartford; he also mentioned the specific immediate cause for this—a cause which did not emerge in the hearings. He explained that the Spanish government had recently insisted that ITT's Spanish company SESA, which has a monopoly of making telephone equipment, should provide them with three years' credit for the new electronic equipment, in place of the customary three months—a credit which would cost ITT around $100 million; and the French government were likely to follow. Kleindienst made a note of this :

ITT's Spanish Co. Sesa sells equipment to the Spanish gov't

—they want 3 yrs—payment vrs. 3 mos.—have to—good credit—same thing in *France*—

This, then, was what was meant by 'cash-short foreign customers', and the significance was considerable. ITT were saying that they must keep the cash, or the borrowing power,

Richard Kleindienst's notes about ITT's difficulties with the Spanish Government. (*Kleindienst Hearings*: Vol. III, p. 1274.)

provided, by the Hartford, to finance French and Spanish subsidiaries; their empire was apparently so interdependent that without Connecticut, Spain and France would be threatened. It was precisely the opposite argument to that which Geneen used in Connecticut; according to Rohatyn, ITT was very seriously short of cash; and the Spaniards and French were determined to squeeze them. Therefore, Rohatyn argued, the anti-trust case should be dropped, for the good of both ITT and the nation. ITT's hardship, he warned, might have a 'ripple effect' on the rest of the stock market; and since he had just come from his crisis talks with Mitchell, his warning was ominous.

Rohatyn followed up his presentation with three more visits to Kleindienst in the following three months in the summer of 1971, each time complaining about the rigid anti-trust attitude. Rohatyn's arguments were evidently effective, for in the hearings both Kleindienst and McLaren testified to the dire consequences which, they now realised, would follow the divestiture of Hartford, with such phrases as 'total financial disaster', 'just about break ITT', 'devastating financial impact'. Yet McLaren admitted in the hearings that when he first brought the case against the Hartford merger, 'We could see that if it were successful, this was going to have a massive financial effect'; his attitude then was: 'They made their bed, they could lie on it.'

Anyway by May 12, after Rohatyn had seen Kleindienst again, McLaren had relented sufficiently to commission, through Peter Flanigan at the White House, an independent report from Richard Ramsden. (He also received a report from the Treasury, but the advice from there, they insisted, was minimal.) Ramsden was shown Rohatyn's analysis, but did not agree with it; he thought it was 'dubious', and he did not believe in the 'ripple effect'. He agreed that the divestiture of the Hartford would cause a drop in the market value of ITT shares, by as much as sixteen percent, or $1.2 billion, and that there might be some indirect effect on ITT's contribution to the balance of payments. But he did not think that a fluctuation of a billion dollars would seriously disturb a stock market with a trillion dollars (a thousand million) in security values, and his report was less alarmist than Rohatyn's.

Yet, according to the evidence, it was this that changed McLaren's mind: 'I read the report and found it persuasive.' Was it the arguments of Rohatyn and Ramsden that changed his mind, after the two years of insistence on breaking up the Hartford? Or were there deeper political pressures working in the background, so that the Ramsden Report, in Senator Tunney's words, provided only the thin reed, the crutch, with which to justify the settlement?

While these big guns trained on Kleindienst, the ITT lobbyists stepped up their contacts and 'casual conversations'. ('Practically every important contact that we have heard about here,' Kennedy complained, 'was at these social affairs and these informal kinds of meetings. This has been an extraordinary education in how ITT moves and operates.') One such casual conversation occurred late in

April when Dita Beard told Ned Gerrity that she would be going to the Kentucky Derby, and that John Mitchell would be there. The scene in Louisville, Kentucky, as it emerged confusedly in the hearings, provided a comic cameo of the relentless lobbyist at work. It was in the Governor's palatial mansion, with wide halls and side archways, where forty guests had been asked to a buffet supper party after the race, including John and Martha Mitchell and of course Dita Beard, an old friend of the Governor, Louie Nunn (though he later tried to play that down). She had been drinking Bloody Marys and Mint Juleps all day. In the drawing room Mitchell was chatting with the Governor about his wife Martha and the telephone. Dita Beard (who hadn't met Mitchell before) took her cue from the mention of telephones, and butted in to complain to Mitchell about the 'damn rotten deal' that ITT were getting. Mitchell tried to change the subject, and the Governor moved them on to the buffet supper; but as they walked slowly through the reception rooms into the ballroom, Mrs. Beard kept on getting back to the subject. She joined Mitchell at his small table in the ballroom, still talking about ITT, to a background of organ music, until finally Mitchell burst out, and he said he was sick and tired of the subject and didn't want to hear any more about it. Soon afterwards, according to Nunn, Mrs. Beard passed out, from exhaustion or drinking, and had to be carried away; the next day she came back to apologise.

Whether Mrs. Beard behaved quite so badly, and whether her badgering influenced Mitchell, remained very obscure. Both Mitchell and Nunn insisted that there was no talk of a settlement, and stressed Mrs. Beard's drunkeness, but Mrs. Beard had insisted to Hume that Mitchell had agreed to a settlement, and even during the hearings, after she had denied it, she then told Mike Wallace on television that Mitchell had eventually been awfully sweet, with a twinkle in his eye, and had said : 'I think it'll be worked out fairly, but how I don't know.'

ITT were also deploying their personal contact with the White House, Jack Gleason. Gleason worked for a year in the White House, where in late 1969 he had been visited by Gerrity and Merriam to make the case for ITT; Gleason had put in a word (apparently without results) with a friend of his in the Department of Justice, Kevin Phillips. When Gleason left the White House in January 1971, Gerrity and Merriam asked him to work as a consultant for ITT, to keep them in touch with what the government was doing. When Merriam wanted to find out what the White House was up to over the San Diego convention, he asked Gleason who asked his contact in the White House, William Timmons, the convention co-ordinator; and it was the muddled reply from Timmons to Gleason, relayed to Merriam and thus to Beard, that precipitated the Beard Memorandum and thus the whole scandal. But how close was this link between ITT and the White House never really emerged : for Timmons never gave evidence.

All these salvoes, forays and excursions came to a climax of hectic activity, as the time for the ITT settlement became closer, reaching a peak in July, when the negotiations were at the final stage. And during the same month the Republicans were choosing San Diego as their convention site, armed with the $400,000 pledge from ITT. How many people in government really knew about both negotiations was still obscured, but certainly *some* people in the White House knew. To become indebted to a big corporation just when negotiating to break it up, was not reassuring to the impartiality of justice.

Moreover, it was clear that the $400,000 was only part of a massive assault on every relevant area of government — an assault which encircled and undermined the enemy, and consciously or unconsciously wore down the anti-trust division. Geneen, as he intended, had succeeded in creating an atmosphere in which opposition was simply not worth it. The pressure was literally inexorable.

THE JUDGMENT

After two months most of the fifteen Senators were glad to see the end of the hearings, and many wished they had never started. They had stopped and started so often that the threads were hard to follow; the evidence was increasingly complex, with more and more characters appearing, and it was hard to remember who was being accused of what. On the penultimate day, Sam Ervin interjected :

> Art is long, and time is fleeting
> And our hearts, though stout and brave,
> Still, like muffled drums are beating
> Funeral marches to the grave.

The Republican Senators, and some of the Democrats, had no desire to cause trouble to Kleindienst in an election year; and it was never likely that the Senate would actually reject Kleindienst's nomination. It was no great surprise when the sub-committee voted by eleven to four to recommend his appointment to the rest of the Senate.

Nine of the Senators concluded in their majority report that Kleindienst was not a party to any deal, and that the 'settlement was reached on the merits after arm's-length negotiations'. Kleindienst's handling of the ITT cases was not, they said, the same as negotiating the settlement, so that he had not told a lie. 'Taken as a whole,' they agreed, 'Mr. Kleindienst's testimony leaves the distinct impression that he had no substantive discussions with anyone at the White House about ITT cases.' It was an impression that was to be abruptly dispelled eighteen months later, by Kleindienst himself, as we will see in Chapter 12.

Two Senators, while endorsing the appointment, reported dissent. Charles Mathias of Maryland, though friendly to Kleindienst, expressed his worries in a colourful report about ITT's pressure on the trust-busters. He blamed Congress for leaving the law vague enough to allow the 'unseemly pulling and hauling' of ITT, but he blamed ITT for its massive corporate assault, and for being willing to stoop to conquer, with 'furtive appeals and unworthy demands'. 'It does not require any confirmation by Dita Beard to explain to me the relationship between a $400,000 commitment to a political party whose incumbent president is likely to be re-elected and a corporate giant which must deal with some level of government every day. It was like a wind-storm insurance premium . . .'

Philip Hart also dissented, while approving the appointment. He tried to analyse honestly McLaren's predicament. 'The division does not operate in a vacuum. The perennial ties between Washington and big business constantly threaten vigorous anti-trust enforcement. We must bend our efforts to isolate these pressures, to challenge their inevitability, and to minimise their impact—whether conscious or subliminal—on the decision-making process. But while they undoubtedly were part of the context for this major litigation, as they have been for every other, such stones are not first cast lightly. . . . Would Judge McLaren have weighed these complex factors with exactly the same result, if he had been analysing the policy choice in the groves of Academe, far from Washington? Probably none of us, including him, can say. But I have concluded that he reached the best judgment he could . . .'

In the meantime Kennedy and his allies (Tunney, Bayh, Burdick), all voting against Kleindienst, prepared a report of unprecedented length which came out a month later, with 384-pages of text and appendices and a fold-out chronology, four and a half feet long—a masterpiece of Senatorial research. It analysed the contradictions, prevarications, and unanswerd questions, and insisted that the committee should hear further witnesses, including Timmons of the White House, and Bud James of Sheraton. But it was already clear, they said, that Kleindienst 'played a determinative role in the events leading to the settlement of the ITT cases, and that, beginning last December, for reasons yet unknown, he attempted to withold from the public and the committee the full facts about his extensive participation'.

The question was debated on the floor of the Senate, where the Senators, now more overtly political, droned on to an almost empty chamber. Roman Hruska complained that the whole delay had been a political trick. Senator Fannin read out a letter from Senator Goldwater, extolling Kleindienst's honesty and his fight against crime. Marlow Cook complained that the hearings were an all-time record for irrelevancy.

The young Democrats returned to the fray. John Tunney attacked the corporate arrogance of ITT, Birch Bayh lamented the credibility gap. Kennedy as usual talked longest, in a nasal monotone, while his aides rushed in and out with facts and papers. He championed the small man against the big battalions of business : 'I do not blame ITT for trying to get across their views, but I do blame those who are willing to give them the extensive attention they apparently received.'

The press fired their last broadsides : since Jack Anderson's first allegations the liberal newspapers had been making the running with each exposure which the Senators took up. The *New York Times* in its last editorial, gave a final pounding : 'What is seriously in doubt is the integrity of his judgment.' The *Washington Post* ran four editorials concluding : 'This is what is at the heart of the Kleindienst nomination — the maintenance of public faith in our processes of government. . . .' But the main body of the Senators were unmoved; and when the vote at last came up in June, there were only nineteen Senators who voted against Kleindienst's nomination. After four and a half months' delay, Richard Kleindienst was at last Attorney-General.

Of course there was plenty of humbug in the outrage of the liberal Democrats. They knew well enough the indebtedness of politicians to big money. As Tunney admitted : 'It is a sad fact but true that no administration is spared the corporate muscle that was applied here.' The $100 million election campaign that followed was to produce plenty of new debts. Many of the relevations of close contacts between business and government were not really surprising : they were just another sign that, as LBJ said, 'It is business that makes the mare go.' In this context it was more remarkable that McLaren should ever have begun his anti-trust crusade than that he should have been eventually frustrated.

Yet the protests amounted to something more than political opportunism; and the ITT affair was more far-reaching than the earlier anti-trust scandals. It was partly that there was a more militant movement to curb the power of the giant corporations; the attackers, whether Anderson, Nader, Robertson or Kennedy, knew that they were speaking on behalf of a formidable constituency. But more important the new kind of industrial power, both conglomerate and multinational, of which ITT was a forerunner and a prototype, presented a more insidious enemy than the earlier trusts and combinations. The world scale of trade and technology had encouraged the growth of giants which could dominate their governments in many ways more effectively, because more pervasively. And the basic question was put by Senator Hart : 'Have we reached a point in our society where there has been permitted to develop a private concentration of power which, because of the enormity of their reach, makes impossible the application of public policy to them?'

The reach extended far beyond the United States; and while the hearings were progressing, a quite separate story had been unfolding about ITT's pressures on a government three thousand miles away; a story which was to have more widespread and longer-lasting repercussions.

11

The Spymasters

What's wrong with taking care of Number One?
Ned Gerrity, in the Multinational Hearings.

IN the middle of the Kleindienst hearings, when the Senators
were preparing to visit Dita Beard in Denver, and when ITT
was already established as an electoral scapegoat, Jack
Anderson published two columns, on March 21 and 22,
which were in the end to have deeper repercussions than the
Beard Memorandum. He announced that secret ITT documents, which had escaped shredding, showed that ITT had
plotted in 1970 to stop the election of Chile's Marxist President, Salvador Allende; that ITT had dealt regularly with
the Central Intelligence Agency to try to create economic
chaos in Chile and to encourage a military coup; and that
Harold Geneen had offered to contribute 'up to seven
figures' to the White House to stop Allende. The documents,
said Anderson, 'portray ITT as a virtual corporate nation
in itself'.

His accusations seemed well-founded. The eighty pages of
memoranda which he soon made available (which had been
leaked from a different source than the Beard Memorandum) revealed the most sinister-sounding discussions between ITT officials, the CIA, and the White House concerning Allende's election. They were written partly by ITT's
men in Chile, partly by their officials in New York and
Washington; and they were remarkable not only for their
revelations about plots, but for the attitude of all the ITT
men involved, who were equally contemptuous of Chilean
politicians and State Department officials. The language was

brutal and callous; the memos might have been written by a Marxist novelist depicting capitalist warmongers. And the correspondence was the more convincing and alarming because it involved the personality of John McCone, the ex-director of the CIA who was now a director of ITT. The memos produced the same kind of evidence of ITT's intervention in foreign affairs as the anti-trust memos had shown in domestic affairs, and the implication throughout was that the American government could and should be pressed to conform with ITT's foreign policies, and that ITT was much more important and well-informed about Latin America than the blundering State Department. As Bill Merriam wrote to Dr. Kissinger : 'Those of us who have been operating in the area for almost a hundred years are intimately aware of these failures.'

To understand the background to the Chile revelations, it is important to look back briefly at ITT's past involvement in Latin America, which for the previous forty years had been a lucrative but vulnerable source of its profits, and which had deeply influenced the company's chameleon character. In the 'twenties Sosthenes Behn had expanded from Puerto Rico to Cuba and then through the whole Latin-American continent, buying up or building up telephone companies under every kind of regime, dealing with dictators and revolutionaries with his customary ingenuity. But as the tide of nationalism rose, the republics not surprisingly resented their telephones being operated by a foreign-owned company; and Behn and his managers, as we first saw in Chapter 2, had to make increasingly awkward contortions, first to maintain their operations, then to extract adequate compensation, as they did in 1946 from Perón in Argentina.

There were widespread complaints from Latin-American politicians about ITT's bribery, and about the incompetence of the telephone systems; many governments insisted on keeping down the telephone rates, so that ITT had no incentive to improve the system. Cuba was an especially notorious example, both of ITT's bribery and of incompetence : a 1950 report by the World Bank on Cuba, under the Batista regime, firmly criticised the antiquated ITT telephone system, in which connections were repeatedly cut off, and subscribers had to shout to be heard. When Castro seized power, he soon expropriated the telephone system without compensation. It was soon after Geneen had taken over as President of ITT, and the shock of this setback contributed to Geneen's pessimistic view of the rest of the world.[1]

It was clear that the business of operating telephones, as opposed to making them, was now in retreat, but in the course of the retreat ITT still made some remarkable deals: in Brazil, for instance, they were paid $7·3 million for their operating company in 1963 and a further $12·2 million in 1967. In Peru, after the military junta came to power, they were able to avoid the fate of the International Petroleum Corporation, which was expropriated without compensation, and they made a deal by which they were paid $17·9 million for the telephone company, on condition that they reinvest $8 million in Peru—which they did, partly in the form of a huge new Sheraton Hotel in Lima. The change from telephones to hotels was symbolic of the new role of ITT, restricting itself to safer and less political investments.

ITT was becoming disillusioned with the future in Latin America, and was investing very little new money there except in Brazil, in which Geneen had great confidence; otherwise they preferred Europe, Australia, or South Africa. But they still were one of the biggest investors, with a network of factories, communications, and hotels; and they were fortified by their intelligence service, which one director boasted was better than the CIA's, which greatly helped their negotiations. It was their custom to hire reporters with access to leading politicians to look after their public relations, and they insisted on regular and detailed political reports to the Washington office. Ned Gerrity himself had graduated via Latin America, and to run their Latin-American intelligence they now had a tough right-wing journalist, Hal Hendrix, who had won the Pulitzer prize for his reporting from Miami of the Cuban missile crisis for which he had excellent CIA sources. Hendrix was assisted by a genial reporter from Mexico, Bob Berrellez; and between them, working with ITT's regular staff and their pet politicians, they provided a flow of information and gossip to Gerrity and Geneen. In Washington they had many other

1. see Chapter 3.

sources, co-ordinated in their own office by Jack Neal, the 'anti Communist war-horse,' as Gerrity described him, who had spent thirty years in the State Department.

ITT always did its best to insist that the American government pursue a tough line with Latin-American countries, to assure that it got proper compensation. Geneen himself was an active lobbyist; and he was proud of his role in pressing for the Hickenlooper Amendment, which enabled the American government to cut off aid to any country expropriating without compensation. Geneen had an important ally in Dr. Noobar Danielian, the remarkable Armenian economist who had promoted the St. Lawrence Seaway and then founded the International Economic Policy Association, which pressed successive governments to drop aid programs. Dr. Danielian was a fervent admirer of Geneen, and he was much concerned with Latin America; he also had very good contacts on Capitol Hill.

After the nationalisation in Peru, ITT was operating telephone systems in only three parts of the world : in Puerto Rico, where it had begun, in the Virgin Islands, and in Chile. The Chilean operation was much the most important economically and politically; by 1970 it employed 6,000 workers and was valued by ITT at $150 million. Colonel Behn had bought the company from the British in 1930, and since the original fifty-year concession had been signed it had produced very high profits, with a stipulation that ITT should be paid in gold. For a long time Chile had seemed a secure base, protected from the revolutionary nationalisms around it, and there were new hopes with the election in 1964 of the Christian Democrat President Eduardo Frei, who promised reforms, without antagonising the big corporations; he was the moderate's answer to Castro, an example for the rest of Latin America. Geneen put much hope in Frei, and, before his election, he and other American industrialists had offered a campaign fund to support him, through the then director of the CIA, John McCone [1] (who became a director of ITT a year later). McCone turned it down, on the grounds that the CIA does not accept private money, but in Chile at that time there

1. Confirmed by McCone's and Geneen's testimony, March 21 and April 2, 1973.

were allegations that a good deal of money had mysteriously arrived in the country. After his election, ITT was on good terms with Frei : when in 1966 the Chileans wanted to extend their telephone system, the Swedish Ericsson company made a bid for the contract, and submitted a report pointing out the faults of the existing ITT system; but ITT got the contract, with a much higher bid installing 144,000 lines for $186 million.[1] Frei also agreed with ITT on a plan for gradual nationalisation, with the government buying control.

Frei however was soon in political difficulties; his limited reforms could not satisfy the radicals, and Chilean politics were becoming more polarised. The right-wing was splitting off under the previous President, Jorge Alessandri, and the Marxists were still strong under their leader, Salvador Allende; while the Christian Democrats, under Radomiro Tomic, were moving to the left. In the Presidential elections of September 1970, Allende gained only thirty-six percent of the votes, less than he had won in the 1964 elections, but more than either of his divided rivals, Alessandri and Tomic. Under the Chilean constitution, the choice of President thus had to be decided by the Congressmen at the Congressional elections seven weeks later; and there followed a hectic period of intrigue, speculation, and panic to try to prevent a Marxist victory. It was during these seven weeks that most of the ITT memos revealed by Jack Anderson were written.

In Chile, the Anderson disclosures came at a dramatic moment, when negotiations between ITT and the Chilean government had reached a critical stage. Allende by now had taken over the telephone company, by appointing a government manager, and there had been long talks to try to agree on compensation. ITT put the value at $153 million, the Chileans (according to ITT) put it at $24 million. The Chileans proposed a group of international adjudicators, which ITT would not accept. ITT proposed an international auditing firm, which the Chileans would not accept. ITT suspected that the Chileans were trying to make the company bankrupt, to avoid paying anything; the Chileans accused ITT of not wanting a settlement and preferring to collect insurance money. By March 1972 the

1. *Nouvel Observateur*, Paris, May 8, 1972.

Chilean Ambassador in Washington, who was leading his team, had just come up with a new formula to determine the fair value. Then Anderson's column broke, and transformed the whole situation; for the revelations about ITT's plotting seemed to confirm all the Chilean's suspicions.

Allende of course made the most of it. A week after the revelations, the Chilean Congress decided to investigate the past activities of ITT and the CIA. A month later, at a vast pro-government rally attended by 200,000, Allende announced that he would ask the Chilean Congress to nationalise the ITT telephone company, which had been practising 'imperialist penetration.' Allende, whose economic difficulties were rapidly increasing, continued to attack both ITT and the other multinationals. In December 1972 Allende came to address the U.N. General Assembly in New York. ITT, he said, had 'driven its tentacles deep into my country, and proposed to manage our political life. I accuse the ITT of attempting to bring about civil war'. He extended his attack to the big corporations which, he said, had been 'cunningly and terrifyingly effective in preventing us from exercising our rights as a sovereign state'. After his speech, Allende flew direct to Moscow for talks with the Russian leaders; but it could be misleading to regard the speech as inspired by the Soviets; for the Russians had no desire to get involved in aid to Chile, and they were busily themselves negotiating with the multinationals. The *Financial Times* pointed out that 'as Pepsi-Cola disappears from the supermarkets in Santiago it will become available to buyers in Moscow'.

THE MULTINATIONAL HEARINGS

In the United States the Anderson revelations did not fully sink in in the midst of the more intimate quest for Dita Beard; and the revelations at first caused more stir in Latin America and Europe than in America. ITT as usual, promptly denied that it had done anything wrong, and issued a statement that 'ITT has been and continues to be a good corporate citizen in Chile as well as in all other countries where it has operations'. The CIA made no statement; though John McCone confirmed that ITT executives *had* discussed moves against Allende, in co-operation with the United States government. He and Geneen, he said, were filled with regret at the way that the memos were written, and the way they had been treated by the press, 'so that our true policy has been distorted'. But Geneen himself said nothing.

It looked for a time as if the whole Chilean scandal might blow over. Few Americans bothered to read the full text of the memos, which were published in Chile and Britain, but not in the United States, except in the Congressional Record; and though they seemed clearly incriminating, they were hard to make sense of, with big gaps in the story and many questions left hanging. Not even the directors of ITT took the trouble to read them, even though they appeared to accuse Geneen of meddling deeply with foreign politics without their knowledge. They commissioned two law firms to investigate the papers, to make sure they did not prejudice ITT's insurance claim; and Geneen assured the board that he had done nothing illegal.[1]

But the Chilean scandal, it turned out, was a very slow time-bomb. Two days after the first Anderson column appeared, the Senate Foreign Relations Committee, chaired by Senator Fulbright, held a closed session to discuss the allegations. The Secretary of State, William Rogers, assured them that the administration had not acted 'in a wrongful manner'; but the Senators were not satisfied, and they decided to form a special sub-committee to investigate the activities of American corporations abroad. The Multinationals Sub-Committee, as it was called, was duly set up, under the chairmanship of Senator Frank Church. Church is a genial, highly articulate lawyer from Idaho, who looks on big corporations with studied distrust; he is sometimes unfairly labelled as an isolationist, but he is not a crude critic, and he insists only that the American government must uncover the true facts about the multinationals. He took on his new assignment with relish, and he hired an able and passionate counsel, Jerome Levinson, who had worked for the Alliance for Progress in Latin America, and written a very critical book about it. The sub-committee resolved to devote three years to investigating the multi-

1. Rohatyn testimony, March 29, 1973.

nationals, and their first enquiry would be devoted to ITT's behaviour in Chile, and its relationship with the CIA. They were voted powers to subpoena officials from ITT and the government and began amassing still further documents from the ITT files.

There was also a topical subplot, in the shape of insurance; for like other companies operating in developing countries, ITT was insured by the government agency, the Overseas Private Investment Corporation (OPIC); and they were now claiming $92 million for their expropriated Chilean company. But the OPIC claims were not valid if it could be shown that expropriation was the result of provocation by the investor—*unless* it could also be shown that the provocation was at the specific request of the United States government. The Anderson papers appeared to show evidence of provocation, but if the CIA had asked for it, ITT might still get the money; the money would have to come from the taxpayers, since OPIC's premiums could not cover the claims (though part of the liability was reinsured by Lloyd's). The OPIC question also had a wider political touchiness; for there were many, including Senator Church, who suspected that OPIC merely encouraged corporations to involve the government in commercial disputes, and thus to exacerbate the tension between nations. Certainly ITT's concern with OPIC was not merely its immediate need for the money; it was (as Church perceived it) the need to show nations everywhere that in its negotiations it had the American government right behind it.

It was not until March 20, 1973—exactly a year after Jack Anderson's revelations—that the sub-committee began its hearings, the second Senate hearings to have been initiated by Anderson. Church's hearings were much shorter, but much brisker and more formidable, than Eastland's hearings the previous year (*that* committee had now moved on to question the nomination of Patrick Gray to be head of the FBI, which formed a rival attraction, two floors below). There was no doubt or confusion about what the Church hearings were about, or who was being accused. The accused was ITT, with the CIA as a secondary suspect; and the charge was that they had conspired to influence foreign elections, or, to subvert a foreign government.

And this lot of Senators spent very little time rambling or justifying themselves, with the occasional exception of Stuart Symington from Missouri. None of them was prepared to accept ITT without question. The most sympathetic was Charles Percy of Illinois : as a possible Republican contender for the Presidency, his approach to big business was guarded, and he had been president of Bell and Howell while Geneen was comptroller; but even his questions were sometimes double-edged. Clifford Case, the Republican from New Jersey, chewing his spectacles and stroking his cheek, seemed increasingly perplexed and distressed by the constant evasions and often would change from a mumble to a sharp angry question. Among Democrats, Edmund Muskie seemed to have recovered his wits and his anger after his electoral failure; and William Fulbright occasionally looked in to ask an awkward question or reflect on the state of the world. But Church himself dominated the show, shooting the key questions and providing his own running commentary; gazing sternly down at the witnesses, shaking his head, twiddling his glasses, occasionally flashing a wide but disconcerting smile. He was much quicker and more trenchant than Kennedy in the previous hearings.

The mystery unfolded like a far-fetched whodunit, with false trails and comic relief, but always with the central question : what was the million dollars *for?* For the memorandum that Jack Anderson referred to was unambiguous, that Geneen had offered up to a seven-figure sum to the CIA. On the first day the unfortunate Bill Merriam appeared again, like a dazed walrus, and described to an amazed audience how he had several times lunched at the Metropolitan Club with William Broe, the CIA's head of clandestine services for Latin America, though Merriam didn't realise, he insisted, that Broe was clandestine ('We lunched in places with three or four hundred people present'); they had discussed plans for economic disruption in Chile, he said, but nothing had actually been done. On the second day John McCone himself was called, a small white-haired man of seventy-one with sharp eyes and a responsible frown. He described in a cool monotone how he became a director of ITT in 1965 while continuing secretly to be a consultant to the CIA (which even Geneen, he said, didn't know). He explained, while the cameras whirred, how he had discussed the Chilean elections with his successor as CIA director, Richard Helms, and had later seen Helms and Kissinger to offer help to stop Allende; but Geneen's plan for the million dollars, McCone insisted, was not for economic disruption, but to provide constructive projects, like housing or agriculture. The Senators were respectful but incredulous: how could Geneen have believed, asked Clifford Case, that a million dollars in aid could have any effect on the elections, after the *billion* dollars that the United States had already spent on aid to Chile?

Other ITT men still further confused the story. Jack Neal from the Washington office, who had written the fateful memo referring to the million-dollar offer, explained that he hadn't known what the money was for, and that ITT had done nothing illegal. The two field reporters were summoned, led by Hal Hendrix, with a husky voice and weather-beaten face. They insisted that they had no contacts with the CIA and knew nothing about Mr. Broe; they were only reporters, picking up news ('vacuum cleaners', Gerrity called them). On the third day, Ned Gerrity himself appeared, genial as ever, apparently unperturbed, to give another version of the million-dollar promise: it was Geneen's idea, said Gerrity, that ITT should do something to show its confidence in Chile; the million dollars would merely be seed-money to encourage other companies to establish multimillion-dollar projects, including housing and farming. But how, asked Church, was there not a single document written about constructive projects and so much written about economic chaos? Even Charles Percy's tolerance was now strained: 'It just doesn't hang together. It's just unbelievable.'

After a week, the ITT position looked perilous; the contingent of ITT lobbyists and public relations men, sitting in a phalanx through the hearings, looked increasingly glum; ITT stock fell five points; and the prospects of collecting insurance money of $92 million, with the evidence of provocation, looked thin. The tactics of the sub-committee—whatever their views—were clearly to isolate ITT from other multinationals, as a solitary villain; and a succession of bankers, from the First National City Bank, Chase Manhattan, Bank of America, testified piously that *their* policy was never to interfere in the politics of any country where they operated; if *they* had been approached to induce economic chaos, they would have firmly said no. The State Department and the Treasury joined in the general dissociation. For a time it seemed as if the whole plot was no more than a fantasy of the ITT memo-writers; but then, sensationally, Senator Church announced that, for the first time in history, a member of the CIA, William Broe, would give evidence that would be released to the public.

Broe's evidence, when it emerged, was unambiguous; he testified that Geneen *had* offered a 'substantial' amount of money in July 1970 for an election fund for the conservative candidate in Chile, Jorge Alessandri; that he wanted it to be channelled through the CIA; and that Broe had rejected it though Broe had later come back to ITT, with proposals of his own for economic disruption. Broe's testimony made the projects for housing and agriculture look even less probable; and the next day Charles Meyer, the former Assistant Secretary of State in the State Department, denied that Jack Neal, or anyone else from ITT, had offered money for constructive projects. Senator Church made a statement in his gravest manner: 'It is obvious somebody is lying; and we must take a serious view of perjury under oath.'

The next week Ned Gerrity and Jack Neal were recalled to explain the contradictions; this time they both back-pedalled about the constructive purposes; Neal said he had not been told about them by Merriam, and Gerrity said that he wasn't now sure that Geneen had been quite so precise: the vision of the great ITT housing-and-farming project was dissolving as quickly as it had appeared.

In the meantime everyone was waiting for the last witness, Geneen, who alone knew the whole story: how could he extricate himself from the tangle of conflicting evidence? He appeared in the hearing room, brown and tense, protected by two attorneys and a bodyguard, but still sometimes grinning at his colleagues. He seemed now more than ever like some sprite, who had animated and committed everyone else and persuaded them to write down elaborate details, while he himself still hovered in the air, impossible to tie down or commit. He gave his explanation, calmly and confidently;

he had talked to Broe at the Sheraton Carlton, he agreed, but could remember very little about it; he accepted Broe's word that he made a substantial offer, but it was only a suggestion, which was rejected and which died then and there; his real purpose in talking to Broe was simply to find out information about Chile, and to make known his concern. There was no connection at all, he said, between this offer and the later million-dollar offer in September; the second offer was only partly intended to stop Allende coming to power; it was also meant to encourage Allende, if he came to power, to moderate his nationalisation programme. As for any suggestions of inducing economic chaos or military coups, they had been firmly rejected.

Geneen as usual fought back, and never seemed at a loss. He talked once again about ITT's financial achievements, its contributions to the balance of payments, its profits of $450 million a year; but when he was asked what federal income tax ITT paid he suddenly could not remember (Church recalled that ITT paid about $2 million). He complained that it was the publication of the Chile papers, not the writing of them, that had been harmful to multinationals; and he even suggested that the hearings themselves were helping America's enemies. He was firm in support of hard-line policies, and listening to him I was reminded of his attack on the British government's policy towards Rhodesia, when I first encountered him nine months before. It seemed for a time as if Geneen would escape his critics once more; that the white whale, surrounded by the harpooners, would once more suddenly submerge in a sea of froth. But Church and Case gradually pinned him down. Senator Case made it clear that if he were in Allende's position, he would regard Geneen's offer as provocative. And if all that Geneen wanted from the CIA was information about Chile, asked Church, why did he go to the head of *clandestine* services? And whatever happened to the plan for houses and agriculture? There's been a lot of talking about housing, replied Geneen, but really it was no more than a few ideas.

By the end, Geneen did clearly admit that he had on two separate occasions offered money to stop Allende coming into power; the offer to Broe might have been ill-advised, he admitted, but he was shocked by the change in U.S.

foreign policy. Having extracted this much, the Senators refrained from rubbing the wound. After a fortnight's hearings, Church summed up briefly, with a warning that multinationals must be welcome in the countries where they do business. The wider the distance between them and the CIA, he said, the better for all concerned; and he would like to introduce legislation, he said, to prevent this kind of contact. A week later, on April 9, came an expensive consequence of the hearings: the president of OPIC, Bradford Mills, announced that the ITT claim for $92 million would be denied, on the grounds that the company had failed to disclose material information, and had 'increased OPIC's risk of loss by failing to preserve administrative remedies'.

The report of the Senators appeared two months later, a twenty-page pamphlet which had been drafted by the counsel, Jerome Levinson, and then carefully mulled over and edited by the five senators. The language was more cautious than the language of the senators in the hearings, and the senators were anxious to show that they appreciated ITT's problems. 'The company's concern was perfectly understandable. So, too, was its desire to communicate that concern to the appropriate officials of the U.S. government. . . . But what is not to be condoned is that the highest officials of the ITT sought to engage the CIA in a plan covertly to manipulate the outcome of the Chilean presidential election. In so doing the company overstepped the line of acceptable corporate behaviour. If ITT's actions in seeking to enlist the CIA for its purposes with respect to Chile were to be sanctioned as normal and acceptable, no country would welcome the presence of multinational corporations'.

THE PLOT THAT FAILED

The story that finally emerged from the evidence, three years after it had happened, was in some ways a familiar Latin-American epic, in the tradition of United Fruit, of big business trying to dominate small republics. But what made it disturbing was not just that it was out of date and out of keeping with official American policy, particularly after Vietnam. It was also that the plot emerged from the core of a corporation that presented itself as one of the most sophisticated and modern-minded in the world; and which, as a multinational, continually stressed its 'good citizenship' in all parts of the world—a policy which seemed indeed essential to its survival. The story seemed out-of-keeping even with the earlier history of ITT itself, and with the principles of Colonel Behn, who had striven so hard to please any regime with which he did business. There could be no doubt, by the end of the hearings, that ITT *had* taken the initiative to approach the CIA to interfere with the politics of Chile—at the same time that it was so relentlessly lobbying against the anti-trust division. This was the making of the plot, as it emerged from the sworn testimony at the hearings.

Early in 1970 both Geneen and McCone, his fellow director, had become worried about the future of Chile, and discussed it at board meetings; both of them shared the same fixed anti-Communist views,[1] and thought it possible Allende might be stopped. McCone had talks with his close friend Richard Helms of the CIA, both in Washington and at McCone's home in California, and asked Helms whether the United States government intended to do anything to support a friendly Chilean candidate. Helms replied that the 'Forty Committee'—the secret interdepartmental committee under Kissinger, to which the CIA is responsible—had already decided that nothing should be done. There were different estimates of the elections, it seemed, and the CIA had conducted its own opinion poll, which predicted that Alessandri, the favoured candidate, would win the plurality, with forty percent of the votes;[2] but Helms told McCone that he personally thought that Alessandri could not win. He suggested, however, that a 'minimal effort' to oppose Allende *would* be managed within the flexibility of the CIA budget; and McCone proposed that a CIA man should get in touch with Geneen ('it would be a natural thing for me to do'). McCone reported back to Geneen that the CIA could not do much, and Geneen was disappointed.

But Helms duly instructed one of his senior staff, William

1. McCone testimony: 'International Communism has said time and again that its objective is the destruction of the Free World, economically, politically, and militarily . . . That is what Mr. Geneen was thinking of.' (But how does this square with ITT's negotiations in Moscow?—See next Chapter.)
2. Korry testimony.

Broe, a veteran spymaster of sixty. Bill Merriam of ITT got in touch with Broe, and asked him if he could meet Geneen on his next visit to Washington. So at ten fifteen on the evening of July 16, 1970, Broe arrived in the faded, ornate lobby of the Sheraton Carlton Hotel in Washington; soon afterward Bill Merriam came in, introduced himself to the solitary man in the lobby, and chatted with him. Fifteen minutes later, Geneen came in (he even keeps the CIA waiting), and Merriam introduced him to Broe, whereupon Geneen took Broe up to the private suite kept by ITT for their top men, leaving Merriam behind. Upstairs, Geneen quickly grilled Broe about the Chilean political campaign, and the prospects of Allende, Alessandri, and Tomic. Then Geneen came out with his proposal; he was willing (as he had been in the 1964 election) to assemble a substantial election fund for Alessandri, which he wanted to be con-trolled and channelled through the CIA. Broe told Geneen that the CIA could not serve as a funding channel, and that the United States government was not supporting any can-didate in the Chilean elections. But Geneen asked Broe, nevertheless, to keep in touch, after he got back from a trip to Europe. Broe duly called him on July 27, to tell him about the progress of the Chilean candidates; but only for two or three minutes, because Geneen was very busy. Soon afterward McCone talked again to Helms, before McCone went on a holiday to Alaska in August.[1]

Then on September 4 came the Chilean popular elections, and Allende's narrow victory over his two rivals, with thirty-six percent of the votes. Bob Berrellez, the ITT man in Santiago, cabled his interpretation three days later to Hal Hendrix, Ned Gerrity, and others : Allende's election in the Congressional elections, he said, was virtually assured by the support of the Christian Democrats. Alessandri and his brother-in-law, Matte (with whom ITT was in close touch) still hoped that Alessandri might swing the vote, with the help of money and 'influential pressures'; but Berrellez warned against intervention. 'Strong outside political and economic pressures,' he cabled, 'resulting in unemployment

1. McCone testimony, March 21, 1973. Broe testimony, March 28, 1973.

and unrest internally, will certainly strengthen the hand of the left-wing extremists.'

The next day came the monthly ITT board meeting. Geneen said nothing to the board about the contacts with the CIA; but he spoke privately to McCone, and told him that he was prepared to put up a million dollars in support of any government policy to bring about a coalition of the parties in opposition to Allende, the parties 'which stood for principles inherent in our government'. The plan was not (McCone stressed) to be originated by ITT or Geneen. Geneen asked McCone if he supported it, and McCone said yes. A few days later McCone came to Washington to see Helms and Kissinger, both key men in the crucial Forty Committee. McCone passed on the offer. Kissinger said he would get in touch if there was a plan; but (said McCone) he never did.

In the meantime ITT's Washington staff was lumbering into action. Jack Neal, the 'anti-Communist warhorse,' telephoned Kissinger's Latin-American adviser, Pete Vaky, to explain that Geneen was deeply concerned about Chile, and was prepared to contribute up to seven figures, an offer which he asked Vaky to pass on to Dr. Kissinger; Vaky (according to his testimony) didn't take the offer seriously and didn't pass it on. Neal also said something to Charles Meyer of the State Department—though Meyer denied that he had mentioned any sum of money—and he also 'ran into' John Mitchell, the Attorney-General, at a wedding reception at the Korean Embassy, so he mentioned Chile to him, too.

The Forty Committee, meanwhile, had met to discuss Chile. What if anything was decided remains obscure; but there were hints that the United States line towards Chile was hardening, and that some form of intervention was being considered. By September 16 Dr. Kissinger was giving an off-the-record briefing to editors in Chicago, in which he warned them about the problems of an Allende takeover in Chile : 'We are taking a close look at the situation.' But, he added, it was not one where American capacity for influence was very great at this particular moment. The American Ambassador in Chile, Edward Korry, also appeared to be reflecting a harder line; Korry was a tough, outspoken ex-journalist, who himself held right-wing views;

but he clearly had some support from Washington, from the direction of the White House more than the State Department. He was also, it seemed, quite close to the ITT field reporters, Hendrix and Berrellez. Exactly who was making United States foreign policy toward Chile at this time is the crucial unanswered question.

Two weeks after the popular elections, Berrellez wrote another memo from Chile, which, after editing by Hendrix in New York, was sent to Ned Gerrity. The memo, the most bloodthirsty and reckless of all the ITT documents, was hopeful that Allende could now be stopped from becoming President: Alessandri hoped to get a majority of the votes in Congress, whereupon, according to the 'Alessandri formula', he would resign in favour of Frei, who would then call for new popular elections. But the difficulty was that Frei would only step in if there was a serious constitutional threat; so 'that threat must be provided one way or another through provocation', Berrellez told Alessandri, through Matte, that ITT was ready to contribute with what was necessary 'as always',[1] and made some specific recommendations to New York. They included pumping advertising into the conservative newspaper, *Mercurio,* getting propagandists working on Chilean TV and radio, and publicising the *Mercurio* editorials throughout Latin America and Europe.

This drastic report was taken very seriously by ITT in New York and Washington. Jack Neal visited the State Department to reaffirm ITT's willingness to do anything possible; Bernie Goodrich in Washington visited the United States Information Services to urge them to circulate *Mercurio* editorials (which they were already doing) and to tell them that ITT was helping *Mercurio.* He asked whether there was anything that ITT could do that a government could not. The USIS people stressed that nothing should be done that could be interpreted as American intervention; but Goodrich assured them: 'Our people are well experienced in that field.'[2]

1. Hendrix-Berrellez memo to Gerrity, September 17, 1970. Matte confirmed that he had received an offer from ITT, but rejected it. (Associated Press from Santiago, March 23, 1973.)
2. Goodrich to Merriam, September 23, 1970.

William Broe, too, was evidently impressed by the memo; he had kept in touch with ITT, and Bill Merriam had passed it on to him. They lunched together at the Metropolitan Club on September 22, and Merriam asked Broe what he thought of the proposals; Broe said they were all right and that the assessment was pretty good. Merriam said he was under pressure from ITT in New York to get something done in Chile; but Broe realised that Merriam didn't know much about Chile; and most of the time they talked 'about daughters and education and things like that'.

A week later came a remarkable development. Broe, with the full knowledge of the CIA bosses — 'the people upstairs', he called them — went to see Ned Gerrity in New York, while Geneen was away in Europe. It was September 29, less than a month before the Chilean Congressional elections were due. Broe outlined to Gerrity a plan that involved nothing less than the systematic creation of economic instability in Chile : banks were to be asked to delay credits, companies were to be asked to drag their feet in spending money, shipping deliveries, shipping spare parts; savings banks and loan institutions would be pressed to shut their doors; technical help would be withdrawn. All this was part of a CIA 'thesis' that a deterioration in the economic situation could encourage Christian Democratic Congressmen not to vote for Allende. How far this was a thesis, how far a definite plan, remained blurred; but Broe was sufficiently serious to bring with him a list of companies doing business with Chile which could, he explained, participate in the plan for economic dislocation.[1]

How far was Broe's plan inspired by ITT's memos and contacts, how far was it stimulated by the secret policies of the Forty Committee, and the militant attitude of Ambassador Korry? This, too, remains murky. But undoubtedly Broe's plan accorded well with the proposals of the ITT men in the field, and it seemed that ITT's first approach to the CIA had at last borne fruit. But Gerrity, in the meantime, had received at least two reports from Chile which advised caution. One was from a man in the Council for Latin America, Enno Hobbing, who had once worked for the CIA; he had been visited by one of Alessandri's men, who advised,

1. Broe testimony : March 27, 1973.

'Keep cool, don't rock the boat, we are making progress.' The other was a further memo from Berrellez in Chile, who was now pessimistic about the chances of stopping Allende. There were, he said, undercover efforts being made to bankrupt savings banks, which could help to generate unemployment, which might in turn provoke violence; but President Frei was being weak, and 'some businessmen who seemed all gung-ho about stopping Allende are now talking in terms of trying to make deals with him'. Berrellez advised that 'every care should be exercised to insure that we are not identified openly with any anti-Allende move'. After Broe had revealed his proposals, Jack Guilfoyle of ITT in New York claimed to have got in touch with two of the companies on the list, but said they had been given directly opposite advice.[1]

Gerrity, therefore, cabled to Geneen in Brussels outlining the secret plan, but saying that he did not necessarily agree with it : 'Realistically I do not see how we can induce others involved to follow the plan suggested.' Geneen talked to McCone about the plan; they both decided that it 'would not fly'[2]—more because it was unworkable than undesirable —and Geneen told Gerrity, adding that he should be 'very discreet' in handling Broe. Geneen, however, was still thinking about how to stop Allende, including one odd little scheme that throws some light on his way of thinking. In Brussels he had noticed a copy of the London *Daily Telegraph* with a double headline across page 1, describing hundreds of people jailed in Cairo, by the pro-Communist regime. He thought that this kind of scare-story might stir up opinion against Allende in Latin America. So he airmailed a copy by special delivery to New York, where Hal Hendrix carried it down to Chile, to get copies delivered to members of the Congress, and to stimulate editorial comment.

Broe continued to keep in touch with ITT, and on October 6 he called Ryan in the Washington office. He reported that the picture from Chile was not rosy, since the Christian

1. According to Gerrity's memo to Geneen : but the two companies mentioned in Guilfoyle's testimony—IBM and Anaconda—denied having been contacted.
2. McCone testimony, March 21, 1973.

Democrats were likely to support Allende; but he still advised that ITT should keep on the pressure, for instance with a run on the banks, to limit Allende's support; and 'there was always a chance that something might happen later' and 'the military still might do something'. Two days later Merriam had another lunch with Broe, who was now very pessimistic; there had been approaches to the Chilean armed forces to lead some sort of uprising, but with no success; and American businesses were refusing to co-operate to bring on economic chaos. But Broe told Merriam that he thought that the Nixon administration would take a very hard line with Allende once he was elected. Merriam passed all this on to McCone (but not to any other directors), together with a new message from Hendrix and Berrellez. The reporters also reckoned that a defeat for Allende was now unlikely: but thought that economic chaos and unemployment might still (as Broe had suggested) persuade Christian Democrats not to vote for Allende.

By the middle of October the prospects of stopping Allende were rapidly waning. Hendrix wrote to Gerrity describing how an attempted coup d'état by General Viaux had been postponed—it was said on advice from Washington—and the chance of a last-minute change was now slender. Finally, on October 20, Alessandri withdrew from the Congressional elections, leaving the way clear for Allende. Four days later, Allende was elected.

But the ITT lobbyists had not given up; in fact they now attacked on a much broader front, trying to change the State Department's whole policy toward Latin America. Gerrity put together a stirring policy statement called 'U.S. at the Crossroads' advocating an uncompromising line toward Allende, the stopping of aid funds to Chile and perhaps even reducing American diplomatic staff 'in certain Latin-American capitals'. Gerrity sent it on to McCone and Geneen on October 21 and wrote another memo to Geneen called 'Chile: The Aftermath'; he described how the State Department had been consistently wrong about Chile, and proposed that a new hard line should be put to the top people in government, including Dr. Kissinger and the President.

Both memos were redolent of Geneen's ideology, with

references to 'freedom dying everywhere', and returning to the 'fundamental principles on which this country is founded' (the principles, presumably, which Geneen described in referring to his own schooldays in Suffield : see Chapter 4). Also on October 21, there was an important meeting with the Secretary of State, William Rogers, to discuss the Chile situation with other industrialists, including Jack Guilfoyle and J. R. McNitt from ITT : Rogers was encouraging, and mentioned two or three times 'that the Nixon administration was a business administration, in favour of business, and its mission was to protect business'. Chile was only part of ITT's lobbying operation at that time : they were also pressing the State Department—with remarkable success—to withdraw aid to Ecuador, because Ecuador was offering too little compensation—$25,000 too little—for a nationalised ITT company in Quito.[1] But Chile was far more important.

Bill Merriam, too, was busily trying to pressurise the State Department : on October 22 he met with Jack Neal and the invaluable Dr. Danielian, of the International Economic Policy Association, who was planning a meeting of his Latin-American committee to drum up pressures to stiffen the State Department; and his members would also approach Senators Scott and Mansfield to try to make them 'forget' a new appropriation of aid to Latin America. Still more boldly, Merriam wrote directly to Kissinger, saying 'our company knows the peoples of the Americas deserve a better way of life'; he enclosed yet another proposal for re-appraising the whole Latin-American policy. Kissinger replied with a polite note saying he 'had read it carefully', which Merriam noted was 'more than perfunctory'.

At the same time, ITT set about systematically smearing the diplomats who did not share their policy. Hendrix wrote a long memo about Charles Meyer, the gentlemanly liberal at the State Department, accusing him of being the weakest Assistant Secretary in twenty-two years : 'It would be better for us if he returned to Sears Roebuck'; and Gerrity passed it to Geneen, saying, 'Meyer has not done a good job.' They also turned against Edward Korry, the Ambassador to Chile, who had at first seemed to share ITT's tough line; Hendrix and Berrellez told Geneen that he had become petulant, 'a

1. See *Business Week*, August 11, 1973.

sort of male Martha Mitchell', and that his diplomatic career was at an end. He was reported to be 'trolling' for a job with ITT, but Geneen made it clear that he had no intention of helping him.

These orchestrated attacks on American foreign policy continued without any recorded dissent in the memos from anyone inside ITT—except one man, who deserves to be mentioned as uniquely independent. R. R. Dillenbeck, ITT's general counsel for Latin America, was shocked both by the policies being put forward, and by the unwisdom of openly attacking government policy, at a time when ITT was having delicate dealings with the State Department and claiming its insurance money from OPIC when its Chilean company was expropriated. He complained to Howard Aibel, the chief counsel, that he had not been shown the rash letter to Kissinger; and he was so worried by Gerrity's assessment of 'Chile : The Aftermath' that he sent a copy to Robert Crassweller, the liberal Latin-American expert who worked with him, who effectively debunked its theories, particularly the 'domino theory' that Chile would infect the rest of Latin America. Dillenbeck concluded : 'End runs such as this caused by the Public Relations Department are demoralising and eventually self-defeating to ITT's business goals.' [1]

After Allende was installed, ITT was preoccupied by the question of compensation—about which it had forty years' expertise : and its tactics at this stage reveal the full extent of its double-dealing, toward both Allende and fellow-industrialists. On the one hand, ITT was approached by Anaconda, the copper company with a huge stake in Chile, to arrange a series of ad hoc meetings with other interested companies, including Kennecott, the other big copper company, to bring pressure on Chile. ITT agreed, and Bill Merriam held several meetings in his office in early 1971 (ad hoc meetings are 'a form of life in Washington', Merriam explained afterwards).[2] ITT naturally took the lead in lobbying. At a meeting on February 9 Merriam told the others that the Chilean problem was being handled by the CIA and by Henry Kissinger's office and hardly at all by

1. Dillenbeck to Aibel, October 28, 1970.
2. Merriam testimony, March 20, 1973.

the State Department; ITT had already lobbied Arnold Nachmanoff, who had taken over from Pete Vaky on Kissinger's staff, who had assured them that the United States would encourage other countries not to invest in Chile. The ad hoc meeting proposed to stimulate militant speeches on Capitol Hill, and to press the international agencies not to lend money to countries threatening expropriation.[1]

But while ITT was thus standing shoulder-to-shoulder with the copper companies, it was quietly planning to betray them. On February 11, two days after the ad hoc meeting, Gerrity wrote a confidential memo to Geneen, outlining a shrewd new strategy. The idea was simply to repeat their tactics in Peru, where they had cleverly dissociated themselves from other companies. In Chile, they realised that Allende would expropriate the copper companies (as he did) without compensation, and that this would provoke world criticism ITT therefore would approach Allende directly, suggesting that if he gave *them* good terms, 'he can point to us as an example of how a fair deal can be completed if both sides approach the matter sensibly'. In other words, ITT would benefit from the disasters of the copper companies, and leave them in the lurch.[2]

This tactic seemed, in fact, quite hopeful. In March 1971 a delegation of ITT men, including Dunleavy and Guilfoyle, went to see Allende, and found him cordial and relaxed; he talked about making the telephone company a joint venture with ITT, and even mentioned a telephone gadget that he had invented, which would indicate when there was another call waiting to get through (whatever happened to *that?*).[3] In May, Allende announced that he *would* nationalise the company, but in the following months, ITT negotiated with the Chileans about compensation, and though the gap was wide, there still remained a good prospect of a settlement. On July 9 Jack Guilfoyle wrote a memo to Geneen, explaining again the tactic of separating ITT from the copper companies and saying, 'I think the door is cracked open a bit.'

1. Memo to Robert James of the Bank of America, from Ronald Raddatz, February 9, 1971.
2. Gerrity to Geneen, February 11, 1971.
3. Hendrix to Perkins, March 12, 1971.

But in the meantime Allende was under strong pressure from his own left-wing, to take firm action against American imperialists. How far Allende could have remained moderate, if the American government and the companies had been more genuinely conciliatory, is open to question; certainly the harsh measures that ITT advocated—and which were partly implemented—did not make it any easier for Allende to placate his extremists. But in any case, he was becoming more uncompromising. He first expropriated the copper companies, and then, when the talks had reached deadlock in September 1971, he appointed an 'interventor' to manage the ITT telephone company—a discreet form of nationalisation.

ITT now came out with all its guns firing. Geneen had seen it coming, and two weeks before the takeover, he had lunched at the White House with 'Pete' Peterson, the President's assistant for international economic affairs, and with Major General Haig, Kissinger's deputy. He warned them that the ITT company would soon be expropriated. Now he got Bill Merriam to write to Peterson, enclosing an eighteen-point plan which went further than any previous ITT proposal for intervention : for it advocated without any question, the deposing of Allende : *everything should be done quietly but effectively to see that Allende does not get through the crucial next six months.*' The White House should establish a special task force to put pressure on Chile; they should arrange for all loans to be stopped, whether from American or foreign banks. They should foment discontent within the Chilean military. They should disrupt Allende's diplomatic plans. They should subsidise *Mercurio.* And they should discuss with the CIA how to assist the 'six-month squeeze'. It was a far more ruthless proposal than Broe's plan of the year before.

How far this ITT pressure, whether through Peterson or anyone else, took effect is still obscure, for the leakage of memos by this point had dried up. (Peterson insisted when he testified, that he had never seen the eighteen-point plan that Merriam had sent.) In any case, the process of economic isolation of Chile was already under way, and loans were being stopped and aid withdrawn, without need of extra pressure. Yet ITT, while plotting Chile's total disruption, still continued to negotiate for compensation with the appearance of goodwill; and in February 1972, four months after proposing the eighteen-point plan, Geneen sent Jack Guilfoyle to Chile to interview Allende, to search for a formula. It was not till the Anderson columns appeared the next month, that Allende broke off negotiations, and armed with this proof of ITT's intervention and ill-will, asked the Congress to nationalise the telephone company without compensation.

The history of ITT's dealings with Chile shows, in a magnified form, the familiar characteristics of the company —the corporate arrogance, the inexorable lobbying, the two-faced attitudes, the corrupted communications. Throughout the mass of memos that came to light, there is no sign of any employee being concerned with anything except the company's profits; and whoever got in the way of that purpose —whether Charles Meyer, Edward Korry, Pete Vaky or ex-President Frei—was liable to be smeared and intrigued against. And more than ever the company showed itself as the work of one man, driving all the others. Among all the memos, there was not one that came from Harold Geneen; yet his purpose and even his language— 'foundations of our society', 'freedom dying everywhere'—lay behind all of them.

The documents and testimony about Chile pose questions about the nature of the relationship between the company and governments, on a deeper level than the anti-trust contacts; for in this case the relationship was bound up with intelligence. In the first place, the double function of John McCone, as a director of ITT and simultaneously a secret consultant to the CIA, must raise considerable doubts as to who he thought he was working for when he so effectively lobbied Richard Helms. His instructions came from ITT, but his access derived from the CIA; and he could easily confuse—like so many ITT men before him—the national with the corporate interest. That confusion may have been tacitly accepted in the past; but it cannot be permitted for a modern multinational corporation which professes to be a 'good citizen' in all countries. Of course all intelligence services, whether in America, Britain or France, are tempted to use multinational corporations as 'cover' for spies, and there can be little doubt that they do so. McCone, in his testimony, said that the CIA should never use multinational corporations as cover, because : 'I do not see how any company could survive if the cover was blown'; but in view of his own intervention, this warning need not be taken too seriously. Back in 1966, Richard Bissell, the deputy director of plans at the CIA, recommended that spies would be more effectively concealed in the big corporations than in the embassies,[1] and there are many, like Senator Percy at the hearings, who see nothing wrong with corporations co-operating with intelligence. But what is significant about the ITT collaboration is that it came from the very top. The president of ITT and the ex-director of CIA saw a natural community of interest; and why should Geneen first have hired McCone, if not for this kind of assignment?

How much deeper does this relationship go, beyond what has emerged? Surveying the history of ITT—its long, deep involvements with foreign governments, its wartime manoeuvres, its conflicts and reconciliations with its own government, and all its technical expertise in telecommunications, it is difficult, I think, not to conclude that it has had long associations with intelligence, which were passed on from Colonel Behn to his successors, to which Geneen was the heir, and of which the appointment of John McCone was only part. How sinister, or how necessary, that may be, is difficult to judge; but two conclusions, I think, are clear. First, that this intelligence connection has contributed in part to the arrogance of the corporation, and its access to high places. Second, that the influence of ITT's own intelligence system (as it can now be judged in the Chile documents) on the American government's system, has been crude, dangerous and malign.

All the most serious suspicions about the nature of United States foreign policy towards Chile came to a head three years after Allende's coming to power, when in September 1973 a military coup seized power in Chile, Allende lost his life, and the short-lived Marxist experiment was over. There was no visible evidence that the coup was connected with the CIA or with ITT; and Allende's internal problems were

1. See *The Guardian*, March 23, 1973.

so great that he would very likely have been overthrown, even if the United States and other creditor nations had been more helpful. But the evidence of the Church hearings showed very clearly that the CIA and the White House had been preparing three years before to use economic sanctions to prevent Allende's staying in power, with the assumption that this would encourage a military coup; and the figures for aid and loans showed that those sanctions had been maintained (except, significantly, the loans to the Chilean military, which had actually been increased). The economic chaos which preceded the military coup was thoroughly in keeping with the hopes and plans of ITT and its friends in the CIA.

It was not surprising that ITT was blamed for encouraging the coup, and the identification showed itself in an ugly form soon after it took place. On September 16 a bomb went off in the Zurich office of ITT-Standard, the Swiss subsidiary of the company. Ten days later, on the night of September 27, a fire was started in the Rome office of ITT-Standard, and eight hours later bombs went off in one of the ITT offices in New York, in Madison Avenue: twenty minutes before the explosion a voice had rung up the *New York Times*, claiming to belong to the 'Weatherman underground' to say that the bomb would explode 'in retaliation of the ITT crimes they committed against Chile'. ITT had come to be regarded by left-wing groups in different parts of the world as a convenient symbol of the wickedness of international capitalism, and as a scapegoat for the failures of the left, taking over the mantle of earlier bogeys of the developing world, like United Fruit or Unilever. No doubt there was much that was unfair in this characterisation, to the tens of thousands of ITT employees who were doing honest jobs as best they could. But in their ruthless attitudes towards Chile, the adventurers at the top of ITT had been asking for trouble; and they got it.

12

The President's Doorstep

Already while the Chile hearings were in progress, some more evidence was beginning to emerge about ITT's antitrust dealings; and in the course of 1973 the question of the secret contacts between ITT and the Nixon administration was to be further uncovered, layer by layer, in parallel with the intricate Watergate scandals. The two stories, in fact, were complementary in the light they threw on American politics; for while Watergate and its attendant revelations showed how corrupted the administration had become from inside, the ITT revelations showed how inexorable was the corrupting pressure from the outside.

The first new clues to appear came from those thirty-four boxes of ITT documents that had been subpoenaed, two years before, by the Securities and Exchange Commission in connection with the Hartford merger, and had thus escaped the ITT shredder: they included some documents in a manila envelope which were believed to be 'politically sensitive', containing evidence of connivance between ITT and the White House. The chairman of the Commerce Committee of the House of Representatives, Congressman Harley Staggers, was determined to see the papers—urged on by a very effective staff—and in September 1972 Staggers wrote to the then chairman of the SEC, William Casey, a tough Nixon appointee. An acrimonious correspondence ensued. Casey consulted the White House counsel, John Dean, who told him not to give the records to Staggers; and shortly afterwards Casey delivered the thirty-four boxes to the Justice Department, who were (at least ostensibly) still investigating possible perjury by ITT officials in the Klein-dienst hearings. Once buried in the Justice Department, the thirty-four boxes seemed unlikely to see the light of day. But before the boxes disappeared, it turned out, some diligent members of the SEC staff had quickly recorded notes about their contents; so that when the Multinationals Committee began *its* hearings on ITT in March 1973, one of their counsel, Jack Blum, asked the company to provide copies of the more intriguing letters mentioned in the notes.

What these letters revealed was an even wider range of contacts between ITT and the government, particularly the White House, in the critical periods of 1970 and 1971. Ned Gerrity, for instance, had visited Vice-President Spiro Agnew, an old army friend, in August 1970, to persuade him that 'McLaren seems to be running all by himself';[1] and Agnew, according to an internal ITT memo soon after-wards, had undertaken to bring pressure on Kleindienst and McLaren. Ryan, the lobbyist, explained to Merriam that the question was: 'how good a Republican is McLaren?'.[2] Geneen had seen John Ehrlichman and Charles Colson at the White House at the same time as Gerrity's visit to Agnew, and they had assured him that the President had instructed the Justice Department not to enforce a policy of 'bigness is bad'. John Mitchell, too, it turned out, had told Geneen that the President was not against mergers, and Mitchell promised that he, too, would talk to McLaren.[3] At another critical time, in April 1971, Geneen thanked John Connally for his help in obtaining a delay in the Grinnell case[4]—a delay that had never been properly explained in the Kleindienst hearings; and Merriam also thanked Peter Peterson, the President's Assistant for International Econo-mic Affairs, for his help: 'the work you and your associates have done has been highly effective'.[5] Soon after all these

1. Gerrity to Agnew, August 7, 1970. *Multinational Hearings*: p. 551.

2. Ryan to Merriam, August 24, 1970. *Multinational Hearings*: p. 555.

3. Gerrity to Agnew, Memorandum August 7, 1970. *Multinational Hearings*: p. 551.

4. Merriam to Connally, April 22, 1970. *Multinational Hearings*: p. 550.

5. Merriam to Peterson, April 26, 1971. *Multinational Hearings*: p. 551.

letters emerged, Patrick Gray, the acting and very temporary director of the FBI, who was then undergoing the
nomination hearings, revealed that Charles Colson at the
White House had sent Howard Hunt, the plotter in the
Watergate bugging operation, to interview Dita Beard during the Kleindienst hearings; and also that John Dean, the
White House counsel, had passed the original of the Beard
Memorandum back to ITT for examination by the typewriter experts. From all these new pieces of evidence, it was
now evident that the connivance between the White House
and ITT had been far closer than had transpired in the
course of the Kleindienst hearings, and there was strong
prima facie evidence of perjury. At the same time both the
cast of characters and the means of operation in the ITT
cases were beginning to look very similar to those of the
Watergate : and it even emerged that it was the concern of
the administration about the ITT revelations which was one
of the reasons for the original bugging of the Watergate.
The idea, as one of the organisers, Jeb Magruder, described
it, was to find incriminating evidence that the Democrats
had been receiving kick-backs from corporations, to try to
discredit the Democrat chairman, Larry O'Brien, who had
exposed the ITT connection with the Republicans. 'At that
time we were particularly concerned about the ITT situation', said Magruder in his subsequent testimony. 'Mr.
O'Brien had been a very effective spokesman against our
position on the ITT case, and I think there was a general
concern that if he was allowed to continue as Democratic
national chairman . . . he could be very difficult in the
coming campaign.'[1]

By the end of April 1973, the Watergate scandals were
at last coming to light, and on April 30 President Nixon
announced the resignations of four of his closest colleagues
—Bob Haldeman, John Ehrlichman, John Dean and
Richard Kleindienst. All four were closely involved in the
ITT affair as well as in the Watergate. Two weeks later, on
May 19, the Senate 'Watergate Committee' headed by Sam
Ervin, began its hearings, and at the same time the new
attorney-general, Elliot Richardson announced the appoint-

1. Magruder's testimony to the Senate Watergate Committee,
June 14 1973.

ment of the special prosecutor for the Watergate Case, Professor Archibald Cox, from Harvard. Three weeks later, Richardson announced, on June 8, that he had asked Professor Cox to take over from the Justice Department the investigation of all the ramifications of the merger of ITT with the Hartford company, explaining that 'the ITT enquiry has begun to overlap with the Watergate investigation, particularly in the area of subjects for interview'. The Justice Department was supposed to have been investigating ITT ever since the end of the Kleindienst hearings, when the Senate Judiciary Committee had asked them to examine the testimony for evidence of perjury; and the Justice Department had also been supposedly looking into the 34 boxes of papers from the SEC, for evidence of obstruction of justice. But very little that happened, except for a few interviews of ITT officials by the FBI; and the transfer of the case to Professor Cox—with his independence apparently guaranteed—presaged a more aggressive enquiry. Professor Cox hired a special staff of four young attorneys to take over the investigation, as part of his team in his offices in Washington. The 34 boxes were moved over from Justice Department, the White House files were demanded, and ITT and government staff were questioned once again. But this enquiry was much more dreaded by the corporation than the previous ones; for it showed signs of being effectively insulated against corporate pressures. The offices in K Street in Washington were guarded by police at the entrances; security precautions were stringent; and the young attorneys were exasperatingly discreet, whether to corporation executives or to journalists.

But as the Watergate investigations progressed, and the ex-White House aides began to talk, so new material came to light about ITT, too; and it became apparent that the Kleindienst hearings a year earlier had been a mockery. The disappearance of Dita Beard, just before the Kleindienst hearings, and her subsequent mysterious behaviour, was more closely connected with the White House. Robert Mardian, who was formerly a senior official in Nixon's re-election committee, told Senate investigators that it was Gordon Liddy, one of the convicted Watergate conspirators, who had 'whisked ITT lobbyist Dita Beard out of Washington to a Denver hospital'; and John Mitchell, the former attorney-general, later described the removal of Dita Beard from Washington as one of 'the White House horror stories'. In the meantime Charles Colson, the former White House aide, confirmed to the Staggers committee, which was investigating the SEC, that he had agreed that Howard Hunt, should be sent to Denver to interview Dita Beard about the authenticity of the memo: 'it became critical for the administration to know whether it was Beard's memo or that of a forger'. Howard Hunt himself later gave evidence to the Senate Watergate Committee on September 25, 1973, and vividly described how he went about his mission. His two basic instructions from Colson, he said, were to find out why Mrs. Beard had hidden herself away, and whether the memo was fraudulent. He was disguised with a wig supplied by the FBI, and as he described it:

I arrived out in Denver well after dark, probably 9 or 10 o'clock at night, made telephonic contact with her physician, took some time to get in from the airport. I probably got to her bedside no earlier than 11 o'clock that night. I introduced myself under the pseudonym that had been agreed upon and under which she had agreed to see me, having had prior reference to her daughter's guaranteeing of my bona fides. She was initially very suspicious. I also believe that she was under sedation and was not grasping thoroughly the situation. I had a number of questions to put to her. She was reluctant to answer them at first. There came a time, perhaps within the first twenty or thirty minutes, when her physician who was then in attendance upon her suggested that I step into the corridor, which I did. He indicated that he wanted to administer oxygen or some sort of other aid, chemical aid, to her. I chose that time to absent myself to go to a pay telephone and report back to Mr Charles Colson at his home telephone number, which I did. I just want to establish that this is a pattern that occurred throughout the night until perhaps 3 or 3.30 in the morning . . .[1]

The persistent questioning of Mrs. Beard on behalf of the White House, at a time when the Senate Committee were being denied access to her, showed how anxious were the President's staff concerning the memo. Soon further evi-

1. Howard Hunt testimony to the Senate Watergate Committee: September 25, 1973.

dence—perhaps the most damaging of all—was uncovered by the Senate Watergate Committee while they were questioning H. R. Haldeman, the President's former chief of staff. They got hold of a memo written by Charles Colson to Haldeman, at a time half-way through the Kleindienst hearings, on March 30, 1972.[1] In it, Colson described his worries about the way the hearings were developing, how Kleindienst might not be confirmed, and how 'there is the possibility of serious additional exposure by the continuation of this controversy . . . Make no mistake, the Democrats want to keep this case alive—whatever happens to Kleindienst—but the battle over Kleindienst elevates the visibility of the ITT matter . . .'

Colson's long and indiscreet memo went on to describe incriminating documents about the ITT affair that had not then become public, and which would be highly embarrassing to the administration, including one which would 'lay this case on the President's doorstep'.[2] Some of them were the memos which later *did* emerge, at the multinational hearings, including the letter from Gerrity to Agnew, the letters to Peterson and Connally, and the internal memo from Ryan to Merriam, suggesting that Kleindienst was the key man to pressurise McLaren ('We believe all copies of this have been destroyed', said Colson to Haldeman with misplaced confidence). But other memos referred to by Colson had not emerged, and sounded as if they were still more incriminating. There was a memo from Herb Klein, the President's press aide, to Haldeman, written on June 30, 1971, a month before the ITT settlement was announced, 'setting forth the $400,000 arrangement with ITT' which 'put the Attorney General on constructive notice at least of the ITT commitment at that time and before the settlement, facts which he has denied under oath'. There was a memo written by Ehrlichman to Mitchell in September 1970, 'referring to an "understanding" with Geneen and complaining of McLaren's actions', which would, warned Colson, 'directly involve the President'. There was another memo from Ehrlichman to Mitchell in May 1971, 'alluding to

1. Senate Watergate Committee: document made public on August 1, 1973.
2. Ditto.

discussions between the President and the Attorney-General as to the "agreed upon ends" in the resolution of the ITT case and asking the AG whether Ehrlichman would work directly with McLaren or with Mitchell'. And there was also a memo to the President 'in the same period'.

The Colson memorandum was the single most important piece of evidence about collusion between ITT and the White House since the Beard memorandum had come to light eighteen months before; it appeared to confirm the details of the Beard memo, including the reference to $400,000, and including the implication that the President himself was involved. And it revealed again how hectically the White House was trying to cover up the evidence in the midst of the Kleindienst hearings. The counsel to the Watergate Committee, Samuel Dash, asked Haldeman if he had discussed the contents of the memo with the President, and Haldeman replied that he could not recall, and that he was not familiar with the memo. Colson made a statement, saying that he was only acting as devil's advocate within the White House. But the memo, as Dash remarked, appeared to show 'an act of perjury on the part of Mitchell'; and more important, it pointed the way to more evidence. Professor Cox's investigators promptly asked the White House for all the other memos referred to by Colson, and were given them.

The evidence of perjury and obstruction of justice contained in the Colson memo threw so much doubt on the history of the ITT settlement that Senator Tunney—who with Kennedy had been most active in the attack in the Kleindienst hearings—on the day after the memo's disclosure, swiftly asked the Justice Department to re-open the whole anti-trust action. The Attorney-General, Elliot Richardson, turned the question over to the anti-trust division, and six weeks later, on September 12, replied to Tunney that 'on the basis of their advice, I do not believe that a reopening of the judgment, at this time, would give the government any greater relief than it obtained under the settlement. I therefore am of the opinion that the public interest would not be served, and could be injured, by re-opening these cases'.

But the special prosecutor's team continued to burrow

away, picking up new clues to clandestine meetings and perjured testimony; and on August 13 a grand jury was convened in Washington to look into possible perjury and obstruction of justice, both by ITT and by the Nixon administration. Then, in October 1973, came President Nixon's abrupt sacking of Professor Cox, and the resignation of the Attorney-General, Elliot Richardson. In the aftermath it became clear that Nixon's clash with Cox was not so much caused by the overt dispute, concerning the secret tapes of the Watergate conversations, as by Cox's determination to press ahead with surrounding scandals, including dubious campaign contributions in 1970, and including the ramifications of ITT, which were leading ever closer to the President's doorstep.

But Cox's staff, in the meantime, had obtained evidence which could not easily be suppressed, and which any prosecutor would have to take notice of. One of the most important and recurring unanswered questions had always been: who was it that had asked for the delay in sending the ITT Grinnell anti-trust case to the Supreme Court, on April 19, 1971? McLaren, the trust-buster, was against the delay, and Kleindienst, then deputy attorney-general in charge of the case, had at first testified in his hearings that he could not remember why the delay was asked for; later he professed to remember that he had asked for it after a visit from Judge Walsh, one of ITT's attorneys. But this story seemed inherently unlikely, and it became more unconvincing after the 'politically sensitive' memos were published, in which ITT thanked both John Connally, and Pete Peterson in the White House for their help in the delay. There was still a crucial missing piece to this jigsaw, and Cox's staff eventually found it with the help of the one man who knows best—Richard Kleindienst, who voluntarily offered to help them with the ITT case. Kleindienst revealed that in 1971 he had received a telephone call from John Ehrlichman at the White House, asking the Justice Department to stop the appeal in the Grinnell case. Kleindienst replied that he could not, because McLaren had recommended the appeal, and the solicitor-general, Erwin Griswold, had approved it. Ehrlichman hung up, and soon afterwards a call came through from President Nixon himself. Nixon called Kleindienst by an unprintable name, and then said: 'don't you understand the English language?', and ordered Kleindienst to delay the appeal.[1] Kleindienst threatened to resign over the issue, but was dissuaded by his boss, John Mitchell. Kleindienst duly asked for the delay, over McLaren's head, and in the meantime set in motion the events that led to the favourable ITT settlement.

There was now little doubt left as to who it was who had brought such exorable pressure on the Justice Department on ITT's behalf, who had overturned the decision of the anti-trust chief, and on whose behalf all the leading figures in the case—including Mitchell, Kleindienst and McLaren—had perjured themselves. It was the President of the United States.

1. Kleindienst's revelations to the prosecutors was leaked in the *New York Times* (Oct. 30, 1973) as a result of Professor Cox telling two members of the Senate Judiciary Committee, Senators Kennedy and Hart. The White House replied that the account was 'distorted and unfair', and that 'when the specific facts of the appeal were subsequently explained in greater detail, the President withdrew his objection and the appeal was prosecuted in exactly the form originally proposed'. But the White House neglected to mention that Kleindienst had threatened to resign (which Kleindienst himself disclosed after the *New York Times* leak) and as a result of the delay the way had been opened for the subsequent settlement.

13

The Sovereign State

The nation-state is just about through as an economic unit.
                                    Charles Kindleberger, 1969 [1]

The multinational corporation will be disruptive if a political power does not develop to put the economy at the service of man, and not put man at its service.
                                    Jean-Jacques Servan-Schreiber, 1972 [2]

While ITT was so passionately devoting itself to blocking and bringing down a Marxist government in Chile, it was at the very same time eagerly negotiating with the Communists in Moscow, to open up the huge potential new market, as the cold war thawed. This story is revealing, not only of ITT's contradictions, but as an example of the new scale of industrial diplomacy: for the Russians have negotiated with the giant companies as if they were treating with separate states. As Jean-Jacques Servan-Schreiber has written: 'The multinational company will be the tool for opening the Communist countries of the East. The Communists want to do business with large companies because they don't want to deal with a lot of different small ones.' [3] The two sides can reveal a mutual attraction: the Russians need a disciplined and centralised system to deal with, while the multinationals see in Russia the longed-for prospect of orderly markets, strike-free factories, and predictable five-year plans. Russia might realise Geneen's dream of steady growth, uninterrupted by slumps and competition; it could be the ultimate land of 'no surprises'.

1. *American Business Abroad:* Yale University Press, 1969, p. 206.
2. *Business Week:* November 14, 1972.
3. Ibid.

In the last decade ITT has come gradually closer to Moscow, in sharp reversal of their clash in Budapest in 1950; while the Communists, having executed one ITT man and jailed two others, retained their special fascination with ITT, as an arm of American power and technology. ITT kept its office in Vienna, to explore openings in Eastern Europe; and it established personal connections with Communist leaders in Rumania and Poland : in the 'sixties, to the worry of some other ITT men, the Austrian company began to sell sophisticated electronics to the Communist countries. By the late 'sixties the climate was becoming more favourable, and the British and French companies were deployed to make closer contacts with the Russians. The French ITT companies, basking in de Gaulle's reconciliation with Moscow, were especially concerned with selling a telecommunications system called DS4 to the Russian airline Aeroflot. They negotiated for two years, and eventually in October 1972 the system was inaugurated in Moscow by Marc Lauvergeon, the president of CGCT. But as the French sourly noted, ITT in New York had been using the French subsidiaries as their trailblazers and had now caught up with them, as the American-Russian détente developed. While the French ITT team was inaugurating its project at the Metropole Hotel in Moscow, a big American team was mounting a presentation of the whole ITT system to Russian leaders. As the Paris weekly *L'Express* commented : 'The French subsidiaries of ITT have just experienced the limits imposed on their actions by "multinationality." '[1]

ITT in New York and Vienna had in fact been preparing for years for their invasion, with visits of New York executives and an elaborate symposium in Moscow in late 1969. The head of the Eastern office, Jan Garvin, had been cultivating the appropriate Russian leaders, and in December 1971, with signs of a real thaw, there was a major meeting in Moscow, soon after the visit of Maurice Stans, then Nixon's Secretary of Commerce. There were five ITT men,

1. *L'Express:* November 20, 1972.

led by Jan Garvin and Frank Barnes from New York, facing a team from the Soviet State Committee for Science and Technology (SCST), the chief agency for dealing with foreign businessmen. The SCST is not quite what it looks; it is saturated with members of the KGB and other intelligence services, who use it as cover for their surveillance of Western organisations[1]; and its chief role is what is called 'technical strip-tease' — finding out as much as possible about Western technology without actually having to pay for it (the actual contracts can only be signed by the Ministry of Foreign Trade). Here, at last, ITT had met its match in ruthlessness.

The effective boss of the SCST, who headed the talks with ITT, is its vice-chairman, Dr. Gvishiani, Kosygin's son-in-law, a smooth and subtle negotiator : as ITT's man Jan Garvin described him in a confidential memorandum: 'His looks, demeanor, terminology and other attitudes are those of a courteous but dominating, imaginative and sharp negotiator, well versed in the Western business and management philosophy and practices, the key Soviet bridge-builder to the economies of the capitalist world. . . .'

The ITT team described the wonders that the conglomerate could perform, expressed their desire for a co-operation agreement, and promised an audiovisual presentation for the future. Gvishiani on his side showed curiosity about almost every part of ITT's activities; he was interested in Levitt's modular housing, in colour television, in tapes, cassettes, and hi-fi, in frozen foods and convenience foods, in hotels and reservation systems, in scientific publishing; and of course in telecommunications, which ITT regarded as its first priority, to establish an 'inside track' with the Soviet government. Gvishiani expressed a personal interest in the economics of car-rental (which had been a Russian interest since the days of Khrushchev), believing that a rental system could assuage the Russian yearning for cars, until large-scale production was under way.

ITT seemed just what the Russians wanted, to provide a whole package of technologies; but in return, the SCST in-

1. See, for instance *The Penkovsky Papers* (Collins, 1965, p. 112); Penkovsky, himself a double agent, was 'simply astounded' by the numbers of secret service agents in the SCST.

sisted on a balance of trade from ITT's side, by cross-licensing of Soviet technologies, co-production arrangements, and buying manufactured goods. Garvin reckoned that unless ITT could buy from Russia in return, its prospects were thin. Here as elsewhere, the United States government was virtually excluded from the discussion; it was essentially a negotiation between states. ITT's strategy, as Garvin explained afterward, was to create a favourable climate and mechanism 'to foster the bilateral aspect of ITT/USSR trade'.

ITT congratulated itself on its rapport with Gvishiani. It reckoned that it must operate on a man-to-man basis, and have Gvishiani personally involved in all its important projects. Garvin wrote a long report to Geneen on the meeting with the Communists, with not a word of worries about defence, security, or ideology. Yet only a few months earlier ITT had been passionately denouncing the Chilean government's Marxist tyranny, with ideological fervour : 'Freedom is dying everywhere.' The alliance between ITT and the USSR continued to prosper; there is now an ITT office in Moscow, and there have been further visits, with audio-visual presentations. ITT seem well placed to achieve a long-term contract, and the marriage between the state ministry and the conglomerate seems a happy one.

There is, of course, much to be thankful for in the thaw, and the opening up of Russia. The development of consumer industries may at last help to soften the Soviet intransigence, and turn them away from aggression, toward the pursuit of material comforts, and the intermeshing of Western and Russian industry may diminish the dangers of future confrontations. Inevitably much of this penetration will be entrusted to the giant corporations, who alone have the resources.

But these marriages of monoliths are unlikely to be much concerned with the cause of individual liberties. Watching the conjunction of a superstate with centralised technology —above all with communications technology—it is hard not to have some sense of dread at the unfolding prospects of unified planning systems and controlled markets, undisturbed by competition or anti-trust. As the report of the Tariff Commission noted in 1973 : 'In the largest and most sophisticated multinational corporations, planning and sub-sequent monitoring of plan fulfilment have reached a scope and level of detail that, ironically, resemble more than super-ficially the national planning procedures of Communist countries.' Both sides are preoccupied with the techniques of control and surveillance, which have been so expertly de-veloped in the last decade; the techniques are alarming enough in the West, but in the East they have a much more sinister connotation. Both sides have their self-contained bureaucracies, intolerant of eccentrics and rebels. With the dwindling of ideological disputes, the multinationals can look forward to a single global system. They will naturally prefer to place their investments in countries whose govern-ments can ensure their security, and the discipline of the work force—the more so as the scale of their enterprises grows, so that they will be developing whole territories, cities, and coastlines. They will be wary of countries like Chile which seek to operate outside the disciplined system.

In this scenario it would not be surprising if, on both sides of the world, a new generation will revolt against large-scale organisations, whether as employers, producers, or political influences. For however much they may offer the accoutrements of freedom and the financial means to enjoy it, they demand in return an absolute loyalty to their system; and this system cannot, in itself, provide the scope for human expression.

SCANDAL DISCOUNTS

The ITT anti-trust scandal in Washington, like so many American scandals, appeared to die down as quickly as it had flared up, buried in a surfeit of evidence and talk, and over-laid by new scandals—most notably by the Watergate affair —and by the Presidential election. The White House did not obviously suffer from its involvement; Nixon was trium-phantly re-elected, Kleindienst remained Attorney-General, until the Watergate scandal finally unseated him. ITT itself went on as if nothing much had happened. Ned Gerrity remained in charge of public relations. Dita Beard, after a long period of leave, was given the new job of 'sales re-search' in Colorado; but her health was still mysterious, and in February 1973, after she had been visited by officials from the Justice Department, she was reported to have had another heart attack. Bill Merriam was discreetly moved to Rome, to work for international trade relations. As for Geneen, he continued as chief executive officer, and was promoted to board chairman, while Tim Dunleavy became president, with the mysterious new title of 'chief operating officer'; but key reports went direct to the chairman.

Gerrity and his men maintained that the anti-trust scandal had helped their campaign for corporate identity, putting ITT on the map. As one of the PR men assured me, people would soon forget what the publicity was about; they would just remember the letters ITT. But when I asked one senior ITT executive how much the scandal had cost the company, he replied: 'Between one and one and a half billion dollars.' That, indeed, was roughly the fall in the market value of the shares, below the figure that might have been expected: the 'scandal discount'. The multinational hearings on Chile in March 1973, and the further evidence that emerged about the anti-trust case, sent the share price down still further, and the Chile hearings had a wider impact on ITT's credibility abroad, being extensively reported in the world's press. Geneen, with his secret contacts with the CIA, was becoming increasingly embarrassing to the board. Yet they were in an awkward dilemma; for whatever the political embarrassments of Geneen, they knew that no-one else came near him in ability to manage the company. He had built it up, and he alone knew how to run it. And none of the elaborate meetings, systems, or reports would be the same without his eagle eye.

Geneen's American empire was somewhat diminished by the anti-trust settlement. Avis was being gradually and profitably sold off; Canteen was offered for sale with much less success (both divestitures were handled by Lazards, who had arranged their acquisition). Levitt, too, was preparing to be sold, though the most profitable part of it, the development in Florida, was kept within ITT: they plan to invest $750 million in the 100,000 acres of Palm Coast, to build a complete retirement community, a self-contained ITT-land. But the other four-hundred-odd companies remained, including the Hartford, which continued to increase its profits, and provided the flood of cash which ITT had so desperately needed. Geneen could still buy companies worth less than $100 million; and he continued to accumulate them; in January 1973 he bid $16 million for the 135-year-old publishing firm G. P. Putnam's Sons (including Coward, McCann and Berkley) to add to the existing ITT publishers. But the fall in ITT stock put off this deal, in May 1973.

In Europe, there was no formal restriction on acquisitions, and Geneen still bought anything he could find, from perfume to dogfood. In Britain, ITT caused a stir in January 1973 by bidding for an Insurance group, aptly called Excess Holdings, which had become overextended. There was some opposition from the London underwriters, and the president of the Federation of Insurance Brokers, Gordon Hayman, described it as 'a debt to the devil'; but ITT promised to inject $22 million in cash, which the company urgently needed, and the stockholders were relieved to sell it to ITT for $16 million.

Europe, for the time being, was a refuge from anti-trust laws; and Geneen, having striven so hard to shift the balance from Europe to America, was now forced back to the continent whence the companies' fortunes had first come. In spite of his worries about the Common Market and leftist movements, Geneen now regarded Europe as a better 'business environment' than America. But he knew he must move fast, for resistance to American investment was growing, not only in France, but in Germany and Britain. The trustbusters in the Common Market were beginning to flex their muscles, under a resolute new chief, Willy Schlieder. His department, he said to me, is more effectively insulated against political pressures than his American counterparts, since the commission of the EEC does not have to seek votes or accumulate political debts. But the anti-trust team in Brussels is very small compared to Washington's, and they too have great difficulty in legally defining the case against the conglomerates, which operate outside the normal definitions of monopoly and restraint of trade. It is of the nature of conglomerates that they raise social and political issues, as much as legal ones, and that any limitation of them must have an element of arbitrariness. Moreover, the prevailing European attitude toward the American giants is not so much to try to restrict them, as to build up their own giants to compete with them, both in Europe and abroad. In this they have become increasingly successful, so that giant companies are becoming less an American than a world phenomenon.

In the extent of its controls, as in its other features, ITT is a caricature of a multinational conglomerate, not a typical example. Its whole history, as it has emerged in this study, has given it a maverick character, first formed by the offshore activities of the 'wild Behn', and then reinforced by the defiant ambitions of his successor, Geneen : the two entrepreneurs both had the strengths and limitations of the classic outsiders, possessed with great drive, but not knowing when to stop. No other multinational corporation has the same wildness and placelessness, cut off from any sense of community or belonging; most of them have a far more solid and visible background, based on interrelated products and research rather than accountancy. Yet the case of ITT has, I believe, some lessons for other giant companies; for some of its traits, whether as a conglomerate or as a multinational, are ones which others are tempted to follow. And many of the questions which arose from the ITT scandals and hearings have a wider relevance. Has private power, as Senator Hart asked, now extended its reach so far that no government can control it? Does the scale of world trade necessitate giant conglomerates, which their home government cannot afford to defy? Do they have the right, and the power, to create their own foreign policy? The other multinationals may be tempted to close their ranks, and to ignore the embarrassments of the ITT scandals. But the questions cannot be ignored.

Firstly, do such vast conglomerates serve any purpose? The necessity for huge units may be accepted for many single-industry companies, which have to operate on a global scale—for oil, or steel, or automobiles, or computers—though even here it is increasingly disputed. But Geneen has developed to its extreme the new concept of the conglomerate, acquiring hundreds of scattered companies connected only by their common contribution to profits. His technical achievement has been astonishing. The Geneen machine held together, surviving the slump which collapsed so many conglomerates; and however much Geneen owed to secret accounting and concealed assets, his survival depended on his capacity to control. Many of his methods—the ferreting out of facts, the management by meetings, the insistence on 'no surprises'—are inevitably being followed by others; for in one sense he was right when he said to me, 'It's the only way.' Only by the most rigorous cross-checking, only by a deep distrust of the human element, can such a complex empire be prevented from dissolving into chaos. But what is the point, either economically or socially, of putting together this extraordinary jumble in the first place? Or, as Emmanuel Celler put it, 'I wonder whether the Good Lord has given anybody the prowess and the expertise, the ingenuity, to be able to control all those operations. . . .'

Geneen's most convincing justification is that the conglomerate's spread of interests makes it more secure against the storms of the economic climate. He has not only swings and roundabouts but a complete fairground to balance his business, to enable his earnings to grow always steadily. Yet this concept of the impregnable corporate castle comes close to a rejection of the whole risk-taking basis of the free-enterprise system. It excludes the stockholder from any involvement with the individual industries, for no outsider even knows how profitable or unprofitable they are. The 'only system' which Geneen advocates is a system which tries to cut out the element of human choice and chance as far as possible; it aims to make five-year plans and projections and stick to them, and to press both the managers and the public to conform to its own expectations. To this extent it resembles less the traditional picture of free enterprise than the Japanese type of corporate state, or the Communist planning system.

And inevitably the spread of operations increases the political power of the corporation, to exert leverage and pressure on governments and other companies. A global conglomerate has some connection with every industry, and with every country. ITT is inescapable, and its lobbyists, lawyers, and public-relations men make the most of the fact; for it is in the nature of Geneen's dynamism that he presses his advantages to the limit. Nowadays businessmen on both sides of the Atlantic put Geneen's reputation in two separate compartments : they admire him and perhaps emulate him as a master manager, while deploring his political excesses. But it is in the nature of his system of management—reducing all problems to figures—that it will disregard personal and political factors, and will regard governments, like other obstacles to management, as nuisances to be circumvented or overcome.

It would be absurd to suggest that highly-organised management is inherently undesirable. A company that is acquired by ITT (or any other conglomerate) may gain something in terms of both morale and profitability. Many of the acquired companies, from Sheraton in America to Excess Holdings in Britain, have been in desperate need of new management, which may only be acquired through new ownership. British firms, in particular, often require a drastic shock treatment to cure them of lethargy. But it is very uncertain how long this improvement can last. If ITT were to buy companies, reorganise them, and then sell them again (as it has been forced to do with Avis, Levitt, or Canteen) it might provide a useful purging bath to cut out waste and incompetence. But Geneen insists that his system is an enduring one, like General Motors, with the same unassailable logic; and it is in the long term, I suspect, that the weakness of the ITT method will show itself. For it cannot, by its nature, allow room for more than one entrepreneur, and it cannot tolerate the original eccentrics and stubborn researchers who are essential to real innovation. Imagination and hunches are anathema to Geneen and his comptrollers, for they spring surprises. Yet surprises, good or bad, are essential to invention and genuine enterprise.

It is likely, I believe, that after Geneen retires the ITT empire will prove impossible to hold together, without the drive and iron control of the master. There will be an awkward aftermath, as after the departure of Colonel Behn; the separate entities will reassert themselves, and the faults in the system—the lack of innovation, of entrepreneurs, and of logical connections—will begin to emerge. Eventually probably the major components will break apart, but it will not be easy, and they will leave a tangle of loose ends behind. Whether the separate components of ITT were better managed inside or outside the corporate fold may never be established; for the records defy the analysis of experts. But the strain, the expense of the superstructure, and the human cost of controlling this jumble, have been all too apparent.

MULTINATIONALS

It is ITT's multinational activities on top of its conglomerate capers, that raise the most disturbing political questions. For its conduct, as it emerged in the memos and hearings, does not at all square with the generalised accounts of the role and responsibilities of the multinationals. Many articles and books have emerged in the last few years, analysing the behaviour of the global giants, and the problems of the 'asymmetry' between them and small countries. Mostly, they explain that the giants are sensitive; but there is a striking absence of case histories of individual companies. 'The multinational firm seeks to be a good citizen of each country where it has operations,' says Professor Charles Kindleberger.[1] 'Contrary to the common impression,' writes Professor Raymond Vernon, 'large enterprises are remarkably reluctant to invoke the support of the U.S. government in overcoming the obstacles created by other governments.'[2] Into this reassuring world of theory, ITT has stampeded with the subtlety of an angry elephant, leaving a trail of memos behind it to leave no doubt about its motives and intentions.

The development of multinational corporations is as irreversible and inevitable as the internationalisation of railways and telegraphs in the nineteenth century. As I type with an Olivetti typewriter, listen to a Grundig recorder, pick up an ITT telephone, rent an Avis car, how can I believe otherwise? But like all sudden acquisitions of power, it is subject to abuse; and the story of ITT provides a catalogue of nearly all the potential dangers and excesses.

From the beginning, ITT had a unique opportunity for buccaneering with its new communications. It could appear

1. *American Business Abroad:* p. 180.
2. *Foreign Affairs:* July, 1971.

and disappear in different parts of the world, adopting a heightened rhetoric to suit the time and place, with breathtaking confidence; first willingly pro-Nazi, then piously anti-Nazi, then fiercely anti-Moscow, then busily trading with Moscow, sometimes simultaneously adopting opposite attitudes in different parts of the world. This adaptability is defended as being part of a proper neutrality; but ITT vigorously takes sides.

When it suits it, ITT adopts the posture of defending a national interest, as in the Deep Freeze lobbying, while ruthlessly pursuing its own interest. ITT's relations with the American government have been particularly inscrutable because of its involvement in espionage; but while it has been undoubtedly used by the CIA and its predecessors, it appears likely that it has used the CIA rather more, in return. In foreign affairs, particularly in Latin America, it has made policy as much as it has followed it.

With governments ITT men have made full use of their special facility, belonging to a multinational conglomerate, to say one thing in one place, another in another. In the antitrust case, they pleaded in Connecticut that Hartford needed ITT's money, while in Washington they insisted that ITT needed Hartford's money; just as, in bidding for the ABC network, they told the FCC that they would pour money into ABC, while telling their own staff that they would pull money out of it. The subsidiaries pretend to be autonomous one moment, centralised the next—the trick that came in so useful in San Diego, when Geneen could give money to the Republican convention, in the guise of a local hotelier. When necessary, ITT can appear quite tiny, but when the time comes, it can deploy all its resources on one spot—as it deployed them on Cotter in Connecticut, or on Kleindienst and McLaren in Washington.

Consistency and truthfulness have never come naturally to ITT. It is expert at deliberate concealments, at the kind of 'nonpublic relations' which it practised in Puerto Rico, and at the kind of undercover lobbying which the Washington staff explained in their memos. ITT's record of mendacity and doubletalk, which so clearly emerged in the ABC hearings, implies a deep irresponsibility : and the prospect of its being any further involved in communications, whether in publishing, television, or telephone systems, must be viewed with dread.

The sovereignty of a multinational corporation has emerged through this book in many facets—in its independence of governments, in its self-contained organisation and trade, in its private diplomacy and communications, in its avoidance of taxation, and in the secrecy of the company records. The sovereignty can be exaggerated; the host nations, after all, retain the right to nationalise, or to limit investment, which gives them bargaining power. The national corporations, like GEC in Britain or Michelin in France, can sometimes be harder to control than the multinational ones. Governments still have formidable weapons, and the United States government was in the end able to break up part of the ITT empire. In some obvious respects ITT is much less powerful than the early trusts of Morgan or Rockefeller. But the global diversity, in the context of world competition, has given it a new kind of invulnerability. For it now appears as a crucial engine of trade which a nation will limit at its peril. Geneen's persistent argument is, in effect, that what's good for ITT is good for America, and good for the world. World competition is increasingly the justification for huge organisations at home, so that we must ask, like Senator Bayh, 'Have we gotten ourselves in the position that if the merger is big enough, it doesn't make any difference what the law says?'

Does this matter? Why should we regret the diminution of national sovereignty, when nationalism appears to many people as outdated and frequently dangerous force, associated with prejudice, aggression, and wars? The most ardent supporters of the multinationals portray them, both economically and politically, as benign forces for peace, leading us into a new world society, and breaking down the bigotry and narrowness of local rules, as the early traders broke down the power of benighted chieftains or petty principalities. There is some truth in this portrayal. The multinational companies have progressed further than anyone toward a global organisation. Their own managers, united in their common purpose, inhabit a world in which differences of nationality seem often hardly recognisable. For Europeans accustomed to murdering each other each generation, the achievement is not to be sniffed at, and the multinationals have played some part in the process of intermeshing the nations of Europe, which was the ideal of Jean Monnet and the founders of the Common Market.

But the internationalisation of business will not in itself produce a world society. The railways in nineteenth-century Europe were acclaimed by the bankers as the forgers of a new unity; but they proved, in 1870 and 1914, to be merely the means of far more dreadful destruction. Commercial expansion brings only a small sector of nations together, and unless that sector is widened, it can provoke a bitter nationalist or regionalist reaction among those who feel threatened, as it did in the nineteenth century. The multinational corporations cannot, of their nature, set themselves up as guardians of social welfare, security, or the environment; for their whole justification rests on profitability and change, which depends on rejecting those areas and businesses which cannot be profitable. If uncontrolled, they can undermine the basis of welfare and security, through evading taxes, stimulating inflation, or speculating in currency.

Multinational corporations do not necessarily *want* nations to unite too closely. Geneen himself, rather tactlessly, made clear that he regarded the development of the Common Market as more a threat than a benefit; and ITT's telecommunications, their biggest business in Europe, profit more from the non-co-operation between governments than they would from a common European policy, which would lead to regulation and stiffer competition. Multinational corporations must always be tempted to play the game of divide and rule. Once they have established their factories inside each country they may prefer to support protectionism, for higher tariffs worry them little, and may offer them more secure markets and safer prospects for planning. The role of global companies as barrier-breakers is much less sure than it was a decade ago.[1]

That multinational companies need a more effective control is accepted by many of their own employees. But who can control them? The conventional remedy is for the

1. See Hugh Stephenson: *The Coming Clash*, Weidenfeld & Nicolson, 1972, p. 90.

nations to organise themselves into greater units, and eventually into some kind of world government, in order to limit the abuses; the multinational enterprises would thus stimulate world society through a contained process of conflict. That process is indeed gradually beginning, notably in the European Common Market; in the words of Pierre Malvé, the EEC economic counsellor in Washington in 1972, 'Co-operation among governments is needed more than ever to avoid the excesses of the multinational corporations.' The anti-trust department in Brussels, under Willy Schlieder, is becoming more watchful of restrictions on free trade. The trade unions, too, are slowly coming closer in international federations, to check the power of global employers. (ITT has become a favourite target for trade unionists: when ITT's Spanish company, SESA, retaliated against a strike in Madrid in 1971 by having the leaders arrested, workers in France, Germany and America held meetings and collected funds; and the International Metalworkers Federation in Geneva now has a special study group to watch ITT's activities.)

These counterforces will doubtless grow. But no-one who has watched the development of the Common Market can expect them to grow quickly. A major catastrophe, like the bankruptcy of a major multinational, might compel more urgent action; but even the collapse of Bernard Cornfeld's Investors Overseas Service did not provoke effective controls (such as a European counterpart to the Securities and Exchange Commission). As for the world front, it is hard to envisage any effective countervailance in the face of the disunity of the third world, as demonstrated at UNCTAD. Professor Kindleberger envisages an international ombudsman to ensure fair play among multinationals, and to prevent them from playing nations against each other,[1] but how would the ombudsman acquire the necessary authority? The prospect of effective global control is as distant, it seems to me, as the prospect of world government itself: a goal not to be abandoned, but not to be expected in anyone's lifetime.

The ideal of world controls is attractive, but it can easily become an excuse for postponing more realistic action. Even if it were attainable, it would not be sufficient; for the great

1. *American Business Abroad:* p. 207.

part of the welfare of individuals must continue to reside with the nation, around which the whole apparatus of taxation and the welfare state has been constructed. Nationalism, in this function, is far from outdated; and the advanced nation nowadays is less linked to the idea of military power and defence than to social security and protection—to education, hospitals, old-age pensions, child allowances. The nation, in fact, has become much more a protective organisation, much less an aggressive one; and its citizens will not readily entrust this protection to any larger unit.

This security must inevitably be threatened by the dynamic and disruptive energy of the global concerns, and the nation is bound to fight back. The resulting conflict, it seems to me, is both inevitable and desirable; for both sides need the balance of the other. The national leaders know quite well, though they may not admit it, that they need the resources and skills of the multinationals : the failings of the telephone systems are one example of the national limitations. Most multinational managers accept that they cannot by themselves safeguard the whole range of men's lives: they know as well as anyone that the nation is the guarantor of most elements of what we regard as modern civilisation. And the personal attitudes of the multinational managers themselves betray this; for however denationalised they may have become, in late middle age they look, like everyone else, for a resting place where they can benefit from the stability of the nation and a settled environment. Even within ITT, whose managers seem often to despair of the British worker and the pound, it is noticeable that many of them—including Geneen, Lester, and Bergerac—look to Britain for a background of security and calm in their own lives.

The nation is the only institution strong enough to stand up to the multinationals, and to instil comparable loyalties, for the foreseeable future; and it is only the nation that can redress the present imbalance. The concept of sovereignty may seem an old-fashioned and misleading one, but it expresses well enough the basic conflict and political question : who is going to provide the context and shape of men's lives? Geneen has said (see page 114) that the large corporations have become the custodians of making the entire system work : it may be true that they make it work, but the recent history of ITT shows that they cannot be allowed to be the custodians.

Any honest discussion of the effects of the multinational corporations must end, I believe, on a note of bewilderment. It is no more possible for a contemporary to understand what they are doing to the world than it was for a mid-nineteenth-century Englishman or American to understand what the Industrial Revolution was doing to his country or his community. It is easy both to exaggerate and to minimise their impact. On the one hand, the giant companies encompass the world, forging new systems of communication and organisation, demanding new disciplines, centralisations, and personal restrictions, whose social significance may take some decades to become clear. Yet the new organisations have themselves great limitations : they are caught up in means, not ends, and are too preoccupied with holding themselves to see far ahead.

It is tempting for any critic to depict multinational corporations as planned conspiracies, plotting to rebuild the world in their image, and there are parts of the ITT history that give credibility to this view—from Sosthenes Behn's secret bargains with the dictators to the memos of Dita Beard and Hal Hendrix, and Geneen's campaign to defeat the anti-trust laws. Yet even in ITT's case the conspiratorial view cannot, I believe, be maintained : throughout its history ITT has been precariously balancing on tightropes, protecting its assets, and covering its risks; and its plots and campaigns have stemmed more from its continual sense of insecurity than from a grand master plan—an insecurity that helps to account for some of its crassest mistakes. The executives of ITT—and of other multinationals—are as confused about the implications of their operations as anyone else; and perhaps more so.

But without need of much plotting, the multinationals have achieved over the last twenty years, with the opening up of world communications, a position of sudden dominance : they have found a vacuum and filled it. Their skills and technology have brought new benefits, and paved the way for others to follow; but they have also produced a serious imbalance between their centralised drive and the fragmented and confused state of the countries and communities with which they deal. This imbalance should be gradually rectified, as the nations catch up with the new state of the world, and begin to come together to form their own communications and controls. But in the meantime the multinationals themselves must open themselves up, and allow themselves to be inspected and questioned, if they are not to find themselves in a bitter conflict with their hosts. The behaviour of ITT as it emerged by accident to the public is not, I hope, typical of multinationals; but it is an example of how deeply communications can be corrupted, like a poisoned well; and how easily, without countervailing power, the strength of multinationals can be abused. The worries it induces can only be allayed by the corporations (including of course ITT) taking the initiative, in exposing themselves more honestly before the public, before they are compelled to.

CHILE EARLY 1970-AUG 1970	ANTI-TRUST EARLY 1970-AUG 1970	SAN DIEGO EARLY 1970-AUG 1970
	(Early 1970) Geneen talks to Commerce Secretary Stans about anti-trust.	(Early 1970) Geneen goes fishing with Bob Wilson near San Diego.
	(Early 1970) Gerrity sees McLaren, who insists on ITT divesting Hartford.	(Early 1970) New Sheraton hotel begun in San Diego: Tolle Agency, connected with Wilson, handles PR.
	(Early 1970) Geneen and ITT men descend on Hartford, Connecticut, to convince Commissioner Cotter about merger.	(March 8) Bob Finch of White House discusses idea of Republican Convention with reporters.
(May 1970) Geneen and McCone worried about Chile elections. McCone of ITT talks to Helms of CIA.	(May 19) Commissioner Cotter asks ITT for help with Hartford Civic Centre.	
(June) McCone has further talks with Helms about Chile; Helms agrees to send CIA man to see Geneen.	(May 23) Cotter approves Hartford merger with ITT.	
	(May 27) Geneen sees Mitchell at White House dinner.	(Mid-1970) Geneen has more talks with Wilson, who puts him in touch with Port Commission, for land for ITT cable plant.
(July 16) Geneen meets Broe of CIA at Sheraton-Carlton hotel in Washington: offers 'substantial sum' to stop Allende.		(Mid-1970) Dita Beard negotiates with Port Commission for land for cable plant.
	(Aug 4) Gerrity sees Agnew, discusses anti-trust cases. Agnew presses Kleindienst?	
(August 1970) McCone talks to Helms on telephone about Chile. McCone later holidays in Alaska.	(Aug 4) Geneen sees Mitchell on anti-trust cases.	
	(Aug 6) Chaffetz (ITT lawyer) sees McLaren about Canteen case.	(August 1970) ITT cable plant gets lease from Port Commission.
	(Aug 7) Geneen and Merriam see Colson and Ehrlichman of White House.	
	(Aug 7) Gerrity asks Agnew how to pressure McLaren.	
(Aug 17) Neal of ITT discusses Chile with State Dept; talks with Gerrity.	(Aug 10) Gerrity alerts ITT lobbyists against McLaren.	
(Aug 18) Gerrity tells Dunleavy of ITT: 'I am instructing Hendrix to make 50 percent commitment' (unexplained).	(Aug 19) Ryan of ITT sees Stans, who suggests 'some tangible starting-point' re anti-trust.	
	(Aug 24) Ryan to Merriam: hopes of Agnew influencing McLaren: 'this may be the break'.	

CHILE SEPT-DEC 1970	ANTI-TRUST SEPT-DEC 1970	SAN DIEGO
(Sept 4) *Allende wins popular election in Chile.*		
(Early Sept 1970) Forty Committee meets on Chile: discusses options?		
(Sept 9 and 10) ITT board meeting. Geneen and McCone agree to make second offer to stop Allende.		
(Sept 11 and 12) McCone explains offer to Kissinger and Helms of CIA.		
(Sept 14) Neal of ITT tells White House of million-dollar offer.		
(Sept 17) Hendrix reports how to stop Allende: passed to CIA.		
(Sept 22) Gerrity memo to Geneen, approving Hendrix strategy.		
(Sept 29) Hendrix reports 'aura of defeat' in Chile.		
(Sept 29) Broe of CIA tells Gerrity of plan for economic chaos in Chile.		
(Sept–Oct) McCone and Geneen agree: Broe's plan won't fly.		
(Oct 7) Broe tells ITT: picture not rosy.		
(Oct 9) Merriam lunches Broe, reports to McCone.		
(Oct 15) Neal sees Ambassador Korry: discuss hard line.		
(Oct 21) Secretary Rogers meets ITT and others on Chile: says that Nixon's is 'a business administration'.		
(Oct 24) *Allende wins Congressional elections.*		
(Nov 1970) Anaconda suggests Ad Hoc committee of companies against Allende.	(Nov 25) ITT proposes settlement, retaining Hartford. McLaren rejects.	
(Nov 9) Kissinger thanks Merriam for hard-line memo.	(Dec 31) District court decides against government in Grinnell case.	
	(continued)	

ITT's WONDER-YEAR

This chronology shows principle events mentioned in the second half of this book, in three fields of action – in San Diego, concerning the Republican Convention; in the anti-trust negotiations; and in Chile. It shows some of the 'inexorable pressure' that was brought to bear by ITT on the Administration, both to modify the anti-trust settlement and to adopt a hard line towards Chile. And it shows too the remarkable coincidence of the most intensive anti-trust lobbying with the offer of money to the San Diego convention.

(The chronology is adapted from Senator Kennedy's report on the Kleindienst hearings, with the addition of later evidence from the S.E.C. files about the anti-trust lobbying; and also from the Senate hearings on ITT and Chile, in March–April 1973.)

CHILE JAN-MAY 1971	ANTI-TRUST JAN-MAY 1971	SAN DIEGO JAN-MAY 1971
(Jan 1971) First Ad Hoc meeting in Merriam's office: ITT, Anaconda, Kennecott, etc.	(Before February) Geneen sees Secretary Kennedy on anti-trust.	(Jan–Feb 1971) Lt-Gov Reinecke (according to Beard) asks Beard to check out San Diego as possible convention site.
(Feb 5) ITT meets Nachmanoff, of Kissinger's staff, who advocates 'quiet pressure' on Allende.	(Feb) Geneen sees Flanigan on anti-trust.	(Early 1971) Mayor Curran of San Diego refuses to bid for Republican Convention.
(Feb 9) 2nd Ad Hoc meeting: ITT advises pressure on Kissinger.	(Feb 2) Bob Wilson attacks McLaren in Congress: other Congressmen follow.	(Jan–April 1971) Dita Beard checks out San Diego facilities for convention.
(Feb 11) Gerrity advises Geneen to deal separately with Allende, ditching Anaconda, etc.	(March or April): Ryan of ITT at neighbourhood party, meets Kleindienst, who agrees to see ITT man on anti-trust.	(March or April 1971) Bob Dole, Republican chairman, suggests a San Diego bid to Wilson.
(Mar 5) Ad Hoc committee meets again.	(Mar 18) ITT briefs lawyers and lobbyists on anti-trust.	(March 19) San Diego declines to bid for Democratic Convention.
(Mar 10) Dunleavy etc. of ITT see Allende in Chile, who discusses joint venture: very friendly.	(Early April) Geneen asks Rohatyn to prepare economic case for keeping Hartford.	
(Mar-April) ITT negotiate with Allende's team about compensation for nationalisation, and joint venture.	(April 8) Geneen asks Judge Walsh to urge government review of anti-trust policy.	(April 26) Lt-Gov Reinecke sees Mitchell at Justice Department.
	(April 16) Walsh writes Kleindienst, asking for review, and delay on Grinnell case.	(April 27) San Diego reception in Washington, including Reinecke: convention discussed.
	(April 16) Geneen meets Peterson of White House about anti-trust.	(Late April) Reinecke, etc, working with San Diego officials.
	(April 19) Kleindienst asks for delay on Grinnell, against McLaren's advice.	(Spring 1971) Bob Finch and Herb Klein from White House visit San Diego.
	(April 20) Rohatyn sees Kleindienst, who arranges for ITT presentation.	(Early May) Timmons from White House in San Diego for 2 weeks, checking convention facilities.
	(April 20) Geneen thanks Peterson for help in delay.	
	(April 20) Merriam thanks Secretary Connally for help in Grinnell delay.	(May 12) Finch tells Wilson that Nixon wants convention in San Diego. *Wilson tells Geneen, who pledges $400,000 for convention.*
	(April 29) Rohatyn sees Mitchell, then presents ITT case for keeping Hartford to Kleindienst, McLaren.	(May 12–June 3) Wilson and Reinecke line up local support for San Diego convention.
	(May 1) Beard meets Mitchell at Kentucky derby party.	
	(May 10–12) McLaren asks Flanigan to contact Ramsden, for report on Hartford.	(May 17–22) Reinecke sees Beard in Washington, discusses convention commitment.
	(May 17) Secretary Connally advocates restructuring anti-trust laws.	(May 22) Reinecke at White House.
(May 26) Chilean government tells ITT that it intends to nationalise the telephone company, quickly.	(May 20) Ramsden delivers report to Flanigan (McLaren in Europe).	(Late May) Merriam of ITT contacts Timmons of White House about convention.

CHILE JUNE-JULY 1971	ANTI-TRUST JUNE-JULY 1971	SAN DIEGO JUNE-JULY 1971
		(May–June 1971) Beard talks with Governor Nunn about Mitchell and ITT's 'noble commitment'.
		(June 2) San Diego asks to submit bid for convention.
	(June 10) Flanigan delivers Ramsden report to McLaren in Kleindienst's presence.	(June 3) Wilson announces $400,000 in pledges.
	(June 17) McLaren memo to Kleindienst: *agrees to let ITT keep Hartford.*	(June 11) Wilson and Dole visit San Diego.
		(June 24) Wilson sees Geneen in New York, discusses convention financing.
		(June 24) Merriam has call from White House about convention: is muddled; Beard is cross.
	(June 25) Secretary Stans advocates modifying anti-trust policy.	(June 25) *Dita Beard writes memo implying link between convention and anti-trust settlement.*
	(June 29) Rohatyn sees Flanigan and Kleindienst, complains about McLaren.	(June 28) Wilson at White House, discusses convention.
(July 8) ITT meet with OPIC: suggest that telephone company already expropriated; ask for guarantee.	(Early July) Flanigan passes Rohatyn's complaint to Kleindienst.	(June 29) San Diego council authorises convention bid.
(July 9) ITT board meeting discusses Chile. Guilfoyle proposal to Geneen to make deal with Allende, capitalising on Anaconda nationalisation.	(July 15) Rohatyn again complains to Kleindienst.	(July 3) Reported that Geneen provides 'Lion's share' of $400,000.
	(July 1–30) ITT directors sell ITT stock.	(July 11) Wilson visits Geneen's fishing camp in Maine.
	(July 31) *Settlement announced, allowing ITT to keep Hartford.*	(July 21) ITT-Sheraton cables Wilson, committing $200,000 for convention.
		(July 23) *Republicans approve San Diego for convention.*
AFTER JULY 1971	**AFTER JULY 1971**	**AFTER JULY 1971**
(Sept 14) Geneen lunches with Peterson and Haig at White House.	(Sep 21) Reuben Robertson asks Kleindienst about connection between anti-trust settlement and convention. Kleindienst denies.	(August 5) Wilson confirms that pledge comes from ITT-Sheraton.
(Sept 29) Allende appoints manager for ITT telephone company.		
(Oct 1) *Merriam writes Peterson, with 18-point plan to bring down Allende.*		

Index

292

294

298

299

302